Modern Language Association

Approaches to Teaching World Literature

Joseph Gibaldi, Series Editor

28. Sidney Gottlieb, ed. *Approaches to Teaching the Metaphysical Poets*. 1990.
29. Richard K. Emmerson, ed. *Approaches to Teaching Medieval English Drama*. 1990.
30. Kathleen Blake, ed. *Approaches to Teaching Eliot's* Middlemarch. 1990.
31. María Elena de Valdés and Mario J. Valdés, eds. *Approaches to Teaching García Márquez's* One Hundred Years of Solitude. 1990.
32. Donald D. Kummings, ed. *Approaches to Teaching Whitman's* Leaves of Grass. 1990.
33. Stephen C. Behrendt, ed. *Approaches to Teaching Shelley's* Frankenstein. 1990.
34. June Schlueter and Enoch Brater, eds. *Approaches to Teaching Beckett's* Waiting for Godot. 1991.
35. Walter H. Evert and Jack W. Rhodes, eds. *Approaches to Teaching Keats's Poetry*. 1991.
36. Frederick W. Shilstone, ed. *Approaches to Teaching Byron's Poetry*. 1991.
37. Bernth Lindfors, ed. *Approaches to Teaching Achebe's* Things Fall Apart. 1991.
38. Richard E. Matlak, ed. *Approaches to Teaching Coleridge's Poetry and Prose*. 1991.
39. Shirley Geok-lin Lim, ed. *Approaches to Teaching Kingston's* The Woman Warrior. 1991.
40. Maureen Fries and Jeanie Watson, eds. *Approaches to Teaching the Arthurian Tradition*. 1992.
41. Maurice Hunt, ed. *Approaches to Teaching Shakespeare's* The Tempest *and Other Late Romances*. 1992.
42. Diane Long Hoeveler and Beth Lau, eds. *Approaches to Teaching Brontë's* Jane Eyre. 1993.
43. Jeffrey B. Berlin, ed. *Approaches to Teaching Mann's* Death in Venice *and Other Short Fiction*. 1992.
44. Kathleen McCormick and Erwin R. Steinberg, eds. *Approaches to Teaching Joyce's* Ulysses. 1993.
45. Marcia McClintock Folsom, ed. *Approaches to Teaching Austen's* Pride and Prejudice. 1993.

Approaches to Teaching Joyce's *Ulysses*

Edited by
Kathleen McCormick
and
Erwin R. Steinberg

The Modern Language Association of America
New York   1993

Library of Congress Cataloging-in-Publication Data

Approaches to teaching Joyce's Ulysses / edited by Kathleen McCormick
and Erwin R. Steinberg.
     p.   cm. — (Approaches to teaching world literature ; 44)
    Includes bibliographical references and index.
    ISBN 0-87352-711-9 (cloth) — ISBN 0-87352-712-7 (pbk.)
    1. Joyce, James, 1882–1941. Ulysses. 2. Joyce, James, 1882–1941
—Study and teaching. I. McCormick, Kathleen. II. Steinberg, Erwin
Ray. III. Series.
PR6019.O9U557   1993
823'.912—dc20   93-736

Sections of Jeffrey Segall's article originally appeared in the *James Joyce Quarterly*
(Univ. of Tulsa, pub.), in *Joyce Studies Annual 1991* (Univ. of Texas, pub.), and in
his book *Joyce in America: Cultural Politics and the Trials of* Ulysses (Berkeley: U
of California P, 1993) and appear here with permission of the publishers.

An earlier version of Kathleen McCormick's "Reading *Ulysses* within the History of
Its Production and Reception" appeared in *College Literature* (1992); the revised
version appears here with permission of the publishers.

Cover illustration of the paperback edition: Photograph of Joyce manuscript.
Reproduced with the permission of the Poetry/Rare Books Collection, University
Libraries, State University of New York, Buffalo.

Published by The Modern Language Association of America
10 Astor Place, New York, New York 10003-6981

Printed on recycled paper

CONTENTS

PREFACE TO THE SERIES

In *The Art of Teaching* Gilbert Highet wrote, "Bad teaching wastes a great deal of effort, and spoils many lives which might have been full of energy and happiness." All too many teachers have failed in their work, Highet argued, simply "because they have not thought about it." We hope that the Approaches to Teaching World Literature series, sponsored by the Modern Language Association's Publications Committee, will not only improve the craft—as well as the art—of teaching but also encourage serious and continuing discussion of the aims and methods of teaching literature.

The principal objective of the series is to collect within each volume different points of view on teaching a specific literary work, a literary tradition, or a writer widely taught at the undergraduate level. The preparation of each volume begins with a wide-ranging survey of instructors, thus enabling us to include in the volume the philosophies and approaches, thoughts and methods of scores of experienced teachers. The result is a sourcebook of material, information, and ideas on teaching the subject of the volume to undergraduates.

The series is intended to serve nonspecialists as well as specialists, inexperienced as well as experienced teachers, graduate students who wish to learn effective ways of teaching as well as senior professors who wish to compare their own approaches with the approaches of colleagues in other schools. Of course, no volume in the series can ever substitute for erudition, intelligence, creativity, and sensitivity in teaching. We hope merely that each book will point readers in useful directions; at most each will offer only a first step in the long journey to successful teaching.

Joseph Gibaldi
Series Editor

PREFACE TO THE VOLUME

Ulysses is generally recognized as the most influential of all modernist literary texts. It has dramatically altered how fiction is read and written, yet seventy years after the book's publication, Joycean parody, pastiche, fragmentation, and self-referentiality can still tease readers out of more familiar, seemingly "natural," ways of perceiving both the word and the world and into more complex modes of apprehension in which uncertainty, multiplicity, and over-determination reign.

Joyce's work has also had a major effect on literary criticism and theory. Not only have his books, and particularly *Ulysses*, spawned intense interpretive debate, but they have also had a significant influence on the development of narrative and linguistic theories as various critics attempt to account for the experience of reading the Joycean text. Jacques Derrida remarks, "Deconstruction could not have been possible without Joyce" (qtd. in Jones 77). Indeed, as Joyce predicted, *Ulysses* looks as if it will "keep the professors busy for centuries" (qtd. in Ellmann, *James Joyce* 521)—between 1968 and 1990 alone the Library of Congress cataloged over six hundred books on Joyce, over three hundred of them specifically on *Ulysses*.

But the *Ulysses* that critics have talked and argued about has changed over the years as the dominant assumptions about reading within different societies—what Tony Bennett usefully calls "reading formations"—have changed ("Texts" 7–11). To some extent changes of this kind occur in the reception of any text from one historical period to another, but they have been more extreme with *Ulysses* than with any other modernist text. *Ulysses* therefore poses a unique challenge to teachers, who are faced with a stylistically complex text whose ways of being read and whose literary status have undergone vast revisions. Whereas in the 1920s *Ulysses* was seen by many as an unreadable, vulgar, even obscene book, over the last fifty years it has come to be regarded as perhaps *the* classic modernist text. Most recently, it has been lauded by poststructuralists for some of the "unreadable" qualities that initially provoked attack. This change makes us recognize that reading formations are not monolithic: at any given point a particular position may be considered dominant, yet tensions among competing and contradictory positions always exist, and out of such tensions change often occurs.

It is a commonplace that Joyce's work was hailed within the circles of avant-garde writers, artists, and publishers in Paris and Zurich, even as it was neglected or scorned in England, where Eliot's or Woolf's work was more easily integrated into the developing modernist canon. Early British responses to *Ulysses* included the characterization "underbred" (Virginia Woolf, *Diary* 199) and complaints that "he has remarkably little taste" and that he uses "obscene words" (Rebecca West 431).

Ulysses presented a challenge to the emerging orthodoxies of modernism and to changes in the field of English studies, which nevertheless proceeded to assimilate it—another example of the tensions within a reading formation. Key moments in the history of the reception of *Ulysses* are Eliot's influential "mythological" reading, first published in 1923; the exploration of the naturalistic or literal relation between *Ulysses* and Dublin, which took hold with Richard Kain's demonstration that Joyce frequently consulted *Thom's Dublin Directory* when writing *Ulysses* (*Fabulous Voyager* [1947]); the gradual move in the 1940s and 1950s by such critics as Kain, Harry Levin, and Stanley Sultan to the study of humanistic themes in the novel; Hugh Kenner's ironic readings of *Ulysses*; interpretations that focus on biography and the composition process, made possible with the publication of Joyce's letters (1957; 1968), Stanislaus Joyce's *My Brother's Keeper* (1958), Richard Ellmann's *James Joyce* (1959; rev. 1982), and A. Walton Litz's *The Art of James Joyce: Method and Design in* Ulysses *and* Finnegan's Wake (1961); and the proliferation of studies in the 1970s and 1980s on style and narrative techniques, which, of course, continue even with the advent of poststructuralist criticism. Looking back, we can see that all these approaches use assimilative strategies to make *Ulysses* readable—to naturalize and tame the work to fit acceptable concepts of literature. In time *Ulysses* came to be seen as an example of triumphant aesthetic wholeness—despite its apparent fragmentation. This view of the text dominated Joyce criticism, teaching, and scholarship from the 1950s until the 1970s, and many still regard it as the normative way of reading *Ulysses*.

These readings of *Ulysses* are not "objective" but rather are complexly linked to cultural, literary, and institutional forces, and they both open up and close off ways of apprehending the text. Its very status as a "classic"— its shift from a book for underground reading to a monument of high culture—has fundamentally (and in some instances unfortunately) changed how *Ulysses* will be read and received by readers today. The text's canonical reputation often intimidates students, who fail to enjoy much of the humor of the book, at least in part because they assume that a "classic" must be "serious." Reading early reviews of *Ulysses* may shock these students almost as much as *Ulysses* shocked early reviewers, yet glimpsing *Ulysses* from the perspective of a somewhat different reading formation may demonstrate to students that classics are not instantaneously produced by an author but are created over time by a variety of historical conditions. Similarly, the teacher of *Ulysses* today is in a position different from that of a teacher forty years ago. Then considered rebellious, even subversive, reading and teaching *Ulysses* are now generally seen as complicit with dominant academic culture.

Increasingly in the last twenty years or so, critics such as Colin MacCabe, Derek Attridge, and Umberto Eco have reversed both early disparaging dismissals and many favorable modernist readings and have opened the possibility of a postmodernist (or a poststructuralist) Joyce. Precisely those characteristics that had to be explained away or smoothed over to produce the triumphantly canonized *Ulysses* of modernism—including unreadability, scatology, parody, intertextuality, and pastiche—are now making the book seem a triumphantly "decentered" postmodernist text.

Recent feminist studies also call into question many aspects of the modernist views of *Ulysses*. Critics like Suzette Henke, Bonnie Kime Scott, and Elaine Unkeless problematize the masculinist and modernist tendency to interpret women characters in *Ulysses* as symbols or archetypes, especially when male characters are frequently particularized as "individuals." Many feminist critics situate Joyce's representations of female characters within the larger cultural context of the dominant attitudes about women that prevailed when Joyce was writing the novel.

These revisionist interpretations point up the historically situated nature of any reading. What were once thought to be universal significances are now seen as the product of particular reading practices that, far from being transcendent, are rooted in historically definable conditions and assumptions. Current theory argues, therefore, that canonization is not a process that discovers the intrinsic greatness of a book but rather one that attributes to it particular qualities—whether mythical allusions, symbolic structure, unity, polyvalence, self-referentiality—believed to constitute greatness. Such qualities can shift dramatically from one reading formation to another, but multiple and conflictual ones are always vying for dominance within any formation. The meaning, the status, indeed the very "literariness" of a literary text are thus not fixed but repeatedly negotiated within a reading formation whose concerns are both contemporary and in part determined by the history of the text's past reception. The colleges and universities where *Ulysses* is read, taught, and written about provide the primary arena for these activities of negotiation, assimilation, and contestation.

Such recognitions compel us as teachers to realize (and inform our students) that the questions we help them ask of *Ulysses* are historically and culturally situated. That these questions were not always asked of the text does not make them arbitrary or subjective: rather, particular questions are important at a given time for particular social and historical reasons. A book on the teaching of *Ulysses*, then, must suggest different ways of teaching the text as well as help teachers raise questions about the history and implications of those approaches. This volume will, we hope, encourage the teacher to ask not only such questions as What does the text mean? or What is the dominant symbol of this chapter? but Why does the text mean this to some readers today? or Why am I less (or more) interested in symbols than in discourse conventions or the status of women in the novel? and, further, What are the implications of my encouraging students to ask one set of questions over another?

To elicit comments from a wide variety of teachers on their practices of teaching *Ulysses*, the MLA sent questionnaires to randomly selected members of its Division on Twentieth-Century English Literature, and the volume editors sent questionnaires to randomly selected members of the James Joyce Society; questionnaires were also circulated at the 1989 James Joyce Conference in Philadelphia. We are indebted to those teachers who responded: their comments helped us to formulate part 1 of this volume, "Materials." Respondents also proposed most of the essay topics that appear in part 2, "Approaches."

We have tried to represent a range of approaches, some traditional, many innovative, that indicate the tensions and contradictions in Joyce studies today. In addition, the essays interact on the level of practical pedagogy. From the wealth of suggestions for teaching *Ulysses*, a teacher may pick the one or two that seem the most promising and follow them through. Indeed, a teacher may want to use different approaches as opportunities to teach *Ulysses* recur over the years.

KMcC and ERS

Part One

MATERIALS

Editions

The publication history of Joyce's *Ulysses* is long and tangled. Between March 1918 and August 1920, Joyce published versions of the first fourteen chapters (of a total of eighteen) in the *Little Review*, an American journal edited by Margaret Anderson and Jean Heap, and in the *Egoist*, a British journal edited by Margaret Weaver. The United States Post Office confiscated and burned four issues of the *Little Review* containing episodes of *Ulysses*, and in February 1921 the two editors were convicted of promulgating obscenity and were fined fifty dollars each.

When publishers, alarmed at the possibility of being tried for obscenity, hesitated to publish *Ulysses*, Sylvia Beach, owner of Shakespeare and Company, in Paris—where Joyce was living at the time—offered to publish the novel; and Joyce accepted. Because English printers were afraid of obscenity charges if they set the type, Beach gave the project to a French printer, in Dijon, who had done a book in French for her. The first two copies of *Ulysses* arrived in Paris the morning of 2 February 1922, Joyce's fortieth birthday.

In the United States between July and October 1927, Samuel Roth, without Joyce's permission, included a slightly expurgated version of the first fourteen chapters of *Ulysses* in his *Two Worlds Monthly*. The piracy ended with an injunction from the Supreme Court of the State of New York that enjoined Roth from using Joyce's name, and the litigants entered a consent decree that allowed Roth to escape without paying damages.

Finally, early in 1932 Bennett Cerf, at Random House, offered Joyce a contract for *Ulysses*, which the novelist signed in March. The inevitable trial for obscenity was held in the United States District Court in November 1933, and on 6 December, in a famous decision, Judge John M. Woolsey declared that the book should be admitted to the United States. Woolsey's decision was reprinted in Random House's 1934 and 1961 editions of *Ulysses*. (See Ellmann, *James Joyce* 497, 504–08, 523–26, 641–42, 666–67 for a detailed publication history.)

Since the first publication in 1922, there have been ten other editions. The most recent is Ulysses: *A Critical and Synoptic Edition*, edited by Hans Walter Gabler with Wolfhard Steppe and Claus Melchior, published in 1984 and revised in 1986. The bibliography lists all the previous editions (1855–56). Few editions appeared without controversy; and this last has raised the greatest furor among scholars and critics because it is allegedly a "recovered, ideal" text compiled from many of Joyce's drafts.

Such a recovery from the various drafts was deemed necessary because the typescript for the original edition of *Ulysses* has been lost, so that we do not have the actual final version of *Ulysses* as Joyce intended it. Possible corruptions crept into the first edition for various reasons. The many typists who worked on the manuscript found Joyce's handwriting hard to decipher and introduced many words and phrases he did not intend. Because Joyce's eyesight was bad, he did not necessarily notice the changes when he read the typescripts and, later, the galleys. Furthermore, Joyce did not read galleys against his copy text, and he often corrected typographical errors with something different from what he had originally written; in several instances he did not correct them at all. Particularly in the final chapters, he made many additions on the galleys in a spidery hand that was difficult to read—especially for French printers who knew little or no English.

For readers who are interested in the composition process of *Ulysses*, Phillip Herring's *Joyce's* Ulysses: *Notesheets in the British Museum* provides insights into the early stages of Joyce's thinking about the last seven episodes of the novel. Two other books are also helpful: *The Art of James Joyce: Method and Design in* Ulysses *and* Finnegans Wake, by A. Walton Litz; and Ulysses *in Progress*, by Michael Groden.

Ulysses: *The Corrected Text*, edited by Gabler with Steppe and Melchior, published by Random House in 1984 and revised in 1986, derives from the *Critical and Synoptic Edition*. Given the circumstances of the writing and first publication of the novel and the changes that crept in with some of the succeeding editions, it is not surprising that many of the Gabler "corrections" were challenged. The story of those objections has been widely told in the public press. See, for example, Edwin McDowell, "On the Eve of 'Blooms-day': Scholars Level Attack on Corrected *Ulysses*"; John Kidd, "The Scandal of *Ulysses*"; Charles Rossman, "The New *Ulysses*: The Hidden Controversy." Articles have also appeared in various scholarly journals. A symposium held by Joyce scholars in 1985 resulted in a volume entitled *Assessing the 1984* Ulysses, edited by Clive Hart and C. George Sandulescu. Philip Gaskell and Hart have reviewed the available manuscripts, typescripts, and proofs for *Ulysses* and, in Ulysses: *A Review of Three Texts*, provide lists of alterations for the 1922, 1961, and 1984 editions that they believe will produce a version of *Ulysses* closer to the one Joyce might have intended in 1922.

The controversy continues to simmer. Random House now publishes both the 1961 edition and the 1986 *Corrected Text*. The writers in this volume cite *The Corrected Text* not because they prefer that edition but because it was the only one available when they were writing the essays. A table for converting page numbers between the two editions can be found in the appendix.

Manuscripts and Prepublication Materials

The Garland Publishing Company has issued in sixty-three volumes *The James Joyce Archive* (Groden, gen. ed.), which consists of facsimiles of all

Joyce's notes, drafts, and manuscripts and all the available typescripts and proofs. Since the prepublication materials for *Ulysses* are widely scattered, having them available in one place is useful; but anyone doing careful work on the writing of *Ulysses* that involves those materials would do well to consult the materials themselves, since the Garland *Archive* contains reproductions in which penciled notations are not always clearly discernible from Joyce's handwriting. Indeed, one of the charges made against the 1984 *Ulysses* is that its editors sometimes relied on the reproductions in the Garland *Archive* instead of consulting the originals. Groden has also edited *James Joyce's Manuscripts: An Index to the James Joyce Archive.*

The availability, at various university libraries, of Joyce's manuscripts and of other prepublication materials, as well as of collections of books from Joyce's library, is cataloged by Thomas F. Staley in *An Annotated Critical Bibliography of James Joyce* (24–27). This selective bibliography is invaluable for those interested in any aspect of Joyce's life and work. The schemas for *Ulysses* that Joyce gave to Carlo Linati and to Stuart Gilbert are reprinted in Richard Ellmann's volume Ulysses *on the Liffey.*

Joyce's letters, not included in the Garland *Archive*, are available in separate volumes, the first edited by Stuart Gilbert and the second and third by Ellmann. Ellmann also edited *Selected Letters of James Joyce*, a selection from the three volumes plus ten letters not published before. Since Ezra Pound was an important influence in Joyce's life and commented extensively on Joyce's writing in correspondence, *Pound/Joyce: The Letters of Ezra Pound to James Joyce, with Pound's Essay on Joyce*, edited by Forrest Read, is also of interest.

Biographical Materials

When questioned about biographical reading for themselves and for their students, most teachers mentioned Ellmann's *James Joyce*, which they often characterized as "monumental." No student of Joyce can afford to ignore it. Indeed, the book is so well regarded that it probably accounts for the paucity of other serious attempts to write a biography of Joyce. The feeling is growing, however, that having other full biographies would be beneficial, since any biographer can provide only his or her understanding of a life.

In the meantime, other biographical materials are available. Joyce's longtime friend Frank Budgen offers biographical information and details about the writing of *Ulysses* in a book now available in a revised edition with additional recollections of Joyce, *James Joyce and the Making of* Ulysses *and Other Writings*, compiled by Hart. Before his death, Joyce oversaw the writing of a biography by Herbert Gorman, *James Joyce*. Although it contains much of import, Joyce's close connection makes it suspect. Joyce's brother, Stanislaus, published *My Brother's Keeper*, and Stanislaus's *Dublin Diary* for the years 1903–05 has been edited by George Healy. In *The Exile of James Joyce*, Hélène Cixous uses biographical data as a setting for her reading of Joyce's work. Brenda Maddox's *Nora*, a biography of Joyce's wife, views Joyce from a new vantage point.

Staley catalogs other "biographical studies and memoirs by contemporaries" that present useful information about Joyce and the times and places in which he lived (7–19). He also documents similarly important "background and milieu studies" (19–23), many of which contain photographs of interest to teachers and students of *Ulysses*. A short chronology of Joyce's life can be found in Patrick McCarthy's Ulysses: *Portals of Discovery*.

Textual Aids

Since *Ulysses* is replete with references and allusions—to turn-of-the-century Dublin, to Catholicism, to international events, to diverse works of philosophy, theology, and literature, and to other matters not often known to contemporary readers—the teachers were asked about the background materials that best enable them and their students to read and comprehend the novel. Two books are considered particularly helpful: Weldon Thornton's *Allusions in* Ulysses: *An Annotated List*; and the revised and expanded edition of Ulysses *Annotated*, by Don Gifford and Robert Seidman.

Many teachers also recommend Stuart Gilbert's *James Joyce's* Ulysses: *A Study*, a critical commentary and chapter-by-chapter analysis that emphasizes Homeric correspondences. This book both gains and suffers because it was written with Joyce's help. A number of teachers mention Harry Blamires's *The New Bloomsday Book: A Guide through* Ulysses, which gives a page-by-page reading and commentary. Other highly readable introductions to Joyce and *Ulysses* are David Hayman's Ulysses: *The Mechanics of Meaning*; Patrick McCarthy's Ulysses: *Portals of Discovery*; and *The Cambridge Companion to* Ulysses, edited by Derek Attridge.

Cultural and Aesthetic Contexts

For those interested in a study of Irish history relevant to understanding *Ulysses*, Mary E. Daly's *Dublin, the Deposed Capital* provides an excellent detailed social and economic history of that city from 1860 to 1914, and Cliona Murphy's *The Women's Suffrage Movement and Irish Society in the Early Twentieth Century* fills out a part of Irish history often neglected by more traditional accounts. Joseph Lee's *The Modernization of Irish Society, 1848–1914* provides a shorter, more general history. Among the best visual presentations of Joyce's Dublin is William York Tindall's *The Joyce Country,* which features eighty-three photographs of Dublin with appropriate references to Joyce's texts.

Although many critics in the past have contended that Joyce's works are apolitical, a number of recent books attempt to situate Joyce and his texts with respect to larger cultural and political forces. *Joyce's Politics,* by Dominic Manganiello, discusses the relation of Joyce's politics—in his life and literary texts—to Irish and European political thought. In *Joyce's Anatomy of Culture,* Cheryl Herr explores the linkages between Joyce's texts and Irish popular culture, especially the newspaper, the stage, and the sermon. Jennifer Wicke's *Advertising Fictions: Literature, Advertisements, and Social Reading* contains a substantive chapter on the connections between advertisements and the writing of *Ulysses.* For further discussions of Joyce's work with reference to Irish politics, traditions, and other Irish writers, see also Richard Brown's *James Joyce and Sexuality; James Joyce and His Contemporaries,* edited by Diana A. Ben-Merre and Maureen Murphy; Seamus Deane's *Celtic Revivals: Essays in Modern Irish Literature, 1880–1980;* and James M. Cahalan's *The Irish Novel: A Critical History.* The relation of Joyce's work to Catholicism is investigated in William T. Noon's *Joyce and Aquinas,* Kevin Sullivan's *Joyce among the Jesuits,* and J. Mitchell Morse's *The Sympathetic Alien: James Joyce and Catholicism.*

Joyce is a major figure in the period now labeled modernism, roughly from 1910 to the beginning of World War II. While there is considerable disagreement about that period, even about when it begins and ends, various critical anthologies can help teachers and students make up their own minds about such matters: Malcolm Bradbury and James McFarlane's *Modernism, 1890–1930;* Ellmann and Charles Feidelson, Jr.'s *The Modern Tradition: Backgrounds of Modern Literature;* Irving Howe's *Literary Modernism,* also published as *The Idea of the Modern in Literature and the Arts* (see esp. Howe's introductory essay, "The Idea of the Modern"); and Eugen Weber's *Paths to the Present: Aspects of European Thought from Romanticism to Existentialism.* See also Terry Eagleton's "Capitalism, Modernism and Postmodernism" in his *Against the Grain.*

Several other works explicitly discuss Joyce's place in literary modernism: *James Joyce and Modern Literature,* edited by W. J. McCormack and Alistair Stead (from a New Left position); Maurice Beebe's "*Ulysses* and the Age of Modernism"; *James Joyce and Modernism,* edited by Heyward Ehrlich; and Anthony Cronin's *A Question of Modernity.*

Critical Works

Joyce's works and *Ulysses* in particular have been widely examined by scholars and critics. This critical examination, which has come to be dominated by Americans, has changed dramatically over the years, and a number of collections of essays document or analyze these changes. The most complete collection of early commentaries on *Ulysses* is Robert H. Deming's *James Joyce: The Critical Heritage* (2 vols.), which excerpts responses to Joyce's work from 1902 to 1941. Seon Givens's *James Joyce: Two Decades of Criticism* compiles early full-length essays on Joyce's texts, including T. S. Eliot's "*Ulysses*, Order, and Myth" (also in Ellmann and Feidelson), as well as a significant number of American reactions to the novel. Bernard Benstock's *Critical Essays on James Joyce's* Ulysses offers a wider-ranging collection of historical essays—from early essays by Ezra Pound and others to contemporary theoretical pieces. The essays in Thomas F. Staley's Ulysses: *Fifty Years* each present a fifty-year perspective on a particular critical issue in the novel. Janet Dunleavy's *Re-viewing Classics of Joyce Criticism* looks at major critical studies of Joyce from 1929 to 1960.

Traditional studies of *Ulysses* tend to focus on such issues as the significance of symbols, myths, and other literary texts; the novel's relation to the real Dublin; its stylistic devices; and its humanist themes (see Attridge and Ferrer, introd.). These studies have substantially altered the way *Ulysses* is currently received: initially viewed by most as inscrutable, idiosyncratic, and pornographic, *Ulysses* has come to be seen as an apparently readable and ordered classic.

The critical work employed most often by the teachers polled was *James Joyce's* Ulysses: *Critical Essays*, edited by Hart and David Hayman, a collection of eighteen interesting, useful—and idiosyncratic—discussions, one for each chapter of *Ulysses*. Zack Bowen's essay "*Ulysses*," in *A Companion to Joyce Studies*, edited by Bowen and James Carens, provides a shorter chapter-by-chapter analysis. The same book has articles on Joyce's biography, his letters, his publishing problems, his critical writings, and his poetry, plays, and earlier and later fiction, as well as on the history of Joyce criticism and scholarship. Monographs on single chapters of *Ulysses* include Robert Janusko's *The Sources and Structures of James Joyce's "Oxen,"* Richard Madtes's The *"Ithaca" Chapter of Joyce's* Ulysses, James Van Dyck Card's *An Anatomy of "Penelope,"* and Kathleen McCormick's Ulysses, *"Wandering Rocks," and the Reader: Multiple Pleasures in Reading*.

Three books by Hugh Kenner were also cited frequently: *Dublin's Joyce, Joyce's Voices*, and Ulysses. In the first—a highly influential book—Kenner argues that all Joyce's works are fundamentally ironic. Although the second book opens with a discussion of some of Joyce's short stories, Kenner's main purpose is to explain how Joyce began *Ulysses* in naturalism and ended it in parody. In the third Kenner deals with such matters in *Ulysses* as rhetoric, style, the narrator, the Homeric parallels, and other issues that have continued to interest him and other students of Joyce. Kenner's books and articles read easily, always include useful insights, and are often provocative.

A pair of books by Ellmann, another respected scholar of the modernist period, also received repeated mention: Ulysses *on the Liffey* and *The Consciousness of Joyce*. In the first book, Ellmann examines *Ulysses* on four levels: literal, ethical, aesthetic, and anagogic. The second book traces Joyce's responses to his principal sources, especially Homer, Shakespeare, and the aesthetics and politics of Joyce's time. Ellmann's books and articles, like Kenner's, are accessible and profitable to read.

Other critical works that emphasize symbolic or mythical readings of *Ulysses*, relating it specifically to Homeric action, are William York Tindall's *Reader's Guide to James Joyce* and the more recent and sophisticated *Epic Geography: James Joyce's* Ulysses, by Michael Seidel. Books that emphasize the naturalistic detail of *Ulysses* include Robert Adams's *Surface and Symbol: The Consistency of James Joyce's* Ulysses and Richard Kain's *Fabulous Voyager: James Joyce's* Ulysses. Stanley Sultan's *The Argument of* Ulysses offers a close symbolic and thematic reading.

The style of *Ulysses*, particularly the narrative strategies, has been of major interest to critics throughout the history of the reception of the text. Among such studies are Melvin Friedman's *Stream of Consciousness: A Study in Literary Method*, which provides a historical study of the stream-of-consciousness technique in fiction and its development in *Ulysses*; Erwin Steinberg's *Stream of Consciousness and Beyond in* Ulysses, which examines the psychological stream of consciousness and how Joyce simulates it in *Ulysses*; Dermot Kelly's *Narrative Strategies in Joyce's* Ulysses, which relates the development of narrative strategies in *Ulysses* to character development; Herring's *Joyce's Uncertainty Principle*, which investigates the ambiguities of plot, language, character, and motivation in Joyce's texts; Sheldon Brivic's *Joyce the Creator*, which studies the way in which Joyce authoritatively designed himself into his texts; Michael Patrick Gillespie's *Reading the Book of Himself: Narrative Strategies in the Works of James Joyce*, which explores the effects of narrative style on the reader's response; and Vicki Mahaffey's *Reauthorizing Joyce*, which critiques the diverse and contradictory representations of authority in Joyce's texts from a poststructuralist perspective, with a particular focus on the relation between language and authority.

Joyce's works, and *Ulysses* in particular, have attracted the attention of innovative literary theorists. Teachers often use Bonnie Kime Scott's *Joyce and Feminism*, which analyzes the feminist intellectual milieu of Joyce's time, Joyce's familial and professional relationships with women, and his female characters. Of similar interest are *Women in Joyce*, a collection of essays edited by Suzette Henke and Elaine Unkeless; Scott's *James Joyce*;

and the feminist essays in *New Alliances in Joyce Studies*, edited by Scott, and in *James Joyce: The Augmented Ninth*, edited by Bernard Benstock.

Teachers also recommended Karen Lawrence's *The Odyssey of Style in Ulysses*, which blends reader-response theory, psychoanalysis, and narrative theory to interpret the effects on the reader of the narrative developments in the novel. Other studies on the role of the reader are Wolfgang Iser's *The Implied Reader*, which develops a theory of reader response and contains two chapters on *Ulysses*; Brook Thomas's *James Joyce's* Ulysses: *A Book of Many Happy Returns*, which extends Iser's theories; Marilyn French's *The Book as World*, which studies the effect of changes in style on the mind of the reader; and the *James Joyce Quarterly's Structuralist/Reader Response Issue*.

Psychoanalytic studies include Brivic's *Joyce between Freud and Jung*, a discussion of the mind of Joyce as it is reflected in his work; Mark Shechner's *Joyce in Nighttown: A Psychoanalytic Inquiry into* Ulysses, an extensive Freudian analysis of the characters in *Ulysses* with reference to Joyce's life; and Christine Van Boheemen's *The Novel as Family Romance*, a psychoanalytic genre study with two chapters on *Ulysses*.

Colin MacCabe's *James Joyce and the Revolution of the Word* approaches the language of Joyce's texts and its effect on the reader from a Marxist, semiotic, and psychoanalytic perspective. Patrick McGee's *Paperspace: Style as Ideology in Joyce's* Ulysses combines deconstructive, psychoanalytic, Marxist, and feminist thought to reread the style and characterizations of *Ulysses* from a postmodern perspective. Anthologies of essays written explicitly from diverse contemporary theoretical orientations include Attridge and Daniel Ferrer's *Post-structuralist Joyce*, Bernard Benstock's *The Seventh of Joyce*, MacCabe's *James Joyce: New Perspectives*, and Morris Beja and Shari Benstock's *Coping with Joyce: Essays from the Copenhagen Symposium*.

Audiovisual Aids

William S. Brockman

Joyce's life and works, especially *Ulysses*, have inspired dozens of sound recordings, films, and video recordings. Many, distributed on a limited basis, are now difficult to obtain. The twenty-eight described here meet two criteria: they offer particular insight into *Ulysses*, and they are available from libraries or commercial distributors.

The sound recordings consist of critical examinations and dramatized readings of *Ulysses*. Joseph Campbell's *Imagery of Vision* depicts Bloom as the Wandering Jew, points out correspondences of detail within the novel, and demonstrates multiple examples of the influence of language on style, particularly in "Oxen of the Sun" and "Circe." Hugh Kenner's pithy *Sound Portrait* uses dramatic readings from *Ulysses* to illustrate matters of style, consciousness, and character. The recorded lectures by Thomas Staley, Bernard Benstock, and Hugh Staples attempt to establish introductory critical attitudes toward the novel. Readings and dramatizations of parts of *Ulysses* include those by Siobhan McKenna, E. G. Marshall, and Milo O'Shea as well as Joyce. Joyce's own striking performances, recorded in the 1920s, include MacHugh's recitation of John F. Taylor's speech from "Aeolus" in *Ulysses* and the ending section of "Anna Livia Plurabelle" from *Finnegans Wake*. The Radio Telefís Eireann production of *Ulysses* records a live performance of the entire novel on Bloomsday, 1982, in Dublin. Performances of the musical pieces that are integral to *Ulysses* can be found in Zack Bowen's dramatic readings of five episodes, in John McCormack's recordings of songs from the period, in Maura O'Connell's rendition of "Love's Old Sweet Song," and in the songs and operatic arias of *The Joyce of Music*.

Visual materials are especially useful to students and scholars alike for the documentary material they make readily available. *Faithful Departed* shows photographs of turn-of-the-century Dublin taken by Robert French. *Is There One Who Understands Me?*, closely following the Ellmann biography, contains a particularly rich collection of scenes from Dublin, Trieste, Zurich, and Paris; interviews with Maria Jolas, Sylvia Beach, and others who knew Joyce; and rare material such as the home movies made of Joyce in the 1930s. *James Joyce's* Ulysses combines biography with staged excerpts from the novel. In *James Joyce's Women*, Fionnula Flanagan plays Nora, Sylvia Beach, Harriet Shaw Weaver, Gerty MacDowell, Molly Bloom in "Penelope," and a washerwoman in "Anna Livia Plurabelle," creating characters who take on lives of their own. *Joseph Campbell on James Joyce: Wings of Art* explores the roles of myth and symbol in Joyce's major works. Bruce Arnold's *The Scandal of* Ulysses interviews Hans Walter Gabler, John Kidd, and other contestants in the battle over the 1984 edition of *Ulysses*. In *Silence, Exile and Cunning* Anthony Burgess tours Dublin (including 7 Eccles Street, on the verge of being razed) and admires Joyce's transmutation of "the ordinary stuff of life" into something eternal. Joseph Strick's motion picture of *Ulysses* severely condenses the novel yet makes imaginative uses of voice-over, rapid cuts, and other cinematic techniques. *Walking into Eternity* introduces places in and around Dublin that feature in *Ulysses*.

Sound Recordings

Count John McCormack, the Gentle Minstrel. 6 LPs. GEMM 185 includes the 1927 recording of "Love's Old Sweet Song." Pearl, GEMM 183–GEMM 188, 1980.

The Imagery of Vision in the Novels of James Joyce. 4 3¾" reels or 6 audiocassettes. Lecturer, Joseph Campbell. Pacifica Tape Library, 1969. Distr. Big Sur, 3397, 3092, 3093, 3094.

Introduction to James Joyce. Audiocassette. Lecturer, Thomas Staley. Everett / Edwards, Cassette Curriculum, 3910, 1976.

Introduction to Joyce's Ulysses. Audiocassette. Lecturer, Bernard Benstock. Everett / Edwards, Cassette Curriculum, 3903, 1976.

James Joyce Reads James Joyce [formerly *James Joyce Reading from* Ulysses *and* Finnegans Wake; *Cyril Cusak Reading* Pomes Penyeach, Chamber Music, *"Ecce Puer"*]. Audiocassette or LP. Original recordings of Joyce from 1924 and 1929. Caedmon, CPN 1340, formerly CDL 51340 (cassette); TC 1340 (LP).

James Joyce Soundbook. 4 audiocassettes or 4 LPs. Collects four previously issued recordings, including Cyril Cusak reading from *Portrait*, poems, and *Finnegans Wake*; soliloquies of Leopold and Molly by E. G. Marshall and Siobhan McKenna; and Joyce's own readings. Caedmon, CDL 51340, 51110, 51063, 51086; together SBR-112 (LP), SBC-112 (cassette).

The Joyce of Music. Audiocassette and booklet. New Hutchinson Family Singers. Notes by James Hurt. U of Illinois P, 1983.

"Love's Old Sweet Song." *Just in Time.* LP or audiocassette. Sung by Maura O'Connell. Philo, PH-1124, 1988. Distr. by Rounder Records.

A Sound Portrait of James Joyce. Audiocassette. Prod. Natl. Public Radio with Radio Telefís Eireann. Writ. Hugh Kenner. NPR, QP-801009.02/13-C, 1980.

Stately, Plump Buck Mulligan: Ulysses, *Chapter One.* Audiocassette or LP. Read by Milo O'Shea. Caedmon, TC 1460 (LP); SWC 1460, formerly CDL 51460 (cassette), 1956.

Ulysses. Audiocassette. Lecturer, Hugh Staples. Everett/Edwards, Cassette Curriculum, 2915, 2916, 1974.

Ulysses. 20 audiocassettes. Dir. William Styles. Prod. Micheál O hAodha. Radio Telefís Eireann, 1982.

Ulysses: *"Calypso."* LP. A dramatic reading. Perf. students and faculty members of State Univ. Coll. New York, Fredonia. Prod. and dir. Zack R. Bowen. Folkways, FL 9835, 1963. Distr. on audiocassette by Smithsonian/ Folkways.

Ulysses: *"Hades."* LP. A dramatic reading. Prod. Zack R. Bowen. Dir. Bowen and J. Tyler Dunn. Folkways, FL 9814, 1964. Distr. on audiocassette by Smithsonian/Folkways.

Ulysses: *"Lestrygonians."* 2 LPs. A dramatic reading with original music. Perf. students and faculty members of State Univ. Coll. of New York, Fredonia. Prod. and dir. Zack R. Bowen. Folkways, FL 9562, 1961. Distr. on audiocassette by Smithsonian/Folkways.

Ulysses: *"Lotus-eaters."* LP. A dramatic reading. Perf. students and faculty members of State Univ. Coll. of New York, Fredonia. Prod. and dir.

Zack R. Bowen. Folkways, FL 9836, 1963. Distr. on audiocassette by Smithsonian/Folkways.

Ulysses: "Sirens." 2 LPs. A dramatic reading. Prod. Zack R. Bowen. Dir. Bowen and Oscar Brownstein. Folkways, FL 9563, 1965. Distr. on audio-cassette by Smithsonian/Folkways.

Ulysses, *Soliloquies of Molly and Leopold Bloom*. Audiocassette or LP. Read by Siobhan McKenna and E. G. Marshall. Caedmon, TC 1063 (LP); SWC 1063, formerly CDL 51063 (cassette), 1956.

Films and Video Recordings

Faithful Departed. 16mm film or VHS or Beta videocassette. Dir. Kieran Hickey. Writ. and prod. Des Hickey. Prod. BAC Films, 1970. Distr. Intl. Film Bureau. 10 min.

Is There One Who Understands Me? The World of James Joyce. VHS, Beta, or U-Matic videocassette. Prod. and dir. Seán O Mórdha. Prod. Radio Telefís Eireann, 1982. Distr. Films for the Humanities and Sciences, FFH 897. 120 min.

James Joyce's Ulysses. The Modern World: Ten Great Writers series. VHS videocassette. Prod. and dir. Nigel Wattis. Prod. London Weekend Television with RM Arts and Radio Telefís Eireann, 1987. Distr. Films Inc. 58 min.

James Joyce's Women. Beta or VHS videocassette. Dir., prod., writ., and adapt. Fionnula Flanagan. Prod. Rejoycing Co., 1985. Distr. MCA Home Video, BTA 80206 (Beta); VHS 80206 (VHS). 91 min.

Joseph Campbell on James Joyce: Wings of Art. 6 VHS videocassettes. Dir. Roy A. Cox. Prod. Mythology Ltd. and William Free Productions, 1969. Broadcast on PBS Adult Learning Satellite Service. Distr. Brightline. 6 1-hr. segments.

The Scandal of Ulysses. VHS videocassette. Dir. Ian Graham. Prod. Bruce Arnold. Prod. Roundtable Productions with Radio Telefís Eireann, 1990. Distr. Roundtable Productions. 60 min.

Silence, Exile and Cunning. Monitor series. 16mm film. Writ. and narr. Anthony Burgess. Dir. Christopher Burstall. Prod. BBC-TV, 1965. Distr. Time-Life Films. 43 min.

Ulysses. VHS videocassette. Dir. and prod. Joseph Strick. Writ. Strick and Fred Haines. Laser Film Corp. 1967. Distr. Mystic Fire Video, M1181. 120 min. Soundtrack, 2 audiocassettes. Caedmon, SWC 328, 1968.

Walking into Eternity: James Joyce's Ulysses: A Dublin Guide. VHS video-cassette. Prod. and dir. Seán O Mórdha. Ryan McCarthy Productions, 1988. 28 min.

Part Two

APPROACHES

Introduction

Because of its length and difficulty, *Ulysses* cannot be easily assigned in a course without a significant time commitment by teachers and students. Only a third of the teachers who responded to our questionnaire said that they teach *Ulysses* in a large survey course open to freshmen and sophomores. Two-thirds teach *Ulysses* to English majors in a seminar—generally a course on Joyce, modernism, or Irish literature. Regardless of the setting, however, teachers usually spend a substantial amount of time on *Ulysses*. Almost fifty percent of our sample reported that they spend from fifteen to twenty-one hours in class teaching the novel; over thirty-five percent spend twenty-two to twenty-five course hours; but less than fifteen percent spend only nine to thirteen hours. The time one can devote to *Ulysses* affects the issues one raises about it. This volume, therefore, includes a representative sampling of essays from teachers working in a variety of classroom situations, but most of the approaches can be adapted to various types of courses.

While over half the teachers reported that they spend approximately fifty percent of class time on close textual analysis, many requested an Approaches volume that would apply the insights of contemporary critical theory specifically to the teaching of *Ulysses*. Others asked for essays that would address ways of encouraging students to become more involved in classroom discussion and to enjoy their reading of *Ulysses* more fully. Still others wanted short background essays on a variety of subjects, from aesthetics to politics. We were fortunate that a number of respondents proposed writing just such essays.

The essays that follow are divided into three sections: "Backgrounds," on the literary, political, and historical contexts of the writing and reception of *Ulysses*; "Theoretical Approaches in Practice"; and "Successful Classroom Strategies and Techniques."

In this volume, "background" refers not to something objective that the text merely reflects but to a complex dialectical relation of production and reception. It is now commonplace to recognize that we have no direct access to the past, which is always mediated through the present. Further, even if we could directly access the past, the literary text would not stand outside history, telling us something about it or about life in general, but rather would be a part of that history, helping to produce it. Literary texts do not just "reflect" social conditions or ideology but *produce* ideology as an acting company produces a play (Eagleton, *Criticism* 65–78), both "staging" and contributing to the major ideological conflicts of their times. The study of *Ulysses* needs to be grounded in a study of the historical circumstances of turn-of-the-century Dublin and pre- and postwar Europe; but in order to consider this "historical background," what traditionally were seen as "influences" now need to be regarded as a complex web of overdetermined forces, which *Ulysses* does not so much reflect as rework. The construction of these forces at particular historical moments is the product of the changing questions asked by historians and critics.

Another part of the background of a text is the history of its reception. A text is not a fixed and timeless entity but something whose meanings may change according to cultural circumstances. This is not to say that we can interpret texts in a haphazard, subjective fashion; rather, real, material circumstances exist that determine how a text functions in different historical periods, and critical reading involves the investigation of these circumstances.

The "Backgrounds" section includes three complementary essays. Hugh Kenner sets *Ulysses* in the context of Joyce's total work and sets Joyce's total work in the context of modernism by pointing at what Kenner sees as modernism's two primary characteristics—ambiguity and extreme specificity—and by relating Joyce to other major modernists. A rumination, this essay invites the reader to see *Ulysses* variously as a collection of printed pages, as a work of fiction, as a novel among other novels, as a modernist text, as a work by Joyce. Experienced readers will recognize it as one reader's attempt to "place" the novel. In a lower-level course teachers can use Kenner's ideas to introduce the concept of contextualization. In an upper-level course the essay can serve to show students how they might ruminate, might write personal essays placing the novel in the world of books, of interpersonal relations, of politics, of religion.

Cheryll Herr and Chris Connell contextualize the production of *Ulysses*, Jeffrey Segall its reception. Arguing that all aspects of the text—from characterization to narrative style to theme—are profoundly shaped by the political contexts of Joyce's Ireland, Herr and Connell explore *Ulysses* as itself a production of Dublin's responses to British colonialism. Of major significance in the production and reception of *Ulysses* was the modernist movement. Segall investigates the effects of cultural and political values on the early reception of *Ulysses* in the United States, Britain, and the Soviet Union. This triad of essays in "Backgrounds" is important because there is no single source to which teachers can turn for such analyses of both the production and reception of *Ulysses*.

Because of the current significance of literary theory and because of the emphasis placed on theoretical issues by the teachers who completed our questionnaires, the next section, "Theoretical Approaches in Practice," presents essays written from a self-consciously theoretical perspective. Since instructors may be less familiar with Roland Barthes or Jacques Lacan than they are with Joyce, these essays offer specific examples of ways of reading *Ulysses* and explain not just how particular theoretical concepts are taught but how theory actually informs pedagogical practices. As much as possible the contributors emphasize what and how they teach and how they learn in the process of discussing *Ulysses* with their students.

All our contributors are committed to a student-centered approach even though they recognize that to pose problems they may sometimes need to do some lecturing. The essays offer many guidelines for developing diverse teaching strategies that promote analytical and critical discussion.

Bonnie Kime Scott offers five feminist approaches to teaching various episodes of *Ulysses* in a general-education course, Great English Writers, and includes sample student assignments that are compatible with nonauthoritarian, feminist pedagogy. Other essays, notably those of Richard Pearce, Kathleen McCormick, and Vicki Mahaffey, provide further examples of feminist analyses.

Sheldon Brivic introduces various psychoanalytic concepts, particularly the notion of the "other," explaining how they can be used not only to analyze aspects of *Ulysses*, such as the relationship between Bloom and Stephen, but also to help students in a Joyce seminar confront *Ulysses* and their own responses to it.

A major issue in the teaching of *Ulysses* is studying the text in history. Mary Lowe-Evans's new-historicist approach opens *Ulysses* to ideological and historical analysis in a modern prose fiction course by exposing students both to new-historicist theories and to texts contemporaneous with *Ulysses*. In a complementary essay, Joseph Heininger discusses teaching *Ulysses* in a Joyce seminar, in which he focuses on avenues of popular culture and combines traditional approaches to literary and social history with various applications of cultural studies methods. McCormick extends Lowe-Evans's and Heininger's emphasis on the conditions under which *Ulysses* was written, but she further argues that since the text is being continually reproduced by later cultural formations, students need as well to analyze the history of the changing reception of *Ulysses* and the cultural circumstances that have given rise to different interpretations.

The next three essays explore the problems of teaching first-time undergraduate readers of *Ulysses* how to deal with narrative ambiguity. Pearce suggests, from his experience teaching a course in modern fiction, that students be taught to confront directly, rather than to domesticate or naturalize, the disruptions, contradictions, absences, or "holes" in the text. Scott Klein relates students' reading experiences to the interpretive issues of the characters. He suggests ways of helping students to focus on the novel's treatment of epic themes in order to lead them to read *Ulysses* as a narrative that enacts a falling away of textual authority for readers and characters alike. In the third essay, Erwin R. Steinberg explains how he encourages students in his course in modernism to acknowledge both the diverse narrative voices in *Ulysses* and the various and potentially contradictory hypotheses critics have developed to explain those voices.

With a novel as difficult as *Ulysses*, many teachers reported that they assign various "guides," such as Stuart Gilbert's *James Joyce's* Ulysses or Harry Blamires's *The New Bloomsday Book*, and place on reserve Don

Gifford and Robert J. Seidman's *Notes* and Weldon Thornton's *Allusions*. Many wondered, however, about the extent to which these guides, while providing useful information, may interfere with or interrupt students' reading experiences. Thornton addresses this issue in the final essay in this section. In contrast to a number of the above approaches, Thornton argues for the importance of immersing first-time readers in the text of *Ulysses* itself and suggests that secondary materials be used in moderation in the undergraduate classroom.

The third section, "Successful Classroom Strategies and Techniques," reinforces notions of interactive teaching. These essays emphasize that the students who read *Ulysses* should be taken as seriously as the text itself or as the instructor's theoretical inclination. The authors focus on making the classroom a place for discussion not only between teacher and students but also among students, who often have much to teach one another.

Following Joyce's schema, Morris Beja provides a short orientation to *Ulysses*, which he distributes to students instead of requiring them to read any of the guides. Mahaffey discusses strategies for helping students to see the humor of *Ulysses*, maintain motivation, and confront and analyze the racism and sexism in the book. Austin Briggs presents techniques for encouraging students to recognize their own "expert" knowledge and to draw on personal experience. He considers the advantages of having students read aloud in class and presents questions for discussion and papers. James J. Murphy discusses how his students come to see reading *Ulysses* as a communal activity by writing essays on individual chapters of the book, which they share with the entire class. He presents suggested topics and bibliographies for these essays and offers several examples.

Some readers may feel we should have invited papers on other aspects of Joyce criticism. However, although such readers may not find entire papers devoted to their interests, we think they will find those issues addressed substantially in the volume. No paper, for example, is devoted exclusively to Joyce's use of language—a matter of admiration and even awe for generations of scholars and critics, and to some, perhaps, a matter of consternation—but Klein, Mahaffey, and Steinberg, among others, discuss the subject. So, too, with topics like Joyce's aesthetics or the relation of *Ulysses* to Joyce's other work.

BACKGROUNDS

Joyce and Modernism
Hugh Kenner

How the big book we're facing came to get written down, moreover with undeniable narrative skill, is a question creators of fiction used not to urge us to confront. For we were to be drawn beyond the printed words into sheer illusion; yet the arranged existence of those words that drew us in remained to be accounted for. First-person narrative is especially tricky; pseudoautobiographies exist in such quantity as to imply surprising numbers of people, especially in the past two centuries, who somehow grew up to be *writers*. They include one-time writers, too, not just "novelists" engaged in a profession; for the premise of the first-person novel is a narrator with but the one story to tell, just as you could narrate your own life, or I mine. (So, since this is the writer's one book, explain how it is written so skillfully? Is "skill" perhaps to go unnoticed, to be understood as but second nature?)

Fiction does normally imply that but one story matters: this one: for instance, the one David Copperfield has to tell. It begins, "I AM BORN," and what David can report about the time and place of that event is subject to an "as I have been informed." That Dickensian drollery strikes close to what we're canvasing, how implausible it is that these written pages even exist. David fills out Chapter 1 with pages of dialogue he can't possibly have heard while still in the womb. In Chapter 2 he's recording his very earliest memories, including the night he and Peggoty were sitting by the parlor fire: "I had been reading to Nurse Peggoty about crocodiles." It's remarked, by the way, that *crocodiles* is a word beyond Nurse Peggoty's compass; she imagines a kind of vegetable and says "Crorkindills"(1, 11–16).

So how did "I" learn to read? That's not gone into, no more than how "I" have come not only to scrawl my name but to write fluent prose. (David did learn the alphabet, he does tell us later, at his mother's knee; but that doesn't explain nearly enough.) And it's notable how, ever since *Goody Two-Shoes*— a pioneer children's book and a piece of propaganda for literacy—fiction's child protagonists, well, they simply read, and they do so as easily as they walk. Thus Goody gets hold of books and is soon reading them, as though access to a book were all that mattered. Her vocation, before the tale's over, will be the teaching of reading. Curiouser and curiouser: Dr. Frankenstein's monstrous creation—a prototype graduate student, so to speak—learns English by turning the pages of *Paradise Lost*.

Yes, the explanations are unsatisfactory once attended to, and fictionists have used other devices. Lemuel Gulliver, Master Mariner, spent three years at Emmanuel College, Cambridge, and later read "the best authors" while at sea. So it's plausible that he might cover many sheets with dreary circumstantial Emmanuelese. A testy Cousin Sympson next edited the mess toward readability. He then destroyed the original, so no use our asking to inspect it. As for the script from which the printer worked, it was dropped, by arrangement with Mr. A. Pope, at the publisher's house, "in the dark, from a hackney coach," after Jonathan Swift had left England. That would gravely complicate any skeptic's effort to connect the physical evidence with Dr. Swift, whatever gossip might be alleging (xi, xiv, 3, 4).

And Abraham (Bram) Stoker achieved a ne plus ultra in 1897, when he arranged that the sole authority for *Dracula*—after, as the novel narrates, all the first-person records, the diaries, the letters, the dictaphone cylinders even, had gone up in flames—should be a pile of perfectly inscrutable typescript. Is it relevant, or not, that, like Dr. Swift, Bram Stoker (1847–1912) was a Dubliner?

Or like James Joyce? For two themes are intertwined here. One is a strange avoidance, by fictionists, of what would seem primary facts: that a written, then a printed, text somehow came into existence and that we're "reading" it. The other is what can only be described as an Irish ambivalence about writing and reading. A Dubliner named Pat Norton, so little averse to literacy that he made his living setting type, once stepped into another room, out of sight, to scan a page I had brought him. We'll be coming back to amiable Pat Norton.

"Modernism"—say 1904–90, to date it from Joyce's beginnings to the last pages of Beckett—may be described along one of its cross-sections as a coming-to-terms of printed language with print, thus with our consequent problems as readers. "Obscurity" wasn't modernism's perversity, it was virtually modernism's theme. Why anything, for instance, a voiceless page of the *Times*, is less impenetrable than it is: that is something truly obscure. Modernism has been succeeded by postmodernism and deconstruction and the cult of "text," bogeys that need not concern us just at present. And its coming is heralded when the narrator of "The Sisters," the first version of which Joyce published in the 13 August 1904 *Irish Homestead*, remembers himself as a boy, pondering the mysterious word *"paralysis" (Dubliners* 9), the way Peggoty, who was after all tired, didn't really ponder the still more mysterious word *"crocodiles."*

Paralysis, by the way, is a stranger word than the boy can imagine. The *lysis* is Greek for "loosening," as of muscle control; but *para?* The root means "beside," the way parallel lines lie alongside one another or a parody sits beside another poem. The *Oxford English Dictionary* adduces Greek *paralu-ein* and hopes to content us by muttering "to loose from beside, disable, enfeeble." The *Greek-English Lexicon* coedited (with Robert Scott) by Alice-in-Wonderland Liddell's father, Henry George, says the Greek connotes "a loosening by the side, or secretly"; hence "a breaking open illicitly," which leads to "disabling the nerves in the limbs of one side." That does still have a certain conjecturing feel. Walter W. Skeat's *Etymological Dictionary*, which commenced publication in the year of James Joyce's birth, occupied Stephen Hero "by the hour" (*Hero* 26, 30). Yes, words, a century ago, were newly mysterious, and so were attempts to explain them. Humpty-Dumpty (modeled on Dr. Liddell) had already said as much.

Less arcane, but still less penetrable, is the conversation "The Sisters" next adduces:

> —No, I wouldn't say he was exactly . . . but there was something queer . . . there was something uncanny about him. I'll tell you my opinion. . . .
> —I have my own theory about it, he said. I think it was one of those . . . peculiar cases. . . . But it's hard to say. . . .   (*Dubliners* 9–10)

By this time the reader is no less in the dark than the nameless boy. Suffice it further to say that readers for some ninety years have been screwing tight their attention to make out exactly what it was that mattered so much about the broken chalice, about why Father Flynn could be called "a disappointed man," about what had gone through his mind just before he was found "sitting up by himself in the dark in his confession-box, wide awake and laughing-like softly to himself" (18).

The next story is about a disturbingly sinister man, of whose ravings our boy can make nothing, though access to the word *sadistic* does perhaps help modern readers. But that word, not present in the story, is first recorded as late as 1892, moreover in a translation of Richard von Krafft-Ebing's *Psychopathia Sexualis*, not meant for general consumption. So Joyce, when he wrote "An Encounter" in 1905, seems to have envisaged a readership most of which would have access to no terms in which to think about it.

How far we are, already, from Dickens and Jane Austen! If it's an overstatement to say that the point of each *Dubliners* story is our inability to be sure what's been going on, still that does highlight many of the endings: the small gold coin, for instance, at the end of "Two Gallants"; the disorientation of Joe at the end of "Clay." And what of sailor "Frank" in "Eveline"? Has he really come to Dublin for a bride whom he plans to spirit away to Buenos Aires? Would you believe that, outside of pulp fiction? What, for that matter, of the sentence, late in the story, when Eveline catches a glimpse of "the black mass of the boat" (40)? What tells us that *Black Mass* is not a relevant phrase, tells us, too, so rapidly that we're not even conscious of discarding such an option? Was it perhaps by a parallel mechanism that Eveline overlooked the implausibility of Buenos Aires?

"People seemed [to Stephen Hero] strangely unconscious of the value of the words they used so glibly!" (*Hero* 26). Such a word, for instance, is *grace*, something gratis, freely given, as by God. And in the story called "Grace," which is about fumbling efforts to bring grace to Tom Kernan, we find the word used as follows:

> Mr Kernan was a commercial traveller of the old school which believed in the dignity of its calling. He had never been seen in the city without a silk hat of some decency and a pair of gaiters. By grace of these two articles of clothing, he said, a man could always pass muster.
>
> (*Dubliners* 153–54)

Here "dignity," "calling," "decency," "gaiters," "grace," "articles" all open onto theological possibilities. But, "By grace of these two articles of clothing . . ."—somehow the theological gate clangs shut. Mrs. Kernan, by the way, likes to recall her wedding day, when she left the church "leaning on the arm of a jovial well-fed man who was dressed smartly in a frock-coat and lavender trousers and carried a silk hat gracefully balanced upon his other arm." Yes: "gracefully"! And "jovial" connects her bridegroom, that day of all days, to Jove, a pagan god never acknowledged at "the Star of the Sea Church in Sandymount" (156).

If the modernists introduced the discipline of writing English as though it were a foreign language, they expected readers to exert a like attention. Drafts of three *Dubliners* stories appeared in the *Irish Homestead*, where stories were meant to be glanced at between the advertisements for cream separators and milk pumps. Unsurprisingly, the contracted-for series of ten got discontinued, after letters of complaint. T. S. Eliot long afterward remarked of the early hostility to Wordsworth, that it arose from readers who found the poems difficult but called them silly (*Use of Poetry* 150). Complainers against "The Sisters" or "Eveline" would have found them difficult but called them unsettling. It was both Joyce's liability and his enablement that, unlike his great compatriot Yeats, unlike his contemporaries Eliot and Pound, he was not, till after he was forty, protected by any presupposition of "art." Short stories have since come to exemplify an art form, but the ones in *Dubliners* could be mistaken for attempts at by far the most prevalent literary genre in those years. Not a periodical but sported its weekly story; reflect that the *Homestead* was an agricultural journal. And *A Portrait of the Artist as a Young Man*: what was that but a bungled attempt at a book about a boy growing up, in the manner of *David Copperfield*, of *Nicholas Nickleby*, of *Oliver Twist*? In 1916 one publisher's reader thought it had been dashed off. It needed "time and trouble spent on it"; needed "pruning," "pulling into shape." (Joyce had spent a mere ten years shaping it.) (See Ellmann, *James Joyce* 402–03.)

And on the first page of *Portrait* we may be persuaded we behold modernism being invented.

> Once upon a time and a very good time it was there was a moocow coming down along the road and this moocow that was coming down along the road met a nicens little boy named baby tuckoo. . . .

To punctuate that sentence is to destroy it. While its rhythm sustains it, it's artful too in recapturing the awareness of a child still innocent of punctuation. And "moocow," "nicens," "tuckoo": for such a child's ear those are no more neologisms than are "coming down" and "along the road" and (for that matter) "Once upon a time": as mysterious a phrase as our idiom affords.

Still, "Once upon a time" is the right way for such a story to begin, though Dickens wouldn't have seen how to work it in; *David Copperfield* commences, "Whether I shall turn out to be the hero of my own life, or whether that station will be held by anybody else . . . ." "Station," forsooth; and the sentence wants to ring like a sixpenny Cicero. Which is not to denigrate Dickens, only to remark that he furnished what his readers and he were used to. The truth that fiction is a gestalt of words on a page was one we've seen his contemporaries evading.

But Irish Pat Norton, whom I mentioned several pages back, would have taken the opening of *Portrait* into another room for maybe an hour. Not that Joyce's Irish readers did in fact prove more perspicuous than others, though Joyce clearly trusted they would. The more scrupulous ones, though, still think print merits close attention. And Joyce did come to view his calling not as "telling a story" but as issuing instructions to printers. Put this, for instance, in italics:

> *O, the wild rose blossoms*
> *On the little green place.*
> (7)

Make it exist, so, in a different dimension, that of song. And hope, too, for the fit audience though few who will know that someone (mother?) is euphemizing. That last word shouldn't be "place"; no she's avoiding "grave."

And so that opening continues, all of 313 words, followed by three arrayed asterisks. And No Explanations. Joyce's first "novel" (perhaps his only novel, if you conceive of *Ulysses* as something else) is nowhere more radical than in eliminating the guide and prop of every novel-reader, the comforting narrative voice. Through the length of book after book the Narrator had been your companion, telling you the tale, supplying helpful information, making sure that you always knew where you were and when and that you were never confused. But, depending on our susceptibility to clues, it can be quite a few pages before we grasp so simple a datum as that *Portrait*'s events are set in Ireland.

The lack of a narrating guide increases the emphasis *Dubliners* places on interpretation: on the fact that reading is always an assembling of clues. How we do that is perhaps the most mysterious skill we literates possess. We've seen Joyce, age twenty-two, demonstrating (should we chance to notice) that *Black Mass* is not operative in the phrase "black mass of the boat." In *Ulysses*, commenced about 1914, this principle is extended wholesale; we can't even feel quite sure, it's been pointed out, if the first word, "Stately," is adjective or perhaps adverb. It's certain that the last word, "Yes," runs through "Stately" backward, though to notice that, we have to let "Stately" dissolve into one of the things it is, a string of letters. And—something of which Homer was innocent—"words" are blocks delimited by spaces. So we can count them. The word count of the first sentence of *Ulysses* runs to twenty-two; of the third sentence, to eleven. Eleven is the book's magic number throughout; at one point we may even find ourselves counting paragraphs, to ascertain that episode 14, which is set in a maternity hospital, sandwiches forty paragraphs (for the forty weeks of human gestation) between two blocks of eleven paragraphs each.

Not that anyone need feel constrained to count. These novelties exist on a Platonic plane, to affirm that what we confront is an arrangement of letters, of words, of paragraphs, moreover in roman and italic typeface, also small capitals, and with a sparse sprinkling of nonalphabetic signs. Such, whenever we read, whatever we read, is ultimately what we decode. And no newspaper reader is disoriented by a variousness of typefaces or by the fact that the events the paper records are united by nothing more than a common date.

The date of *Ulysses*, 16 June 1904, in a similar way does unite much indeed, including a funeral, a band concert, a footrace, a viceregal cavalcade, one adultery that we know of, the arrival of a ship from England bearing bricks, a thunderstorm, the loss of a trouser button, and on and on. Not that their date is their only commonality. There's "plot" aplenty, even good Dickensian plot, to which it's arguable that no speck, however tiny, is finally irrelevant. We've even the sturdy Victorian convention of a book that seems the sequel to a previous book; for here's the Stephen Dedalus of *Portrait*, present if not alert on this new book's first page.

But the title—well, it seems to ask us to look for Grecian heroes, who are somehow not in evidence. Still, the first nine words fall into a sturdy dactylic hexameter, and Greek words are being adduced by the second page, and soon, here's a wanderer adrift from his (faithless) wife (though Homer's Penelope was famously faithful) . . . That can all be elaborated toward infinity. It remains a job, though, for the reader, the text being sparse with clues. But, throughout the Joyce canon, everything, beginning with the fate of Father Flynn, presents a job for the reader. It's perhaps a comfort to find the word *Ulysses* present four times, even if once in reference to Ulysses S. Grant.

A new novelty, though, should be noticed: extreme specificity. That is one more modernist note: small items of information. Thus, in *The Waste Land*,

> A crowd flowed over London Bridge. . . .
> Flowed up the hill and down King William Street,
> To where Saint Mary Woolnoth kept the hours
> With a dead sound on the final stroke of nine.
> (62, 66–68)

—to which last line Eliot even appended a note: not a poeticism, no, "A phenomenon which I have often noticed" (n68).

David Copperfield does tell us he was born "at Blunderstone, in Suffolk, 'or thereby,' " also that it was on a Friday, at midnight (1–2). But no map discloses a Blunderstone, nor is a firm date stated. Dickens, writing in 1849, is advancing, but not by much, on an older convention that would gesture toward the year 18—, in the city of ———. It's noteworthy how fiction, the genre of the specific par excellence, tended, before Joyce, to shrink from pinning verifiable things down. Here are successive scraps from a page of *Ulysses*:

> Bare clean closestools waiting in the window of William Miller, plumber, turned back his thoughts. (8.1045)

> Against John Long's a drowsing loafer lounged in heavy thought. . . . (8.1066)

> Mr Bloom turned at Gray's confectioner's window of unbought tarts and passed the reverend Thomas Connellan's bookstore. (8.1069)

Mr. Bloom is walking along Duke Street, toward Dawson. Miller's was at 17 Duke, John Long's (a pub) at the Dawson Street corner, as was Gray's confectionery; Connellan's bookstore was one shop up Dawson past the corner . . . A *Thom's Dublin Directory* of that period will verify such minutiae. And their effect alters with time. In 1922, the year *Ulysses* was published, many were alive who could remember 1904 Dublin; such a reader might have experienced a hallucinatory vividness. But few such, if any, read *Ulysses*—Dubliners were warned off the book—and their Dublin is long since gone. Today we may settle, if we like, for the aura of particularity, which would still work if all the details were fictitious (thus 221-B Baker Street, the London address of Sherlock Holmes, never existed, though Baker Street did and does). Or we can visit Dublin and turn through *Thom's*; or we can read the findings of others who have done those things before us: Clive Hart, for instance, Leo Knuth, Don Gifford. We can do, in short, many things no reader of *David Copperfield* feels an incentive to do. One way or another, a gone Dublin will take shape in our minds, some parts as minutely mapped as Dante's cosmos.

It's arresting that Joyce, Pound, and Eliot, the founding fathers of modernism, were all devotees of Dante; as was Beckett, regretful closer of modernism's gates. In a time of few (and hand-copied) books Dante assumed you'd welcome a book that would last you all your life. In a time of too many books (annually, thousands more) the modernists assumed you'd welcome a book you weren't soon about to throw away. So in the second century since Joyce's birth, as in the eighth since Dante's, readers are busy helping one another by making lists, by explicating phrases, by suggesting structural diagrams, by crying, "Now wait a minute!" and threatening to bash heads. Yes, Dante would have understood. Modernism's historians, when they arrive at clear vision, will have to take him into account.

But back to particularity. Joyce thought of it as shorthand; in an urban milieu nothing characterizes you more than your address. That Stephen's people now live in meager Cabra is a measure of their decline from the time when Stephen was born in prosperous Rathgar. Also, in the *Dubliners* story "Counterparts," Joyce moved Farrington from pub to pub—Davy Byrnes's, the Scotch House, Mulligan's—in an orbit of nicely calibrated decline. There a Dublin publisher—Maunsel & Co.—balked. Their overt objection was to the word *bloody*, though they were just then engaged in collecting J. M. Synge's *Works*, where *The Playboy* alone flaunts *bloody* four times. Their real taboo seems to have responded to that overt *naming*. Joyce declined to invent pseudonymous pubs. He offered, to no avail, to get written clearances from the pub keepers. No. *One must not name names!* An impasse. And Maunsel's printing of *Dubliners* got guillotined.

The whole episode has received too little attention. "In the year 19—, in the city of D———": that would have been the decorous way to go about it. Unlike speech, unlike even writing, print has the power to agglomerate superstitions; we still tend to call some words "unprintable," forgetting that by now the *OED*, even, prints them. Oddly, words specifying mundanities that could be verified were among those that seemed not printable. And print was Joyce's medium; more than any previous maker of fictions, he sensed a primary bond less to his reader than to his compliant printer: his disposer of italics, his omitter of bacterial quotation marks, his carefully expressive speller who should faithfully set *thaaan* with three *a*'s to designate a tune being hummed. (But two *a*'s got mislaid by a typist, and Joyce's shade had to wait for Hans Gabler's team to restore them.)

In *Ulysses*, which came to be typeset in Dijon by men innocent of the meaning of what they were setting, he indulged himself in a very orgy of what Maunsel had forbidden him, naming: not just pubs but many hundreds of places of business, even many dozen real people (one of whom, Reuben Dodd, Jr., materialized years later to sue the BBC, successfully). The penultimate episode in particular is resplendent with small facts, not failing even to let us know the name of the chief engineer of the city waterworks (in 1904 a Mr. Spencer Harty, CE).

And, "The facts in the *Cantos*," said Pound (viva voce, June 1948), "are as accurate as I could make them." The inaccuracies that have been reported make an insignificant percentage, so high is the poem's factual density. The following instructions from canto 51 pertain to tying a trout fly:

> Blue dun; number 2 in most rivers
> for dark days, when it is cold
> A starling's wing will give you the colour
> or duck widgeon, if you take feather from under the wing
> Let the body be of blue fox fur, or a water rat's
> or grey squirrel's. Take this with a portion of mohair
> and a cock's hackle for legs.

There's a joy in particulars there that works down into the very joining of consonants ("duck widgeon"). And Eliot, as far back as 1910, had adduced the "smell of steak in passageways" ("Preludes" 2), to be dismissed as "unpleasant," doubtless by such sensibilities as twitched with discomfort when Joyce named those pubs. *Aroma* would have been a nicer word than *smell*. And "passageways" . . .

Information trends toward the impersonal. As the modernist novel eschewed the storyteller, so the modernist poem eschews the Bard.

And *Finnegans Wake*: if it's not dense with information, still its commentaries are, such diversities of information underlie it. By the time drafts were appearing in print, Joyce was instructing the printer not only what words to make visible but how to spell each of them. The first thing the printer must do is avoid capitalizing the first word of the first sentence. The last is to put no full stop after the last word of the last one. In between, he must by no means emend such a thing as "babalong" (103.6) to "Babylon" or "guenesis" (6.27) to "Guinness's" (else we'd lose "Genesis").

And the reader? The reader is back where the boy in "The Sisters" was, pondering impenetrabilities and omissions, getting the feel of voices, committing mysterious phrasings to memory for want (at the moment) of anything else to do with them; clutching, in fact, at alphabetic straws, all in the wavering confidence that something portentous would be making sense if the speakers, and the hidden authority beyond the speakers, weren't so tiresomely *withholding*. (They withhold, in part, because "he wouldn't understand." And it's true that he wouldn't. He'll just have to grow into it. We grow old growing into the *Wake*.)

Or: the reader is in a bar where talk courses eagerly in several languages, but it's never clear which they are. (Something about the porter being full? No, a Frenchman saying, "Comment vous portez-vous?")

Or: the reader is gazing at page after page of Text, unsure even how to pronounce the syllables, how to group them into cadences, how to do what was done so easily when *Black Mass* got discarded from "the black mass of the boat." For here it's unsure on what principle we'd be safe in discarding anything. "That's as semper as oxhousehumper" (107): are we to remember from a big dictionary that aleph was once a picture of an ox, and beth of a house, and ghimel of a camel? In which case (transposing from the Hebrew alphabet to our own), our task is as simple as ABC. And *semper* is Latin for "always," ABC's being what a printed page always (and only?) has to offer. In *which* case (we're never allowed to dodge this question): How much, ever, is our doing, how much the author's?

Yet these letters, make no mistake, are not randomly scrambled. One clue: Joyce was confident in listing copious misprints. So, apart from letters and postcards, the last thing we have from his hand is yet one more sheaf of instructions for a future printer.

But I halt at the boundaries of deconstruction, where the ghost of Priscian beckons from the shades.

Political Contexts for *Ulysses*

Cheryl Herr and Chris Connell

Teachers of *Ulysses* face the same questions again and again. Should we teach the entire text or emphasize certain episodes? Which episodes can be considered representative, both of the novel and of our pedagogic uses of the novel? How far should we engage students not only with the problems facing the characters but also with the myriad details that Joyce mapped into every page of *Ulysses*? How can the highly charged cultural issues of Joyce's Ireland have value and resonance for non-Irish students? What constitutes the minimal amount of historical and cultural information that students must have at their disposal to read the narrative? Finally, if we present this book as somehow qualitatively different from—more historically and politically challenging than—many other works that we teach, do we monumentalize *Ulysses* and thereby directly contradict Joyce's own resistance to established authorities and power structures?[1]

The writers of this essay believe that such challenging questions must be approached with the recognition that all aspects of *Ulysses*—allusion, characterization, style, theme, narrative mode, story line—are profoundly conditioned by the political situation of Joyce's Ireland. We present here what some might regard as background information to the narrative, but we also suggest that the historical context—the colonized status of Ireland in Joyce's day—infiltrates and shapes this putative background. Joyce makes his world available to us in stylized, politicized ways; reading *Ulysses* tutors the reader in a politics of narration, a mode of writing that inscribes the reader's status as subject—as "subjected" by the experience of reading—much as Joyce's Dubliners were produced as social beings in their efforts to read the civil formation in which they lived. Like a colonial subject, the reader works hard to enter into the mysterious and evasive doublespeak of imperial discourse, noticing the points at which governmental control proves unable to withstand the penetrating humor of Ireland, the array of Irish differences from Englishness.

Our essay discusses several related matters: the evolving status of the "fact" in Joyce criticism, the pressures of the colonial situation as evidenced by Joyce's characters, the primarily urban version of Irish history that Joyce encountered, the issues addressed by the Irish cultural renaissance, and Joyce's representation of Dublin's architecture. The city's architecture has a central place because students new to Joyce, particularly American students, often find their initial encounters with *Ulysses* eased by viewing images of Dublin (especially the period photographs in works such as William York Tindall's *The Joyce Country*) and by learning about the historical events associated with various urban sites. Pictures of the National Library of Ireland, Trinity College, the General Post Office, the Martello tower, and other buildings referred to in the narrative help students visualize a coherent material world that their reading experience at first seems to deny them.

These buildings tell in every aspect of their construction, setting, and mate-rial a story of imported design and imperial power, a power sustained by the effacement of native culture, emphasizing the political pressures under which Joyce wrote. The apparent fragmentations of character, style, and meaning represent the life of a nation semierased by British material culture and illustrate the insight of Frantz Fanon that colonial peoples are deprived of their history and situated within structures, both ideological and physical, constructed by their oppressors. In a world that dissolves indigenous culture, the artist's problem is how to achieve independent vision. Fanon lucidly argues that the very situation of struggle signals the vitality of the now estranged tradition (223). It is such a situation of struggle that marks *Ulysses* and makes it an epic of Irishness even though so much that was Ireland was denied, obscured, or remade in a colonial capital built on the English Geor-gian model. The essay concludes by locating the situation of struggle in the "Circe" episode's questioning of all partisan politics.

We began by enumerating many of the questions that the teacher of Joyce faces. One consideration in formulating them is that the terms through which Joycean scholarship has evaluated "information" dramatically shifted in the eighties. In the first wave of Joycean studies, the wealth of factual detail in *Ulysses*—names of people and places; interpolations of musical, dramatic, and journalistic quotations; literary references; historical allusions—was of-ten viewed primarily as background to the movement of the novel and the consciousness of the characters: an attempt to represent the real more fully and complexly than earlier fiction had done. Some Joyce scholars (and we are among them) have since decided that Joyce's allusive web ties much of this detail not only to the thematic and structural concerns of the narrative but also to the novel's political frames of reference and its frontal assault on the censoring mores of this country. As we see it, Joyce knew that the institutions of his day—educational, religious, journalistic, literary, govern-mental—managed, through a system of self-censorship, to produce particular definitions of nationhood, individual identity, gender relations, and moral values. Deviations from those carefully crafted interpretations of life, from narratives that ultimately served the economic interests of the British em-pire, were punished by exclusion. Joyce's *Dubliners* suffered years of delay in publication because of its possibly libelous transgressions of the institution-ally accepted story of life in Ireland. Neither collaborating with radical repub-licanism nor embracing Britain's domination, Joyce potentially offended readers of many political persuasions because his works interrogated the mechanisms by which custom came to be accepted as truth. To read *Ulysses*, we must be able to connect allusions of all kinds to the larger frames of reference that produced political opinion and practice in Dublin.

Another matter that the teacher of Joyce (and digester of Joycean criticism) often reckons with is that Joyce has been appropriated by two overlapping but distinct academic fields—Irish studies and modernist or postmodernist studies. The Irish studies arena privileges a Joyce who demands our close attention to the Ireland that intrigued and tormented him as citizen and as writer. In contrast, the modernist-postmodernist critics of Joyce are generally more interested in transnational concerns about the status of literature; theirs is a European Joyce, whose exile from Ireland signifies almost a transcendence of Irish politics in the process of writing about them. Certainly, both approaches are crucial to any consideration of Joyce's political contexts and preoccupations. He assumed that his readers would know or learn the history of Ireland's colonization, but his writing also anticipates a present like our own when the texts of history and the texts of theory (often Eurocentric) enter into heady dialogue. As a result of this conversation, many critics have come to see Irish culture itself as a narrative composed of various myths and versions of reality, each one produced by institutional needs and conventions, each one serving class interests, patriarchal power, the needs of religion and of the British state. In *Ulysses*, then, Irish history as lived by ordinary Irish people remains multiple and elusive; the controversies of Irish colonialism permeate the novel. As Fredric Jameson would have it, the real is absent, and everything that we come to know has undergone prior narratizing; so it is that *Ulysses* gestures constantly toward its political context, always assuring us that each frame of reference (including the metaframe that *is Ulysses*) is itself a story, both producer and product, ideology in action. What the present reading of *Ulysses* suggests is the impossibility of ever reaching a reality that is not ideologically mediated.

The narrative of *Ulysses* immediately involves us in a politically charged interrogation of art's relation to the real. Talking with Mulligan on the tower, Stephen, after assessing himself in the cracked shaving mirror, says, "—It is a symbol of Irish art. The cracked lookingglass of a servant" (1.146). Stephen attends to a duality within the single imaging surface; he perceives a distortion presenting itself as ineluctable reality. His characterization of the glass brings together connotations of both cultural domination and the compliance in servitude that shapes even innocent daily rituals according to political tensions. As though furthering the subjugation that Stephen attributes to Irish writing, Mulligan suggests that Stephen entertain, and make himself intellectually serviceable to, the Briton Haines. The terms of representation in this novel are stated, then, at the outset: every moment shown to us in the Ulyssean mirror emerges not as reflective of but as fundamentally shaped by political relations. As a character, Stephen feels acutely the demands of church and state, his own complex lack of expressive freedom in that society; he voices the frustrated resistance that moved Joyce to leave Ireland and write elsewhere. The loss of coherence in Irish culture produced by British occupation emerges in the fragmentation of self-image, viewpoint, style, and frame of reference.

In addition to emphasizing the inevitable impress of colonialism on the production of Irish narrative, *Ulysses* assumes that the reader is familiar with the particular political story Joyce grew up with; the narrative is riddled with bits and pieces of historical data that take on meaning not so much in "the" history of Ireland as in the history that Joyce knew. What Joyce recorded with both maniacal precision and canny purpose is a specifically urban and even more specifically Dublin-based version of Ireland's political story from 1800 through Joyce's lifetime. Even though Joyce left Ireland at a relatively young age, he remained a Dubliner and a cosmopolitan for the rest of his life; as the choice of his places of residence indicates (Paris, Rome, Trieste, Zurich), Joyce was far more at home in the city than in the country, and *Ulysses* is a book about a city rather than one about an entire geographic nation. Hugh Kenner's classic *Dublin's Joyce*, seconded by Richard M. Kain's *Dublin in the Age of William Butler Yeats and James Joyce*, demonstrates that to understand *Ulysses* one needs to come to terms with the compact and complex city from which Joyce hailed. Crucially, political events that took place in other parts of the country were often represented on the Dublin stage or in the press in what might be seen as an urbanized record of national issues, so that through theatrical portrayal, journalism, and local debate, Dubliners produced their own story of Ireland. Joyce foregrounds the world of pubs and politicians, prostitutes and publishers, rather than the efforts of the rural populace, during the final third of the nineteenth century, toward land reform. In the countryside, the recurrence from the mid-century mark onward of both famine and fear of famine fueled attention to land ownership and management. But like Gabriel Conroy in "The Dead" (*Dubliners*), Joyce had little firsthand knowledge of the rural world and its concerns.

Nonetheless, such an urban perspective as Joyce's gains national force from the fact that, while symbolizing in its provincial-capital status the continuation of British power, Dublin was also the site of revolutionary energies channeled from all parts of the country. In a way that helps us to understand Joyce's focus on the city and its significance for a historicist reading of *Ulysses*, Joseph V. O'Brien explains, "In the early years of this century, the forces of Irish political disaffection began to gather in and radiate from Dublin to an extent that the Irish capital became sharply distinguished from the rest of Ireland for the sustained vigor with which the idea of British rule in Ireland came under attack" (241). O'Brien here agrees with Irish scholars such as Mary E. Daly and George J. Watson that Dublin and the rest of Ireland were often politically at odds. As the "deposed capital" (Daly 1), Dublin was the somewhat isolated but constantly assimilative site for crusades central to national development. Thus, to enter the Dublin of *Ulysses* is to confront a world defined by contradiction and conflict, by the sedimentation of differing political paradigms, and by the tension produced as these multiple layerings countered the impress of external power.

What specific political issues captured the minds of Dubliners in Joyce's day? First, Ireland was engaged in an ongoing struggle—sometimes armed and always rhetorically charged—for political self-determination throughout the thirty-two counties on the island. Contributing to that distinctly political struggle was a renewed interest in defining Irishness by a return to the previously outlawed Irish language, by the purchase of exclusively Irish products, and by a cultural revival that swept up both antique folklore and contemporary literary and theatrical expression. In addition, the Catholic church, central to a majority of the population's concept of what it was to be Irish, played an important role in promoting an Irish Ireland—spiritually, culturally, and politically.

But there were many impediments to the speedy and seamless achievement of a truly Irish nation. Britain was remarkably committed to retaining control of its first colony, and centuries of English rule had left many parts of Irish society underdeveloped and even impoverished. Further, the church was likely to censure efforts toward national self-determination when such ventures involved a transgression of clerically established rules of conduct. The use of the English language in a country that wanted to reclaim an Irish Ireland militated against the achievement of a unified cultural identity. Despite the efforts of Lady Gregory and William Butler Yeats to put forward in their art the Irish "folk" as a touchstone for authenticity, for example, in their collaboration on *Visions and Beliefs in the West of Ireland*, it remained difficult to imagine what would constitute an indigenous literature that could address many class and cultural interests.

Joyce wrote *Ulysses* in a continuous, complex dialogue with the movements and competing claims of his era. Instead of attempting to produce a political manifesto from such multiple issues, Joyce strategically enabled many institutions and discourses to have their say in his work, depicting class antagonisms, juxtaposing unresolved social and cultural contradictions, and rhetorically fracturing the forces of domination that exert pressure toward a canonical or official history and literature. When Joyce presents one chapter in the form of a newspaper, another as a playscript, a third as a popular romance, and a fourth as a cultural catechism, he directs the reader's attention to those sites of institutional power and to the contradictory messages often purveyed through them. For example, "Aeolus," the episode that includes journalistic headlines or captions and seems to take on the status of a newspaper, may be seen as referring to the *Freeman's Journal*, in the office of which the episode mostly takes place. Dubliners in the know claimed that in 1904 the *Freeman's Journal* was under the thumb of the lord lieutenant's wife and the archbishop of Dublin. At the same time and in strong contrast, the chapter reminds us of many alternative newspapers of the day, including the nationalistic *Scissors and Paste*. The story of journalism comes to us not seamlessly consistent with conservative power but resistant, contradictory, potentially subversive.

The large issues engaging Joyce and other Dubliners emerged from specific historical events that had, over the years, taken on mythic proportions in the popular mind. In coordination with Joyce's strategy of formally immersing the reader in journalism, drama, romance, and other forms of communication, *Ulysses* insists that we imaginatively move as fully as possible into those historical myths. Instead of telling us the story of the 1798 rising, of Robert Emmet, of Parnell, or of 1916, however, Joyce invites us into the minds of Stephen and Bloom and then walks those characters through the streets that witnessed the events in question. The groundwork for Dublin's view of Irish history is literally mapped into Joyce's city as portrayed in *Ulysses*. Belying the anti-English agitation that characterized Joyce's era and earlier, Dublin City architecturally affirms British presence and colonial power, not least in the formal Georgian squares that Bloom passes through during 16 June 1904. As the "Wandering Rocks" chapter illustrates, the personality of that city is as much a character in *Ulysses* as are Molly, Stephen, and Bloom. The very existence of buildings that are British landmarks suggests the hold of the British empire over legislation, education, economic development, and cultural authority. Riding through the streets on the way to the Mirus Bazaar, the viceregal cavalcade constitutes a wandering demonstration of imperialism that denotes a world of power and fashion, however remote from the real capital, London. Like a collective but nevertheless individual consciousness, the city is caught up in unresolved conflicts.

Many of those conflicts emerge from the mythology of the 1798 rising of the Irish against British rule. For example, in the city center stands the old Irish Parliament building, which became the Bank of Ireland after the 1800 postrebellion removal of the government to London. This imposing Georgian structure tells the story not just of the exercise of British imperialism over Irish government but also of the failed uprising of 1798, a rebellion associated with Theobald Wolfe Tone and Lord Edward Fitzgerald. Both patriots gave their lives in the late-eighteenth-century struggle. To a large extent, the rebellion, which was repeatedly memorialized in Irish political melodramas on the stage of the Queen's Royal Theatre, provided a popular template for Dubliners, a model for the downright theatricality of even the most abortive uprising. Only since the mid-1980s have these plays begun to be published, but those that are available make clear the strong influence of a politicized melodrama on Joyce's and Dublin's historical imagination (see Watt; Herr, *For the Land*). Numerous allusions in *Ulysses* to social agitation and to politicoeconomic failure make reference to this most theatrical and eulogized of rebellions, which playwrights tended to represent at the moment just before disaster in order to convey to Irish audiences in Joyce's day the unabated need for revolutionary activity.

A few blocks from the Parliament building is Lord Edward's ancestral home, Leinster House. After talking in the beautifully domed National Library with John Eglinton, George Russell, Richard Best, Buck Mulligan, and William Lyster, Stephen stands on the library steps, which face Leinster House. Far from being applauded by those who have listened to his Shakespearean theory of aesthetic production, Stephen feels at least provisionally defeated at this point in the narrative. The deferring of any resolution of his own emotional and aesthetic crises echoes the mood of political despair that

Lord Edward's death produced in his followers and to which the failure of the 1798 rising contributed. Thus the intellectual, aesthetic, and personal aspects of Stephen's thought merge with the daily fact of political repression, itself subsumed into the burgeoning mythology of specific historical defeat. The continued subjugation of Ireland by England leads Joycean characters like Professor McHugh to see colonization as a virtual definition of Irishness.

Some sad reminders of that imposed definition are the street urchins Bloom notices in "Lotus-eaters" (5.5–10) and the gnawing poverty of Dilly Dedalus, which draws Stephen's compassion (10.855–80.). By Joyce's day, many of the former Georgian mansions had deteriorated into tenements; indeed, Dublin's poverty level exceeded that of any other city in the United Kingdom, and, as Daly explains, the decade following Joyce's birth gave Dublin the record for the highest death rates (2). In 1881, the year before Joyce's birth, the census showed that twenty-three percent of Dubliners could not read (O'Connor 114). By 1911, over forty percent of the deaths in Dublin occurred in workhouses and other institutions (Daly 142). It is no wonder that Joyce shows the effects, especially on petit bourgeois morale, of poverty in urban centers. Irish space as Joyce represents it is triply dominated, then, by the reminder of imperial domination in British architecture, by the failure that some of the buildings like Leinster House represented, and by the tenementation of formerly grand homes.

The Martello tower, where Stephen, Mulligan, and Haines wake up on 16 June, also reminds us of material oppression. It was one of several towers established along the shore by William Pitt, then prime minister of Britain, where lookouts could watch for Napoleon's invading French armies. Stephen comments, of course, that he and the usurping Mulligan pay twelve quid in rent "[t]o the secretary of state for war" (1.540). Britain's surveillance was also directed inland, for both Tone and Lord Edward had been targets for Pitt's secret service surveillance. Living in the tower, Stephen ponders the more daunting aspects of British imperialism; certainly Stephen rues his fate as part of a conquered people. The student of Joyce, shown visual images of the British buildings that give Dublin its gorgeous Georgian formality and provided information about the political events associated with this architecture, can appreciate Joyce's insistence on situating his narrative in a "real" materiality. These buildings serve as reminders of a century or more of rebellion and disappointment, including the unsuccessful efforts of Robert Emmet in 1803 to take over the seat of British government, Dublin Castle, and thereby to stir the citizenry into widespread insurgency.

Hence, the Dublin tale of Irish politics is relentlessly brought forward for the reader who takes note of where Stephen and Bloom meander and of what aspects of the city capture their attention on 16 June. Like Leinster House and the old Parliament building, the main street of Dublin (Sackville Street, later O'Connell Street) could be read by Joyce's Dubliners in terms of historical events that had taken place there and were part of popular mythology. Stephen's "Parable of the Plums" unfolds under the eye of Admiral Nelson on his pillar, then a monument to British naval power and imperial control. The pillar was located not far from the General Post Office, the main building of the several public structures where the Irish Republican Brotherhood took their stand against British rule during the 1916 Easter Rising. In the GPO Patrick Pearse proclaimed the Irish Republic of which he was chosen the nominal leader for the few days of its existence in 1916. So charged is the post office with memories of national aspiration and martyrdom that Joyce encourages our contemplation of political conflict by merely alluding to the building in its prerising setting:

> Under the porch of the general post office shoeblacks called and polished. Parked in North Prince's street His Majesty's vermilion mailcars, bearing on their sides the royal initials, E. R., received loudly flung sacks of letters, postcards, lettercards, parcels, insured and paid, for local, provincial, British and overseas delivery.   (7.15–19)

Joyce's Irish readers would certainly have understood the contextual resonances, which the text highlights by references to the royal British presence.

And yet, as scholars have noted, the pacifist Joyce opposed militant activity, and the Dubliners that he shows us are far from what Ireland knows as "physical force" heroes. The mild Leopold Bloom, who chooses love over violence, admires Arthur Griffith, a Dubliner who founded the separatist *United Irishman* newspaper as well as the Sinn Féin movement (1905), but Bloom would be unlikely to share any of the subsequent Sinn Féin commitment to militant republicanism. And Stephen's own political stance remains far more invested in self-preservation for artists than in the active assertion of civil rights against the British soldiers he encounters in Nighttown. Students who register the fracturing of discourse and desire produced by colonial rule sometimes question this apparent contradiction between the allusions in *Ulysses* to revolutionary activity and ideology and the characters' antiforce stances.

Indeed, two antagonistic and internally vexed political strands intertwine in *Ulysses*, one having to do with the tradition of "romantic nationalism" that honored blood sacrifice (Watson 41) and the other with the parliamentary (that is, talk-centered) means of securing independence and national identity. Joyce, whose sympathies were always with nonviolence (Watson 41), reserves his most severe criticism for a character like the cyclopean Citizen (in the "Cyclops" episode), whose Gaelic frenzy makes him intolerant of Bloom and everybody else. Even though the Citizen could be viewed as "all talk," the violence of that talk threatens the integrity, within *Ulysses*, of a parliamentary politics. And yet, in keeping with Joyce's commitment to

nonviolence, Charles Stewart Parnell (d. 1891), one of Joyce's central historical icons, based his career on a nonmilitant plan for national regeneration,
on a parliamentary politics.

Emmet Larkin affirms what all Joycean readers come to understand, that
Parnell "is the great mythological figure in modern Irish history. . . . The
myth holds that he brought his people to the edge of their earthly kingdom,
only to find that he was betrayed in the great moment of his promise by 'the
priests and the priests' pawns,' who cruelly broke his heart and hounded
him to his grave" (289). Larkin helps us remember that despite the British
Conservative party's ultimate victory over Parnell (using, as they did, his
involvement in a divorce case to weaken clerical support for Parnell's leadership of the Irish Parliamentary party and its bid for Irish home rule), Parnell
was able to form strong coalitions among the church, the Liberal movement,
and nationalist forces. In doing so, Parnell provided the basis for "the modern
Irish state" (Larkin 289). Winning and then losing the support of William J.
Walsh, archbishop of Dublin between 1885 and 1921—himself a figure bulk-
ing largely, though negatively, in Joyce's narrative imagination—Parnell
revealed the complex interrelation of church and state, of censorship and
public revelation, in a society on the brink of independence but not by any
means home free. As Joyce indicates, the frustrating social climate in which
Parnell met his doom also threatened to undo the creative spirit, the artistic
imagination.

Parnell is not a character in *Ulysses*, but he is a moving spirit in Joyce's
imagination, a hero who is first pilloried by the people he sought to liberate
and who is afterward incorporated into the millennialist aspirations of Irish
republicans. Those aspirations were founded in the experience of loss that
Fanon attributes to colonized lands, the loss of a native political center, both
geographic and parliamentary. Parnell is absent from *Ulysses*, which in its
epic attempt to come to terms with national origin and identity must constantly try to recapture the great Irish parliamentarian as the hero of this
modernist saga. Similarly, identity—both national and personal—is negotiated and partly lost in the complex relations of social forces as well as in the
novel's shifting narrational styles. When students try to define what Stephen
is "really like," what Bloom "should do," whether Molly is Earth Mother or
homemaker or both, they begin to comprehend how the political context of
Ulysses, with all of its longing for the missing center that would restore
political self-sufficiency to Ireland, finds expression in matters of characterization and theme—in specific individual losses and longings that do not
always recognize their own determination by political forces.

Many aspects of *Ulysses* examined in this essay come to a focus in the
"Circe" episode. Without endorsing the extravagances of any version of Irish
nationalism, Joyce here directs a grimly ironic glance at the symbols of
English power. It is significant, given the attachments of the Irish theater to

political action, that "Circe" is cast as a playscript. We would argue that this chapter dramatizes aspects of a politically repressed and fragmented nation's cultural unconscious, as apparitions, songs, religious figures, and folk legends materialize to take part in an always unfolding but always doomed reappropriation of the real and the historical. In the final movement of "Circe," we are shown the king of England, himself a pastiche of power and domination, presiding over the carnivalesque action. Edward VII "is robed as a grand elect perfect and sublime mason with trowel and apron, marked *made in Germany*. In his left hand he holds a plasterer's bucket on which is printed *Défense d'uriner*. A roar of welcome greets him" (15.4454–57). The Germanic Edward Rex stands in comic, institutionally insignia-adorned splendor as Stephen confronts Privates Carr and Compton and as the Virago calls out, "Green above the red, says he. Wolfe Tone" (15.4518). Notably, Stephen in "Circe" is not precisely the same character as Stephen in "Aeolus" or Stephen in "Oxen of the Sun." His subjectivity is as fragmented as the stories of Irish history; in fact, Stephen is not at all in control of the terms in which he is represented or of the story line in which he appears. Although properly belonging to Bloom's memory of the day, the Citizen invades Stephen's subworld, wearing an emerald muffler. The Croppy Boy (an Irish version of the rebel) also appears with a hangman's noose around his neck. Each of these figures is a two-dimensional component in the theater of Irish oppression, each a sign of intolerance given or received.

Joyce insists that partisan logic marks king as well as citizenry. Stephen and Bloom critique partisanship more readily than most of Joyce's Dubliners do, but they are also implicated by such logical paradigms. For Stephen, the "brutish empire" (15.4569–70) seeks his life and his money, and in this respect it is almost indistinguishable from the church, from his mother's insistently pious ghost, and perhaps even from Bloom, who would dearly love to take Stephen home as a surrogate son to be remade in his own bourgeois image. Recognizing the apparition of Old Gummy Granny as the Ireland who seeks the blood sacrifice of her sons, Stephen makes the intuitive connection to Hamlet and his quest for "revenge." Stephen refuses to allow politics to become the "third person of the Blessed Trinity" (15.4590–91); but the Citizen eggs him on with an "*Erin go bragh!*" (15.4621), while Private Compton insists that Stephen is "proBoer" (15.4602): 1899–1902 found the British Empire fighting the Boers in the Transvaal in a conflict that captured the colonized Irish imagination. The appearance of Major Tweedy, who exists in Bloom's memory but not in Stephen's, as a sort of pantomime hero produces a visual standoff between grizzled British military might and the venerable Citizen, while "Massed bands blare *Garryowen* and *God save the king*" (15.4630). *Ulysses* teaches us to interpret with a degree of suspicion, to be ready for reversals of meaning and allegiance, to interrogate each of the antagonists present in the collective unconscious of Dublin. Even Lord Edward Fitzgerald, the great martyr of '98, implodes into his own worst enemy, a comical verbal construct, Lord Gerald Fitzedward (15.4686–87).

The Circean redesigning of historical conflict transforms into a Black Mass, an inversion of clerical power that comes to a close only to find Stephen about to be knocked down by the soldiers. This scene is for many readers the explicitly Irish political high point of *Ulysses*, the moment in which all the oppressive forces that Stephen battles psychologically and socially coalesce. We find it extremely important, then, that nothing comes of the "Circe" conflict. The private levels Stephen with one punch, and Bloom extricates him from police prosecution. In "Circe," Joyce deflates all the classic political positions, from romantic Irish nationalism to indigenous support of British rule. For Joyce, the course of Irish history certainly had its infuriating patterns of incitement and defeat, its heady calls to arms or to parliamentary action; and the rhetoric associated with these patterns had its own compelling attraction for Joyce. Nonetheless, the relentless polarization of Irish politics produced by the implicit and explicit censorship of British rule, reinforced by religious hegemony, mobilizes in *Ulysses* a rhetoric that radically undermines all existing positions, clearing space for the alternative *literary* practices that *Ulysses* epitomizes and the alternative political practices that Ireland still, to some extent, awaits.

NOTE

[1]We are indebted to William Chace for his comments on "monumentalizing" *Ulysses* (see Chace).

Culture, Politics, and Ideology
in the Reception of *Ulysses*

Jeffrey Segall

"I hold this book to be the most important expression which the modern age has found; it is a book to which we are all indebted, and from which none of us can escape" ("*Ulysses*" 198). When we read T. S. Eliot's tribute to *Ulysses*, written in 1923, one year after the publication of both *Ulysses* and *The Waste Land*, we are moved as much by the gravity of his pronouncement as by the sweep of his praise. Eliot, not one given to hyperbole, eagerly promoted Joyce's literary experiment and correctly prophesied its influence on his own and subsequent generations of writers. Joyce's novel and Eliot's poem have come to be regarded as the twin pillars of high modernism. *Ulysses* in particular captured the artistic and intellectual energies of its age. Most important, the novel became a symbol of modern thought and sensibility. And Eliot's praise notwithstanding, it suffered more often than prospered under the weight of that association in the early years of its reception.

We must appreciate the symbolic value of *Ulysses* if we are to understand the range and volatility of the response to it during the twenties and thirties. The book that could move Eliot to reverential praise would move others to invective. Many, it seemed, were ready with an opinion about the novel before they had read more than a small portion of it or, in some cases, before they had read any of it at all. Readers were, of course, hampered by the obscurity of the novel (particularly in the years before the publication of Herbert Gorman's biography—written under Joyce's tutelage—in 1924, and Stuart Gilbert's *James Joyce's* Ulysses, in 1930) and by its unavailability, especially in America, where it was legally banned until 1934. Still, as *Ulysses* received wider dissemination and grew in notoriety, critics aligned themselves for or against it with a sense of urgency. *Ulysses* quickly became an issue in a broader debate over the responsibility of literature in a time of tremendous social and political upheaval. Joyce's tour de force would be continually appropriated by critics of different ideological persuasions in sometimes flagrant efforts to advance their own causes or positions. The controversy that erupted soon after the publication of *Ulysses* drew its heat less from disputes over interpretive questions than from disagreements over the array of cultural, social, and political changes the book heralded. The "text" that we argue over today underwent a prolonged latency period in the twenties and thirties, when, in all its rawness and daring and mystery, *Ulysses* inspired more befuddlement and vitriol than perhaps even its maker anticipated.

Eliot's 1923 essay, "*Ulysses*, Order, and Myth," offered Joyce's book a timely conferral of acceptance when those few who had read it were generally expressing puzzlement or outrage. Eliot, who with Ezra Pound had been instrumental in getting Joyce's early work published, further advanced Joyce's career by defending *Ulysses* against the charge by Richard Aldington and others that it was both formless and a "libel on humanity" (Aldington, qtd. in Eliot, *"Ulysses"* 199). In fact, wrote Eliot, Joyce's brilliant use of Homeric parallels gave the novel form and provided a standard by which we might judge modern life. Joyce's "mythical method," as Eliot termed it, was "simply a way of controlling, of ordering, of giving a shape and a significance to the panorama of futility and anarchy which is contemporary history." It was, he continued, "a step toward making the modern world possible for art" (*"Ulysses"* 201, 202). Eliot's bold and lavish praise for *Ulysses* helped establish the novel as a serious and important work. But Eliot, in his eagerness to legitimize the novel and place it alongside *The Waste Land* as the highest expression of the modernist sensibility, rendered it largely in his own image. The judgment of contemporary history that Eliot found implicit in *Ulysses* reflected Eliot's own reactionary sensibility more than it did Joyce's position. Few readers who shared Eliot's conservative politics could find anything praiseworthy in *Ulysses*. More often than not, the book was condemned for its lack of moral perspective. "An absence of meaning, an emptiness of philosophic content, a poverty of new and disturbing observation," was Wyndham Lewis's complaint (119). What was most apparent in Eliot's reading was his own effort to fuse a political conservatism and an aesthetic radicalism. Joyce, unlike other modernists such as Eliot, Pound, and Lewis, never attempted this synthesis. He was, in this respect, something of an anomaly among this group, a fact that he himself acknowledged in a letter from 1928: "[T]he more I hear of the political, philosophical, ethical zeal and labours of the brilliant members of Pound's brass band the more I wonder why I was ever let into it 'with my magic flute' . . ." (qtd. in Ellmann, *James Joyce* 621–22).

Eliot's collegial endorsement of *Ulysses* may, in retrospect, have been a mixed blessing for the novel. For not only did it mislead readers about the novel's political values, but Eliot's imprimatur made it a simple matter for critics on the Left to identify *Ulysses* as yet another example of decadent, bourgeois art. The most egregious instances of such stereotyping were the responses of the Soviet critics, Stalinist ideologues who condemned nearly all expressions of modernism as counterrevolutionary. They quite eagerly seized upon *Ulysses* as an example of the worst tendencies of modern art. Soviets such as Karl Radek and D. S. Mirsky attacked Joyce for his political diffidence, his linguistic experimentation, and his preoccupation with the unconscious life of isolated individuals. "A heap of dung, crawling with worms, photographed by a cinema apparatus through a microscope—such is Joyce's work," sneered Radek in 1934. Joyce was denounced by the Stalinists as a nihilist, a pornographer, an anarchist, a morbid aesthete, and an unredeemable individualist. *Ulysses* was ample proof that "Joyce [was] on the other side of the barricades" (Radek 181): "Joyceism is a most reactionary philosophy of social pessimism, misanthropy, barrenness and doom, a hopeless negation of all creative, fruitful forces" (Miller-Budnitskaya 687).

Though the Soviets in the early thirties exerted considerable influence on American critics aligned with Stalinism, the response to *Ulysses* among American Communists and like-minded intellectuals was neither so monolithic nor so severe. While a faction of Stalinist supporters led by Mike Gold decried nearly all modernist experimentation in favor of socialist realist literature, less doctrinaire Marxists such as Granville Hicks (party member and editor of the *New Masses* during the thirties) and Malcolm Cowley (fellow-traveling editor of the *New Republic* in the same period) would not dismiss Joyce's novel out of hand. They recognized one of the central enigmas of *Ulysses*: though it was the work of a stylistic virtuoso, it celebrated the consciousness of a middle-class Dublin Jew and rendered with naturalistic detail the realities of modern urban life. It was, in short, both highbrow and middlebrow. In *Exile's Return* (1934), Cowley applauded the novel's "richness" and "complexity," while he chastised Joyce for his insularity and his aloofness (118). Though he admitted that at the time he had met Joyce (1923) he had read barely a tenth of *Ulysses*, he could nonetheless declare unequivocally that the book was "great" (116). Still, he could not refrain from scolding Joyce for making "an inverted Faust's bargain, selling youth, riches, and part of his common humanity to advance his pride of soul" (118).

Cowley's portrait of Joyce, tinctured as it was by the Left's disdain for bourgeois art and its idealization of the proletarian artist, would be questioned by more independent Marxists, notably James T. Farrell. Farrell, who in a 1936 essay in *A Note on Literary Criticism* directly challenged Radek and Mirsky, elsewhere took issue with the neurasthenic caricature of Joyce, offering his own impassioned defense of Joyce as a "living inspiration . . . because of his great constructive genius . . . his dignity, his daring, his high artistic courage" (*League* 59). Farrell joined others on the Left who gravitated toward the *Partisan Review* in the thirties out of a shared desire to embrace both Marxism and the aesthetic experimentation of the modernists. Farrell, Lionel Trilling, Dwight Macdonald, and, especially, Edmund Wilson championed *Ulysses* against attacks from ideologues of both the Left and Right. Their resistance to the straightjacketing of cultural life attempted by the Stalinists created an atmosphere in American literary circles in which *Ulysses* could be read seriously and appreciated aesthetically.

Wilson, a respected critic, journalist, and the editor of the *New Republic* during the thirties, became an eloquent and influential defender of the modernists. His favorable assessment of *Ulysses*, which appeared in *Axel's Castle* in 1931, proved enormously important in securing Joyce's future reputation. In introducing Joyce to an American audience, eventually his largest and most devoted readership, Wilson was instrumental in directing critical debate away from the nebulous politics of *Ulysses* and toward its aesthetics, which he more than anyone else labored assiduously to explain. Wilson was not, however, without his own reservations about the modernists in general and about *Ulysses* in particular. As his interest in Marxism deepened, Wilson, in 1928, complained privately that Yeats, Pound, and Joyce tended to be too subjective and resigned; he worried that *Ulysses* became mired at times in allusion, wordplay, and parody, which slowed its dramatic movement and perplexed the reader. Yet Wilson, as a public advocate for the modernists, defended *Ulysses* in print despite his private misgivings.

Wilson undertook a patient explication of *Ulysses* in his *Axel's Castle* essay, probing the novel's intricacies and puzzling over its ambiguities. Though Wilson clearly perceived the revolutionary quality of *Ulysses*, he located both text and author inside a moral, intellectual, and artistic tradition that made them seem less deviant and obscure. Wilson saw *Ulysses* poised neatly between a Flaubertian naturalism and a Proustian symbolism: Joyce vividly re-created Dublin and delved into the unconscious lives of his characters yet never "[falls] over into [the] decadence of psychological fiction." Like Eliot, Wilson refuted charges that the novel was formless; "*Ulysses*," he argued, "suffers more from an excess of design than from a lack of it." And most important, Wilson insisted that the novel was neither nihilistic nor misanthropic: "Joyce is remarkable, rather, for [his] equanimity" (*Axel's Castle* 204, 211, 219).

> [T]o have exhibited ordinary humanity without either satirizing it or sentimentalizing it—this would already have been sufficiently remarkable; but to have subdued all this material to the uses of a supremely finished and disciplined work of art is a feat which has hardly been equalled in the literature of our time.   (*Axel's Castle* 220)

Wilson, moved by his enthusiasm for Joyce's book and provoked by its detractors, may have overstated his case. Yet, his belief in the underlying moralism of *Ulysses* would be corroborated by future readers and supported in part by Judge John M. Woolsey's opinion two years later (printed in the 1961 Random House edition of *Ulysses*) lifting the ban on the novel. Wilson recognized at the core of *Ulysses* an affirmation of enlightened human values: tolerance over bigotry, compassion over indifference, reason over passion. Years later, Delmore Schwartz, Lionel Trilling, and Richard Ellmann, among others, would further promote Joyce's liberalism, with Trilling crediting *Ulysses* for being "unique among modern classics for its sympathy with progressive social ideas" ("James Joyce" 158).

Wilson was acutely aware of his adversaries on both the Left and the Right, whose condemnations of the modernists could at times sound strikingly similar. Irving Babbitt's New Humanists, a small band of conservative critics and teachers who lambasted modernist art in the twenties and thirties, saw *Ulysses* as symptom of a civilization in moral and spiritual decline. Babbitt's ideological ally Paul Elmer More delivered a scathing attack on the "moral slough of *Ulysses"* in a 1936 volume of his *Shelburne Essays* entitled *On Being Human*. More had expressed his antipathy for *Ulysses* to Wilson in 1929, when, before even having read the novel, he vaguely criticized its obscurity and Joyce's use of Homer. In his essay, having by then read at least parts of the novel, More went further, accusing Joyce of presenting a debased and devitalized portrait of modern humanity; of promoting immorality and solipsism; of displacing religion with obscenity. Echoing (no doubt inadvertently) Buck Mulligan's charge against Stephen Dedalus, More assailed Joyce for offering us "religion *à rebours* in *Ulysses*, this faith in the final reality of nature as something so loathsome that man is relieved of the burden of loyalty to any authority outside himself. . . ." (93). *Ulysses* depicted the hellish, God-forsaken world of More's nightmares, and More was not the first or last to condemn the book as blasphemy. Wilson, Cowley, Allen Tate, and others, however, challenged the narrowness, the Puritanism, and the antiaestheticism of More and the New Humanists, with Wilson specifically contesting More's reading of *Ulysses* in his contribution ("Notes") to a volume entitled *The Critique of Humanism* (1930).

Ulysses again became an issue for debate in America in the late thirties and early forties, when liberals such as Archibald MacLeish and Van Wyck Brooks attacked the modernists as "irresponsibles" for insufficiently supporting Western democracies in the battle against fascism. Brooks, declaring that "the literary mind of our time is sick," labeled Joyce, Eliot, and Pound "coterie writers" who no longer understood or expressed the spirit of their age. Joyce represented "the ash of a burnt-out cigar," whose parodies and obscenities in *Ulysses* depreciated tradition "while Joyce settled down complacently in his 'snot-green' world" (231, 225). Dwight Macdonald and others counterattacked furiously in the pages of *Partisan Review* in 1941, accusing Brooks of practicing a form of cultural fascism. Macdonald seized on the example of *Ulysses* to rebut Brooks's charges:

> What blindness to see in *Ulysses*, a work overflowing with genial delight in the richness of human life, a *rejection* of life. What is rejected is a specific historical social order, and it is only by making that rejection that Joyce was able to survive as an artist and to preserve and defend those general human values on which culture depends.   (449)

Macdonald's Joyce was not sour or curmudgeonly but genial and benevolent; *Ulysses* was not a repudiation of life but a heroic defense of human values. Both Brooks and Macdonald, like other American critics before them, were reading *Ulysses* in such a way as to advance their own arguments in the broader, ongoing debate about the proper social and political function of literature. *Ulysses* was sometimes at the center and sometimes at the periphery of this debate, which occupied American criticism during the twenties and thirties. With the ascendancy of the New Critics during the forties and fifties and under the scrutiny of Harry Levin, William York Tindall, and R. P. Blackmur, among others, *Ulysses* would receive the studied attention it had always demanded, and the process of Joyce's canonization in the American academy would truly begin.

The canonical status of *Ulysses* was a matter of less dispute in British literary circles during the two decades after its publication. F. R. Leavis's significant omission of Joyce from *The Great Tradition* in 1948 was a late confirmation of the marginalization Joyce had long suffered in England. Leavis, acknowledging Eliot's praise for *Ulysses*, could not himself find an "organic principle" that fused its tangle of analogy and linguistic experimentation into a whole. "It is rather, I think, a dead end, or at least a pointer to disintegration" (26), the evidence for which Leavis found in *Finnegans Wake*. Leavis, quoting D. H. Lawrence, whom he esteemed highly, castigated Joyce for "a desire to 'do dirt' on life" (26). This comment was in keeping with Lawrence's own privately expressed belief that *Ulysses* was obscene and his public complaint that it was cluttered with trivial detail. "The last part of it is the dirtiest, most indecent, obscene thing ever written. . . . It is filthy" (qtd. in Ellmann, *James Joyce* 615), Lawrence reportedly told his wife.

Joyce's Irishness posed a perpetual problem for him among the British. "[Joyce] is so Irish that the English have no love for him," said Joyce's friend Italo Svevo in Milan in 1927 (355). Edmund Gosse's 1924 review of *Ulysses* could have been cited as confirmation: "There are no English critics of weight or judgment who consider Mr. Joyce an author of any importance" (313). Gosse overstated the situation, certainly, though *Ulysses* was greeted generally with disgust or genteel disdain by the English in the years just after its publication. H. G. Wells had complained as early as 1917 about Joyce's "cloacal obsession" (86), and *Ulysses* only reinforced perceptions of Joyce as an uncultivated, somewhat perverse recorder of Dublin low life. "An illiterate, underbred book . . . the book of a self-taught working man" (*Diary* 189) was Virginia Woolf's private reflection on her first reading of *Ulysses*. (Woolf's published comments on *Ulysses* in 1925 showed a more ambivalent attitude. While she conceded that Joyce's experiment, "difficult or unpleasant as we may judge it, is undeniably important," she expressed disappointment at the constricted scope of the novel, its solipsism, and its emphasis on indecency [*Common Reader* 190–91].) "He's so terribly *unfein*," added Katherine Mansfield (22). "The poet of the shabby-genteel, impoverished intellectualism of Dublin," said Wyndham Lewis (77). But it was not only Joyce's raffishness or immorality that offended. Arnold Bennett offered a more damning middlebrow appraisal of *Ulysses* in 1922, citing the book's sardonic meanness: "The author seems to have no sense of the general kindness of human nature, and not much poetical sense. Worse than all . . . his vision of the world and its inhabitants is mean, hostile, and uncharitable" (221). Here again, we recognize the portrait of our artist as a misanthrope.

The most serious and sustained attack on *Ulysses* was delivered by Wyndham Lewis in *Time and Western Man* in 1927. Counterposing Joyce's "romantic" art against his own "classical" ideal, Lewis condemned *Ulysses* "for its emphasis upon the self-conscious time sense" (84), a defect he ascribed variously and vaguely to the influence of Bergson, Einstein, and Freud. Lewis expressed his own revulsion for modern life by heaping excremental metaphors on Joyce's book, which so studiously re-created contemporary history. This "monument like a record diarrhea" (92) both bored us with its details and psychological explorations and frustrated our longing to find meaning or perspective. "Joyce is above all things, essentially the craftsman," said Lewis (90), damning with faint praise. The author of *Ulysses* failed at art's "business": "to show us how . . . life would be" (Lewis, qtd. in Kenner, *Lewis* 20).

Lewis's criticism of *Ulysses* was reminiscent of attacks by other cultural conservatives who granted that Joyce was clever but not circumspect; prolix but not substantive; fastidious but not armed with a clear or compelling vision. Joyce eschewed the messianic impulse and adopted as his mythological patriarch the labyrinth maker Daedalus. As a result, Joyce was execrated by reactionaries like Lewis, who looked toward art to restore the order and privilege and certainty mythically embodied in the past. Renato Poggioli points out that in considering the avant-garde the Left is as myopic as the Right. Both "contemplate avant-garde art by way of an analogous anachronism; but while one looks at it through a reactionary and retrospective nostalgia, the other looks at it through an anticipatory dream" (168).

Ulysses, by virtue of its radical form and content, provoked readers as few books have, leading some to genuflect and many more to censure. What is most striking when we review early responses to *Ulysses* is how easily and how dramatically the gestalt of the novel could change. The varied readings of *Ulysses* reflect not only the novel's difficulty but the particular cultural, historical, and political circumstances from which these reactions issued. Today *Ulysses* fascinates us equally as a cultural trace element and as a cultural icon. While we have attempted to read the novel in its fullness and complexity, "to be Joyce's contemporaries, to understand our interpreter" (Ellmann, *James Joyce* 3), it has relentlessly and unscrupulously read us, making us uncomfortably aware of our critical and cultural horizons. Before the altar of *Ulysses* we are always humbled, as, Joyce announced with spite and delight in 1923, he meant us to be: "I've put in so many enigmas and puzzles that it will keep the professors busy for centuries arguing over what I meant, and that's the only way of insuring one's immortality" (qtd. in Ellmann, *James Joyce* 521).

THEORETICAL APPROACHES IN PRACTICE

Feminist Approaches to Teaching *Ulysses*

Bonnie Kime Scott

Feminist theoretical approaches can enter into the teaching of any chapter of *Ulysses*, not just episodes like "Nausicaa" and "Penelope" that present women characters centrally. These approaches apply to all levels and contexts for teaching Joyce—whether a widely ranging survey treating one chapter or a senior seminar devoted to *Ulysses* alone. In a course Woman through Literature, I have taught "Penelope" with such diverse texts as *Tales of Inanna*, The Wife of Bath, Genesis, and the romance best-seller *The Flame and the Flower*. In Great English Writers II (which satisfies general-education requirements at my university), I take what the anthology offers, "Proteus" and "Lestrygonians," and include feminist questions and strategies in their treatment. In an upper-level course devoted solely to *Ulysses*, "Penelope" and "Nausicaa" are scheduled slightly out of sequence for the same week and teamed with Joycean feminist-critical readings.

Why make the effort to include feminism in the teaching of *Ulysses*? Because students taking English courses today are mostly women. Some students trained in women's studies bring into the classroom resistances to a canonized male author or to a text based on male heroic myth; they may have heard Joyce or high modernism denounced as misogynist or phallocentric. The introduction of Joycean feminist work can lead them to an exciting and pervasive strain in recent Joyce criticism. Finally, the forms of feminist reading introduced through Joyce can be transplanted to other literary texts and into students' reading of contemporary culture.

Note that I write of "feminist approache*s*" in this essay (see my *James Joyce* 2–14). I shall introduce here five feminist approaches and suggest exercises and sets of questions that are compatible with nonauthoritarian, feminist pedagogy. It is assumed throughout that gender (as opposed to sex) is a variable concept in culture and for individuals, whatever their sex. I conclude with a consideration of nonlinear endings. In the present period of canonical revision, Joyce as a male author is challenged for space on the syllabus by the women writers of his day and the prolific and talented women writers of today. Other minorities and Third World writers also claim attention. Sandra Gilbert and Susan Gubar suggest that, even in his modernist era, Joyce and other modernist males were sensing the competitive pressure of women writers. Gilbert and Gubar feel that they can detect "the reaction-formation of intensified misogyny with which male writers greeted the entrance of women into the literary marketplace" (233). They are unimpressed by his supposed movement toward feminine literary form, as they suspect him of imposing "occulting" paternal structure on the mother tongue (253–62). Taking their "occulting" to include mystical and obscuring devices, I argue that a new Joyce emerges in the company of the women writers who originally surrounded him and that feminist approaches can make Joyce relevant to students' concerns about sex roles and literary representations of women. Application of feminist concepts to a literary text makes these concepts more available to students for application to their own lives. When we ask feminist questions of Joyce's texts, we can develop a sense of variability in the cultural concept of gender within characters of both sexes; we may also see gender as an aspect of and parallel to Irish colonial identity, or functioning in the unconscious realm of dreams.

Although I prefer to spend the bulk of a class session encountering the literary text, a basic feminist treatment of Joyce begins with the history of the women involved in the production of *Ulysses*. It was a novel brought forth with amazing liberty for revision in the extraordinary setting of Sylvia Beach's amicable Paris bookshop–lending library, Shakespeare and Company (see Beach; Scott, *Joyce and Feminism* 85–115; Fitch). The major financial sponsor of the book was Harriet Shaw Weaver, an editor of the feminist periodical the *Egoist*, where Joyce's *A Portrait of the Artist as a Young Man* and several chapters of *Ulysses* were first published. One question to pose to students is whether these women betrayed their feminism or enriched it through this publication. Instead of serving a male, should they have developed their own intellectual and creative talents or sponsored more exclusively the publication of women writers? I like to show slides of the tables of contents of journals like the *Little Review* (edited by Margaret Anderson and Jane Heap) and *Transition*, where Joyce appeared with Djuna Barnes, Kay Boyle, and Gertrude Stein, partially to remind students of the female authorial space he originally shared. Often I read remarks on *Ulysses* by Virginia Woolf, Gertrude Stein, Dorothy Richardson, or Mina Loy (see Deming; Scott, *Gender*). I also cite the Irish and British campaigns for suffrage, along with more familiar historical data concerning the Irish nationalist struggle and the two world wars (see MacCurtain; Gallagher; Foster).

A second, pragmatic feminist approach operates on the text itself, investigating the experience of women in *Ulysses* (a task done very well in many of the essays in *Women in Joyce*, the volume edited by Henke and Unkeless). What were the familial, sexual, economic, and job situations available to a woman in the novel, and how were these conditions inflected by her religion, ethnicity, political state, or class? Students who have read *Dubliners* can be encouraged to recall women's lives as represented in these stories—for example, at the laundry in "Clay" or as shown by the musical occupations in "A Mother" and "The Dead." For a treatment of women's practical experience, the "Penelope" and "Nausicaa" chapters of *Ulysses* offer an abundance of data. But so do incidents where women filter rather quickly through the text. The realistic, scrupulous meanness of recorded fact that characterized *Dubliners* survives best in minor walk-on roles and brief episodes. Students attuned to this aspect of feminism may notice Dilly Dedalus early in "Lestrygonians":

> Dedalus' daughter there still outside Dillon's auctionrooms. Must be selling off some old furniture. Knew her eyes at once from the father. Lobbing about waiting for him. Home always breaks up when the mother goes. Fifteen children he had. Birth every year almost. That's in their theology or the priest won't give the poor woman the confession, the absolution . . .
>
> Good Lord, that poor child's dress is in flitters. Underfed she looks too. Potatoes and marge, marge and potatoes. It's after they feel it. Proof of the pudding. Undermines the constitution.   (8.28–43)

I might lead students to note how Dilly is identified. Why this emphasis on the father? Not only does the daughter bear his name, but in patriarchy she is known through him to the outside world. The mother's death, not his inattention, is to blame for a deteriorating family situation. What do we learn about her health and economic status? Bloom notes the condition of her dress and evidence of malnutrition. What brings her here? It is worth pointing out that Dilly seems to have special ways of coping with her father's irresponsibility and waits for the auction proceeds so that some money may go home to nourish the family. What sort of an observer and recorder of Dilly Dedalus is Leopold Bloom? Mindful of details and compassionate, he likes to fill in the blanks of her story and to generalize about social forces like the church and biological effects like long-term malnutrition. I might ask students whether some of his interests as a recorder seem masculine and others feminine. The discussion then moves beyond this isolated observation of Dilly. How does her presence in the text alter the reader's reaction to her brother, Stephen (whom my students have encountered in "Proteus")? He seems in comparison incredibly privileged in terms of education and independence. In courses where only a chapter or two of *Ulysses* is studied, I may expand on students' knowledge of the Dedalus family situation, going back to domestic scenes in *Portrait* involving Stephen's younger siblings (162–64) and his now dead mother (175, 252). Referring to "Wandering Rocks," I would supply Dilly's most active role, her financial transaction with Simon. While Dilly is cunning, so as to get what she wants, Simon is still authoritarian. He gives orders about her posture—probably the product of her malnourishment rather than a lack of self-discipline (10.643–716). She diverts small change from her father's quest for alcohol, but later in "Wandering Rocks," instead of buying the milk and bun Simon suggests, she purchases a French primer. This purchase is recorded by the mildly remorseful Stephen (10.854–80). What does this series of episodes say about her strategies, priorities, aspirations, and positions in the text? How accurate was Bloom in his perceptions? He certainly detected Dilly's need and set her in a systematic case history, and both of his gestures define his mental dispositions. But Bloom was not able to see Dilly as she might see herself—actively coping.

Some of the same real-world pressures can be found in the representation of Gerty MacDowell, the central female character of "Nausicaa." Marriage remains the leading vocation for women of this era and place, and she must work against the odds to attract a suitor. What sorts of odds can students uncover? There is again a problematic, abusive father, whose work Gerty has attended to in "Wandering Rocks" (10.1025). Another father keeps his bicycling son away from Gerty, probably because of religious and class differences. Since readers are admitted to Gerty's thoughts, they can assess her personality. How well does she get along with the other young women on the beach? Students might want to look at her physical position and her reactions to the other women's statements and movements. Are there differences in style (activity/passivity, outspokenness/reticence) within this little feminine community? Perhaps the scornful remarks Joyce attributes to Gerty merely serve as a stereotype of female competitiveness for available men. Joyce may have no interest in representing what has been called sisterhood. Does Gerty feel that a man's interest can be purchased with an investment in the right hat and ribboned panties? Might fashion be considered a harmless diversion, given her options?

"Nausicaa" also invites more abstract considerations. This brings us to a third feminist approach, centered on language as it is used in the specialized discourses of culture. One might note the unusual narrative voice of "Nausicaa," asking, for example, whether Gerty seems an individual or a construct of ready-made languages or discourses that culture manufactures for women.

Has she become (with her own study and complicity) the stuff of romance novels and advertising copy? I invite students to make contemporary comparisons. Who profits from this identification, Gerty or the fashion and cosmetics industries? Is Gerty a victim of materialist culture? Or, like Dilly, does she represent a survival strategy in operation? Might she be a romance writer herself? Students might be reminded that this is an outdoor scene, set on a beach. The original Nausicaa was a Phaeacian princess who found Ulysses cast up from the sea. Is there any affinity to nature detectable in Gerty's behavior?

A fourth feminist approach concerns female imaging and the role of the male gaze in traditional aesthetics. The French feminist Luce Irigaray, reacting to the psychoanalytic and linguistic theories of Sigmund Freud and Jacques Lacan, suggests that the perspective or gaze in Western aesthetics is male and that it sees the female form as different, or "other" (23–33). In the Lacanian extension of Freudian theory, woman is castrated; she is defined by her lack of a penis. There is a linguistic parallel, in which the transcendental signifier of mature symbolic language becomes the phallus possessed by the father (Irigaray 34–41, 60–62). To compensate for woman's supposed lack, the author uses language to supply her with a fetish in place of a penis. The fetishistic gaze focuses on woman as different and elaborates on her form, perhaps supplying her with a penis in the form of a shoe or a strand of seaweed. Students who have read "The Dead" and *Portrait* can be reminded of several male gazes at female form. There is the boy's gaze at Mangan's sister in "Araby," where she is set against area railings, outlined in light, and plays with her bracelets. In chapter 4 of *Portrait*, Stephen levels a transforming gaze on the wading figure known as the "bird girl." Her tucked-up shirt becomes a birdlike tail, and he is entranced by the rhythmic motions of her foot.

Students can be asked to follow the gazing that goes on in "Nausicaa." Divided into small groups and armed with worksheets, they can be set to collecting evidence that they report back to the class. I might assign the opening narrative point of view to one group, Gerty's gazing to a second, and Bloom's gazing to a third. The worksheets for Gerty and Bloom would have parallel sets of questions:

> How open and direct is the gaze?
> Where is it focused? Where does it wander?
> Is the character aware of other people's gazing, playing to an audience?
> What sorts of stories does Gerty make up for Bloom and Bloom for Gerty?
> What theories about the opposite sex does this character have?

Students working on Gerty will notice that her first action is a distant gaze (13.80, repeated 13.406) but that mentally she ranges over her own appearance, from figure to face to hands to high-arched instep. Her eye motions may seem staged for observation: "For an instant she was silent with rather sad downcast eyes. . . . but then she glanced up and broke out into a joyous little laugh" (13.123–27). She has even practiced crying before the mirror (13.191). Gerty has good peripheral awareness—we learn that she "could see without looking" (13.495). She blushes at Cissy's "unladylike" expression within hearing of "the gentleman opposite" (13.265–67). First missing the ball Edy has sent her way and then lifting her skirt "to let them see" and giving it "a jolly good kick," she mentally accuses Edy of jealousy for "draw[ing] attention on account of the gentleman opposite looking" (13.361–65). She sizes up Bloom's appearance, deciding, "Yes, it was her he was looking at, and there was meaning in his look" (13.411–12). In the section of the text where the exchange of looks is most intense, Gerty can assess Bloom's most penetrating gaze from beneath the brim of her hat (13.515). With her careful selection and use of stockings, knickers, and hat, Gerty can be seen to equip herself with fetish objects. Gerty makes up stories about herself as fashion plate and dutiful daughter but also shapes Bloom into the manly man who can replace Reggy Wylie in her fantasies of a "dreamhusband" (13.431).

Students who have been doing Bloom will overlap in reported gazing, perhaps as early as "the gentleman opposite looking" (13.365) and certainly by the lines, "His dark eyes fixed themselves on her again, drinking in her every contour, literally worshipping at her shrine. . . . It is for you, Gertrude MacDowell, and you know it" (13.563–67). Both these accounts, however, rely on Gerty's interpretation of the received gaze. The first account that seems to come from Bloom attributes "young guileless eyes" to Gerty (13.745). It is possible to go back over Gerty's manipulations with clothing as interpreted by Bloom; for example: "Took off her hat to show her hair. Wide brim. Bought to hide her face, meeting someone might know her" (13.838–39). It will usually be discovered that while Gerty has studied her father and Reggy with some care, Bloom does a lot more generalizing about women, including their desire to be looked at (13.790–800).

The students working on the opening narrative are asked to report on the scope of its view, its tone, repetitions, and overlap and to mark the transition between Gerty's gazing and Bloom's (the most distinct narrative transition is at 13.474, but the borders are fuzzy, and this point can be discussed). Students also keep an eye out for Edy and Cissy as gazers. Usually picked up on is the wide focus on the seascape from Howth to Sandymount, passing by the church, narrowing to three girls and their small male charges on the rocks, and only settling on Gerty after two pages (13.78). The narrator repeats the wide focus, assisted by Gerty's typically distant gaze (13.624). Cissy gets credit for first spotting Bloom, for making sure that he won't see Tommy going to the bathroom (13.76–77), and for performing athletically before him (13.482). Although I provide structuring questions and encourage the elaboration of simple spottings, I turn over the authority of the class session to students, as befits feminist pedagogy.

Joyce has arranged other events around Gerty and Bloom—the fireworks as a specular but absurd phallic sign; the coincident religious service, which evokes another female vocation and identification for Gerty, that of the nun. A crux of the chapter comes with the apparent notice of a limp, first by the narrator and then by Bloom, as Gerty moves away (13.771–75). Why do we discover a limp in this way? Did the framework narrator withhold evidence for dramatic effect? Is the limp equivalent to female castration? Does its impact tell us something about ideals for feminine beauty? As I did in calling attention to the view Bloom takes of Dilly's nutrition, I encourage students to assess Bloom's reactions to Gerty's limp. When he says, "I wouldn't mind" (13.776), he introduces his taste for curiosities, or even perversity. This situation again calls for a bit of Joycean intertextuality, such as Bloom's pornographic postcard of "anal violation by male religious (fully clothed, eyes abject) of female religious (partly clothed, eyes direct)" in "Ithaca" (17.1811–12). Bloom also wants to know whether Greek statues of goddesses—the standard for Western female beauty—possess anuses (8.919–32). Mention can be made of the 1909 letters to Nora Barnacle, in which Joyce offers money for the purchase of drawers and expresses a desire to see these garments, soiled behind, exposing his own anal, fetishistic perversity (*Selected Letters* 183–86).

The gazing of "Nausicaa" continues in "Circe," where the dream consciousness of Bloom feels more imposed on and reversals of gender roles prove alarming. "Leering" Gerty boldly tells him she loves him for seeing "the secrets of her bottom drawer" (15.372–84). To be gendered masculine in "Circe" (as Bella is in becoming Bello) is to possess power and wield it over another. Bloom "feminine" is Bloom submitting to physical correction, unmanned, and forced into "vicelike corsets" (15.2975). Thus Joyce is sensitive to gender variability, even within the male subject.

The concept of gender leads into a fifth feminist approach—feminine writing (*écriture féminine*), a form of language that can be produced by either a male or a female writer. Feminine language is a controversial concept, even among feminists. Some resist the notion that men can write it. Others worry that it deals in the essential feminine, assigning woman to the realm of the womb, or the mother, or the physical and natural as opposed to the cultural world. Feminine language is variously defined and endorsed in French feminist theory. Hélène Cixous finds in a "feminine textual body" an economy of giving and dispersing, rather than acquiring; she sees the feminine text as endless, wandering, and circulating from body to body ("Castration"). A related French concept is Julia Kristeva's category of the semiotic, at the origin of life, existing in a "matrix space" before gender differentiation and characterized by rhythmic, mobile pulsations (93–95). Does Joyce's interest in language carry back to a fluid language of the womb, associated with the primal relationship to the mother? The obvious limits of such a definition of the "feminine" are worth presenting, even as the question is offered. Must feminine language be preverbal and associated with the mother? Feminine language can definitely be found in *Ulysses*, and Joyce's continuing interest in this form of fluid, essential female language is demonstrated by ALP's river speech in *Finnegans Wake*.

"Proteus," labeled as male monologue in the Joyce-approved system recorded by Stuart Gilbert, seems an unlikely place to search for feminine language, but not if it is supposed that the male artist can assume the feminine. Part of what is protean in this difficult chapter is the assertion of fluidity and decomposition against the organizing forces of male philosophy. Aristotle, Berkeley, Lessing, and the Book of Genesis run through classically educated Stephen's head at the start of the chapter and require considerable identifying for students today. But Stephen sees midwives, cockle gatherers, dogs—both pissing and dead—all of which evade these classical systems and the attention of the male philosophers who have dominated his Jesuit training. What does he do as an artist? We find Stephen most moved to writing by the feminine, as we have defined it: "Across the sands of all the world, followed by the sun's flaming sword, to the west, trekking to evening lands. She trudges, schlepps, trains, drags, trascines her load. A tide westering, moondrawn, in her wake" (3.391–93). Here the feminine is associated with tides and the moon, universalized as a burdened gatherer. But Stephen is assembling language (in regard to her load). In a more masculine mode, he wants to "[p]ut a pin in that"—save the composition (3.399). As he resumes, Stephen can be seen to approach semiotic or womb language, and here he is at his most experimental: "His lips lipped and mouthed fleshless lips of air: mouth to her moomb. Oomb, all wombing tomb" (3.401–02). There is more language and action of flow in the chapter, which students can be challenged to find: feminine seaweeds "hising up their petticoats, in whispering water" (3.462). Waves (as heard by Saint Ambrose) grow tiresome: "To no end gathered; vainly then released, forthflowing, wending back: loom of the moon. Weary too in sight of lovers, lascivious men, a naked woman shining in her courts, she draws a toil of waters" (3.466–69). Lest it go unnoticed, Stephen, too, flows, urinating so that his piss merges with "wavespeech: seesoo, hrss, rsseeiss, oos. . . . It flows purling, widely flowing, floating foampool, flower unfurling" (3.457–60). Even as we record these flows, it is useful to think about the author's handling of Stephen, a young man who has not resolved his mother's death or (aside from his role with prostitutes) played the lover; he writes and pisses in rapid succession. Though we certainly find the feminine essentialized as tides in "Proteus," it is also worth pointing out that "Seadeath" is administered by "Old Father Ocean"

(3.482–83), a tradition dating back to Homer and to the Irish sea god, Mananaan, heralded as source of the waves at the start of "Proteus" (3.57).

Molly Bloom and "Penelope" have been treated by critics as the most pronounced expression of the essential feminine in *Ulysses*. To some extent, Joyce prepared readers to interpret Molly as earth. In "Ithaca," she is described as "reclined . . . in the attitude of Gea-Tellus, fulfilled, recumbent, big with seed" (17.2312–14). Joyce told Frank Budgen that *Ulysses* "begins and ends with the female word *yes*. It turns like a huge earth ball slowly surely and evenly round and round spinning, its four cardinal points being the female breasts, arse, womb and cunt" (*Selected Letters* 285). "Penelope," particularly its affirmative coda, has received praise from the start for its flowing language and earthiness.

To give students a sense of the chapter's structure, I like to assign single pages for annotation. Molly's "yes"s and her references to various parts of her own body must be listed and assessed for each page studied. With each occurrence, it is necessary to sense Molly's attitude. How yielding is a given "yes"? What can we learn about her sexuality from the body references? Through comparable data collection in his article "Molly's Flow," Derek Attridge has convincingly challenged the popular critical notion that Molly speaks only a fluid language. For their own study of flow, students can be asked to insert standard punctuation on a given page, identify pronouns, and follow associational chains. Is there still a pulse that makes the semiotic definition of womblike rhythms work for Molly?

Although "Penelope" can be read in great complexity from the perspective of feminine language, it is important also to read it from the second feminist angle presented above, dealing with the women's experience Molly registers. Why does Joyce have her menstruate? This process is both an essential female body function and a practical event requiring sanitary towels and reconsiderations of plans and prospects. In the real world, what were Molly's options as a professional singer? a wife? a mother? a sister to other women? a Jew? a daughter of the garrison? a Dublin consumer of goods? What is she most interested in—career? women's rights? family? lovers? herself? Are women readers attracted to her?

"Penelope" also invites us to think about endings. Students who have read all of *Ulysses* should reflect on how Molly revises their experience of the male-dominated Dublin that precedes the final chapter. What male opinions of herself does she correct? At the end (around 18.1570), the narrative moves into a musical coda, which can be compared with the similar fluid female finale of *Finnegans Wake* and with the different style of ending in *Dubliners* and *Portrait*. Molly inserts herself into nature at Howth. She talks about herself as a flower (following Bloom's concept of her) and records her momentous "yes" of sexual agreement with Bloom. Many novels end with the marriage of the hero and heroine. This one closes with a memory of union.

For years critics of *Ulysses* read Bloom's supposed demand for breakfast in bed as a reassertion of male rights and a resolution of the Blooms' marital problems. Students should be asked whether they have any predictions for the Blooms. Ultimately, they should discuss whether this book concludes an adventure (as did Homer's *Odyssey* and much literature on the masculine model) or introduces us to the (definitionally feminine) flux of existence, which can be handled best through a looping flow of questions.

Consciousness as Conflict:
A Psychoanalytic Approach to *Ulysses*

Sheldon Brivic

Psychoanalysis has long been seen as an especially effective system for apprehending crucial levels of organization in Joyce's *Ulysses*. The affinity of Joyce
to analysis is well summed up at the conclusion of a list of Freudian writers
in Lionel Trilling's essay "Freud and Literature," first published in 1940:

> James Joyce, with his interest in the numerous states of receding
> consciousness, with his use of words as things and of words that point
> to more than one thing, with his pervading sense of the interrelation
> and interpenetration of all things, and, not least important, his treat-
> ment of familial themes, has perhaps most thoroughly and consciously
> exploited Freud's ideas. (37–38)

The early date of Trilling's statement may have kept him from being as
explicit as he could have been about the importance of sexuality in Joyce's
work, but his emphasis on language was prescient. The shifting of analytic
focus toward linguistic operations, which was accomplished in the following
decades, largely by Jacques Lacan, has provided new tools for understanding
mental activity in *Ulysses* through the processes involved in the field of
language.

In a seminar on Joyce with a psychoanalytic orientation, I start with *A
Portrait of the Artist*, which seems to me a necessary prelude, and then
spend seven to eight weeks on *Ulysses*. Teaching a chapter or two of *Finnegans Wake* afterward completes the linguistic and theoretical implications
that grow up late in *Ulysses*. I confine my treatment of psychoanalysis itself
to one class based on several chapters in Elizabeth Wright's short introduction to the psychoanalytic study of literature, *Psychoanalytic Criticism: Theory in Practice*. Half this class is lecture, and I try to stress the fundamentality
of the Oedipus complex as a structural principle and to sketch the linguistic
concepts of Lacan. I also recommend and refer to *Feminine Sexuality*, a
collection by Lacan and his followers, with excellent introductions by the
editors, Juliet Mitchell and Jacqueline Rose. For Joycean guides, I require
Harry Blamires's efficient *Bloomsday Book* and Don Gifford and Robert
Seidman's plentiful Ulysses *Annotated*. I do not use *Ulysses* to confirm
psychoanalysis: I use psychoanalysis to understand *Ulysses*.

Freud and his followers provide models for seeing identity as a process of
interacting forces; for example, if one speaks, what one says is an ongoing
compromise among certain structures. The compromise may be among ego,
id, and superego (the structural topographical system) or among self-interest,
attraction to the mother principle, and conflict with the father principle (the
Oedipus complex). I maintain that virtually every part of *Ulysses*, like the

whole, expresses an interaction of forces represented by the book's main characters, Stephen Dedalus and Leopold and Molly Bloom. I believe that Molly's role goes far beyond the small space she ostensibly occupies, but I have little space to treat her here, so I concentrate on how the principles embodied by Stephen and Leopold interact throughout *Ulysses* and how this interaction is involved in the book's language.

The interplay of forces constituted by Stephen and Bloom may be defined through Lacan's concept of the Other, a term that indicates the external nature of Freud's unconscious. Lacan argues that human discourse (the subject) forms itself only by addressing an unknowable Other that is represented by people with whom one has active contact. I hold that Stephen and Bloom are major representatives of the Other for each other. The interaction of the subject with the Other, as parallel to the dynamic interplay of Freudian personality, is found not only in the characters and plot of *Ulysses* but in its styles. The point of entry into the opposition of forces is the gap in meaning in the text, the point at which a word slips out of clarity and is suspended between one meaning and another, and my class works from close examination of Joyce's words.

To focus on specific details and issues, I give out brief questions for discussion before the class reads chapters of the book. Such questions can bear any number of emphases, and mine try to raise issues that are both fundamental to the novel and germane to psychoanalytic interpretation. For the first episode, for example, I ask what Stephen means when he says of his mother, "Someone killed her" (1.90); why, when Mulligan hails the sea as a "great sweet mother," Stephen sees it as a bowl of vomit (1.80, 107–110); and how Stephen can be both Telemachus and Hamlet. New ideas from students are welcome and can lead in new directions; but having discussed oedipal patterns in both Wright and *Portrait*, students tend to recognize Stephen's obsession with the Father-God who has violated his mother, as well as his embodiment of the archetypal image of the young man (such as Telemachus or Hamlet) whose home is ruled by a usurping or false father. One's attachment to parental forces is fundamental to the unconscious or otherness of one's mind because the parents constitute the primary otherness against which the infant's consciousness is formed.

Because the object of desire represents the mother in this oedipal pattern, what is attractive is forbidden. Therefore Stephen's ambivalence about satisfaction in general inclines him to turn aside from the direct path of desire to alternatives, the "infinite possibilities . . . ousted" (2.50–51) by reality. To demonstrate his persistent focus on alternative possibilities, I have the class look at his "visit" to his uncle Richie Goulding in "Proteus" (3.70–103). This scene is so vividly presented that it is easy to get students to grant that they see it as an actual visit. By examining the context one can then prove that the scene is only imaginary. This class procedure indicates how Stephen dwells in alternatives, and it illustrates the need for caution in framing

Ulyssean "reality." The concentration on alternatives, moreover, reflects a pattern in Joyce, a compulsion toward the many possibilities in any situation—and toward the polyvalence of the text, the multiplying of meanings.

To involve the class in bringing out the existence of simultaneous opposed levels in Joyce's discourse, I ask each student to critique a passage about half a page long from a different episode. Students may pick passages from a list of topics for reports (see app.) or consult with me and choose their own. The student reads the passage aloud in class and spends about ten minutes commenting on its style and significance. Other students are encouraged to respond or add observations. These performances take place once or twice a week and make up about twenty percent of the course, which is some thirty percent lecture and fifty percent discussion.

When different interpretations of a given passage arise, it is important to realize that almost all are correct to some extent on different levels. For example, a passage on Stephen's student Sargent in "Nestor" has Stephen thinking about his childhood and the power of mother love (2.139–169). One student may feel that Stephen has compassion for Sargent, another that he has contempt. One may view the passage as sympathetic to Stephen; another may see it as condemning him for his condescension. All these views represent aspects of a text designed to have multiple intentions. *Ulysses* develops a tendency (expanded in the *Wake*) to teach the reader to be aware of contradictory impulses within each textual unit of consciousness. When we hear several opposing interpretations, recognizing the validity of each, we can feel their interaction within the seminar corresponding to interaction within "the mind of the text" (Kenner, Ulysses 112). And when the text's ambivalence leads us to switch from one view to another that contradicts it, the transition opens up our sense of the vital texture of Joyce's verbal activity. We can sense Joyce's delight in escaping established principles (even his own) and in increasing the breadth and stereoscopic depth of his vision.

Psychoanalysis has played a central role in promoting the opening up of textual contradictions by poststructuralism; unlike deconstruction, however, analysis uses such contradictions not primarily to undermine established values but to approach the unconscious of the subject. The subject of Lacanian analysis always speaks for a large number of private and public voices, including those of relatives, friends, auditors, and cultural codes. While it has to give the effect of an individual human voice, its source, which lies in the Other, is diffused and unlocatable (Ecrits 299, 305). Likewise, the subject of *Ulysses* is impossible to locate because it encompasses the minds of characters, author, readers, and a range of cultures from Homer's to the present (the latest theory to be derived from Joyce).

Many levels of the mind of the text may be seen as engaged in the oedipal pattern, linked above to Stephen, of attachment to a woman who is being violated by an oppressive man. Bloom follows the same pattern in his devotion to Molly. An awareness of the parallels between Stephen and Bloom helps one to see how their viewpoints interact throughout *Ulysses*. Freud's idea of the circulation of libido is modified by the object-relations theories of Melanie Klein, so that personality becomes what Juliet Mitchell calls "a two-way process from inner to outer and back again" (29). Lacan, by refining this process into a system of linguistic transformations called the field of the Other, presents the subject as involved in an interplay with a larger otherness that constitutes that subject. This need of individuals to define themselves through the Other suggests the attachment of the person to a social context, but it also shows how people are moved by their connections with one another. Lacan saw the field of the Other as conveying language through human relations and did not believe in social codes that bypass the unknowable nature of the Other (Ecrits 305). His conception of the subject as a play of voices surrounding an empty center allows us to see the individual as shaped by social forces, but the theory also entails a recognition of how these forces constitute individuality.

I ask my students to explore how the first three episodes, portraying Stephen, are parallel to the next three, showing Bloom. For example, young Stephen confronts the sea, a symbol of birth, in "Proteus" at the same hour that the older Bloom confronts the symbols of death in "Hades." Beginning with their similar reactions to the cloud they each see early in episodes 1 and 4 and continuing through their thinking of the drowned man at the ends of episodes 3 and 6, Stephen and Bloom share many images, which students can be asked to look for.

These six episodes establish an ongoing subtle counterpoint between the two characters. Stephen gains depth by being framed from Bloom's point of view, which sees Stephen's irony with compassion; while Bloom gains humor by being framed from Stephen's perspective, which sees Bloom's compassion with irony. Bloom's compassion is the aspect of life that Stephen cannot face, while Stephen's independence is the aspect Bloom cannot face, and this parallelism indicates why each represents the unconscious of the other. I suggest that what is speaking at any point in the text is usually a combination of their personalities.

We enact this polyphony in class by reading a randomly selected passage and asking whose voice is speaking. Consider the following sentence: "A warm shock of air heat of mustard hanched on Mr Bloom's heart" (8.789). In its syntactical breakdown, this sentence describes Bloom's interior sensations, so it must speak for him. But since the word *hanch* is, presumably, outside his vocabulary—"hanched" in fact sounds more like Stephen than Bloom—the line exemplifies the way that the discourse of Joyce's figures always draws on verbal and stylistic resources far beyond their ken.

What bites Bloom's heart with mustard is Nosey Flynn's reference to Blazes Boylan; this passage thus ironically recognizes Bloom's anxiety at being cuckolded. The extensive development of Bloom's psychosexual problems, as seen here, expresses a probing acuteness that corresponds to Stephen. The aspect of Bloom's mind that suspects (but cannot quite see) that he desires cuckoldry is actively opposed to his consciousness. Insofar as the text draws on knowledge of the unconscious, knowledge that Bloom cannot have, it characterizes him better than he could characterize himself. Much of what is unconscious here matches Stephen's sardonic view of Shakespeare's sexuality.

The aspect of Stephen's presentation that corresponds to Bloom gives his bitterness more emotional depth than it had in *Portrait*. A cue to this new tonality appears at the opening of *Ulysses*: "Pain, that was not yet the pain of love, fretted his heart" (1.102). Stephen's new ache of prelove, which is unlike anything in *Portrait*, is caused by the loss of his mother. The perspective this line introduces so obtrusively remains to make all of Stephen's discourse in *Ulysses* moving. It corresponds to Bloom, the only male figure in the book who possesses love.

In teaching "Scylla and Charybdis," I emphasize the way in which Stephen's theory of Shakespeare as cuckold anticipates Bloom. I ask the class to give examples of parallels between "Shakespeare" and Bloom (a dozen are listed in Schutte 127–30). The parallel complexes and opposing orientations of Stephen and Bloom may be seen in their sections of "Wandering Rocks." Stephen continues to vent hostility toward a Father by whom he feels haunted and controlled (10.824–26), while Bloom, reading *Sweets of Sin*, is excited by the image of an unfaithful wife—Freud, in "A Special Type of Object Choice Made by Men" (52–53), explains that the eternal-triangle pattern of a man attracted to a woman who is attached to another man is a repetition of a boy's childhood relation to his mother, who belongs to his father. These brief, concentrated sections are good subjects for reports by ambitious students, as is Freud's essay.

I ask the class to explain the puzzling fact that when Stephen and Bloom finally meet, they have virtually nothing to say to each other either in "Oxen of the Sun" or in "Circe." They drastically misunderstand each other in "Eumaeus," and their conversation in "Ithaca" is presented only indirectly, as question and answer between unknown speakers. To consider some obstacles that separate the two, we examine the point at which Bloom enters Bella Cohen's music room and Stephen sees him for the first time in "Circe." Stephen must realize that Bloom has followed him, but he refuses to greet him. Instead, Stephen says, "A time, times and half a time" (15.2143), a line from Revelation (12.13–14; see Gifford 488) that enumerates his previous meetings with Bloom and indicates that the end of the world is near. Frightened by Bloom's compassion, Stephen fears that if Bloom touches him emotionally, his independence will be destroyed, and at the end of "Eumaeus," he sings, "*Youth here has End*" (16.1810–11).

A useful view of the misunderstanding between Stephen and Bloom proceeds from the Lacanian principle that all communication is misunderstanding. Insofar as the two men think they understand each other, no contact with the unconscious is possible. The Other can be glimpsed through gaps in discourse; when the two men feel they misunderstand, they confront each other with the unknown that has the power to transform. The climax of their shared incomprehension takes place as they stand in Bloom's garden. Here they are overwhelmed by a sense of the unknowableness of the source of motivation, as represented by the heavenly bodies, including Molly's light, and then they are "silent, each contemplating the other in both mirrors of . . . theirhisnothis fellowfaces" (17.1183).

In a Lacanian perspective, *Ulysses* moves toward the dis-integration of language, the multiplying of meanings and connections for each word that shifts the textual frame of experience into an ongoing semantic displacement. Colin MacCabe's *James Joyce and the Revolution of the Word* traces this progressive opening up of language through Joyce's whole canon. In *Ulysses* such dis-integration tends to proceed on some level even in episodes where it is not evident. "Eumaeus," which seems to be one of the least experimental episodes in the second half of the book, provides a lively way to observe one form of this breakdown: I ask each student to take a few pages of this episode and find an example of a grammatical error that is expressive. The solecisms or slips in "Eumaeus" convey meanings (ambiguities and undertones) that correct English could not, as in this thought of Bloom's:

> [I]t occurred to him as highly advisable to get a conveyance of some description which would answer in their then condition, both of them being e.d.ed, particularly Stephen, always assuming that there was such a thing to be found.   (16.15–18)

The loosening of grammatical connections here brings out alternative meanings, moving toward the polyvalence of the *Wake*. The last eleven words appear to modify Stephen, though they are probably meant for "conveyance." While it seems to be a carriage, this "conveyance of some description" also suggests a mode of discourse that Bloom seeks to sustain in his new relationship with Stephen. This conveyance would both serve their purpose and talk as though its mind were blurred if it "would answer in their then condition." In this discourse the ambiguity of the final misplaced modifier is more meaningful because Bloom is so disoriented by Stephen that he really does have doubts about whether "such a thing" as Stephen is "to be found." This bewilderment fits in with the way "Eumaeus" calls into question the reality of all objects (such as the coffee and D. B. Murphy).

In class, examination of such multilevel slippage can lead to fruitful discussion of association, for *Ulysses* continually shows how paths of conventional discourse steer between many unconscious alternatives, into which Joyce increasingly lapses. The disintegration of meaning is for psychoanalysis a mode not merely of criticism but of access to the unconscious. In the selection of examples of such disintegration for the class to observe, it is thematically and structurally effective to focus on the closing passages of "Nausicaa" and "Ithaca." Here Bloom's language disintegrates into a flow of signifiers, first before he meets Stephen and then before the narrative is taken over by

Molly. The breakdown of language prepares the mind of the text for a new connection.

Freud holds that every person contains both genders, and Lacan sees the genders as linguistic structures imposed on people without biological basis (*Feminine Sexuality* 7, 76–79). In this view, all people use both masculine and feminine systems, and all should be able to develop either side as much as they want at any moment, if they can free themselves from social conventions. Though Molly's lack of punctuation presents her as trapped in a feminine mode of language outside the decisiveness of closure, she asserts her will in relation to Bloom in many ways, especially by taking a lover, and thus shows a strong component of masculinity, which appeals to Bloom. Bloom, like all the men Joyce respects, shows a strong component of femininity, and this appeals to Molly. While recognizing the power of gender roles, Joyce suggests that each person should alternate between the roles to avoid one-sidedness. It may be that feminine sensitiveness is what gives Bloom his strongest grip on Molly and that her masculine aggressiveness is what compels him most, though neither is conscious of the power these reversals exert. Each is held by a part of the other that neither is aware of.

Both with Leopold and Molly and with Bloom and Stephen, who are powerfully driven by the illusion of paternity, *Ulysses* builds on the ways in which characters are attached to each other by their mutual alienation—attached in ways that could not work if they made definite claims. What links them may only be the sense of loss that sunders them, but this may be what links us all to ourselves; for if the subject can never be conscious, if every conscious formulation obscures and denies the subject, then we can never reach our fundamental selves. And our deepest contact with this foundation built on conflict must lie in perplexity. Psychoanalytically, the truth Stephen, Bloom, and Molly find in each other is the unconscious truth of otherness, of suggestions that tease toward what cannot be grasped. This truth is parallel to that of Joyce's constantly withdrawing presence in the text, which keeps suggesting knowledge, purpose, and authority that cannot be dismissed but can never be pinned down.

In relation to teaching, this truth of incomprehensibility corresponds to a prime function of the lecture part of the course: not to be understood. After all, when students discuss Joyce, their common background tends to promote understanding. But because they think I know more about Joyce, I can confront them with an almost ineffable otherness. Of course, I try to be as clear as possible, but going beyond the understanding of the students may be essential to the creative development of their thought. Lecture, however, is only one component, and the rhythm of teaching has to allow time for students to absorb their versions of new ideas and to build on them. When they have assimilated Joyce's ideas into a clear form, they have often drifted away from Joyce, and they need again to be confronted with the incomprehensibility that is central to *Ulysses*. For my part, I find that I usually learn most from students who surprise me by disagreeing with me. As wanderers in Joyce's (and life's) labyrinth of language, we should get not only the feeling of closing in on the truth but the feeling of not quite being able to reach it.

Appendix: Topics

While the topics for reports listed below are for oral reports, I use similar topics (with more explanation) for written ones. By having students write briefly about specific passages, I allow them to try their hand at interpreting *Ulysses* before they finish the novel and write their major papers. My comments on the first paper often are beneficial to the second.

I give one passage, accompanied by a question, for each episode. This list is not universal but personal. Every page of *Ulysses* can be shown to enact psychoanalytic principles; these passages are not supposed to be the best examples, but they are typical. I change my list frequently as my interests change and as I get impressions that some things work better than others.

1. 265–79: What does Stephen's vision of his mother show about his mind?
2. 139–69: Explain the significance of Stephen's thoughts on Sargent and mother love.
3. 45–54: What does the passage about Stephen's conception (and its theological associations) tell us about his conception of himself?
4. 145–64: What does Bloom's trip to the butcher show about his desires?
5. 494–506: How does Bloom see Molly, and what does she suggest to him?
6. 63–84: How does Simon relate to Bloom on the issue of fatherhood?
7. 614–30: How does Myles Crawford affect Stephen as the Other of authority?
8. 897–918: What does the memory of Howth mean to Bloom?
9. 828–45: What is meant by the idea of fatherhood as a mystical estate?
10. 608–24: What does *Sweets of Sin* mean to Bloom?
11. 730–53: How does Bloom's reaction to Simon work to constitute "Siopold"?
12. 1481–1501: Evaluate Bloom's definition of love.
13. 741–53: How do Gerty and Bloom mix in this paragraph?
14. 289–312: How does Stephen relate theology to gender here?
15. 4227–49: What is Stephen trying to do, and what does he actually do, when he breaks the chandelier?
16. 748–84: What can we learn from the disagreement between Stephen and Bloom on the nature of the soul?
17. 2154–94: What do envy, jealousy, abnegation, and equanimity mean to Bloom?
18. 185–206: How do Molly's views of the power and competition of women reflect both her understanding and its limits?

Approaching *Ulysses* through the New Historicism

Mary Lowe-Evans

In an article that might serve as a fine introduction to the new-historicist approach to teaching literature, Brook Thomas characterizes modern students as "alienated from history . . . confined to a series of fragmented, directionless presents" ("Historical Necessity" 510). Many of us involved with bringing students and literature together would agree with Thomas.[1] But literature teachers using new historicist techniques—treating literary works not simply as finely wrought decorator pieces but as vital contributors to a culture's operations—can awaken students to the interrelatedness of all cultural phenomena past, present, and future. By moving in and out of a variety of contemporaneous texts, typically regarding the literary work as a keystone, teachers can lead students to recognize that the constantly shifting values of a culture, indeed of history itself, are produced through the language of all cultural texts.

Those teaching *Ulysses* in this manner may begin by reading materials on Ireland roughly contemporary with Joyce's life, looking for insights into questions that the novel raises and even for figures of speech, repeated in Joyce's works, that might indicate his ideological engagement with the issues of his day. Histories like Emily Lawless's *The Story of Ireland* (1892), Phillippe Daryl's *Ireland's Disease* (1888), L. Paul-Dubois's *Contemporary Ireland* (1908), and Horace Plunkett's *Ireland in the New Century* (1904) contain material on all the major cultural issues in *Ulysses*—from the meaning of Irishness to the historical significance of the Martello tower—using metaphors and attitudinal tags that were part of Joyce's linguistic heritage. Tags include descriptive words or phrases that help us evaluate an author's assessment of a subject. The medical term *disease* in the title of Daryl's treatise on Ireland, implying that the country is an unhealthy organism with the potential of being scientifically diagnosed and cured, is an example of such a tag. Most university libraries will have Daryl's and the other works I've listed or alternative histories of Ireland written during Joyce's lifetime. I place these works on reserve throughout the semester that I teach *Ulysses*, and I require students to read and transcribe passages from them for class discussions or papers.

Emphasis on the linguistic kinship of contemporaneous texts is an important feature of new historicism. Unlike older historicist methods of literary study, new historicism denies that history texts are truer than or even substantially different from literary works, since the common denominator of the two genres is language. Furthermore, language is understood to include all the sign systems of a culture—dress, graphic arts, music, cuisine, and even kitsch—that communicate values at a particular time in a given culture. While new historicists recognize that language systems are governed by grammatical rules sanctioned by the language community, they also know that the language system is, paradoxically, always in the process of transformation—a transformation motivated by ideological shifts, changes in a culture's attitudes about what is normal, acceptable, or preferable behavior. Because historical movements are traced through the constantly adapting system of language, the absolute origins of those movements are virtually impossible to pin down. And the modern critic, caught, like the author of a literary work, in a linguistic cross fire that influences attitudes, cannot view the debates of an earlier period with the supposed objectivity that traditional historicists would have allowed.

Nonetheless, the new historicist understands that momentous changes or transformations do occur in history; and language, whether captured in a history text, novel, or even a women's-magazine article, carries the forces for as well as the resistance to change. The new historicist, then, attempts to account, as far as possible, for historical transformations. In the new historicist's search for historical transformations, the literary author to some extent loses individual identity (though the author's biography remains an important cultural text); language is thought to speak *through* the author to create a work inescapably marked by the myths, conventions, ideologies, and concerns of the language community at the time the work was written. In part, then, new historicism views literature deterministically. But critics disagree about just how trapped authors and critics are in the prevalent cultural debates of their day. Both Michel Foucault, in *The History of Sexuality*, and Stephen Greenblatt, in *Renaissance Self-Fashioning: From More to Shakespeare*, suggest that authors have little choice about the subjects and attitudes of their texts. Jerome McGann, in contrast, emphasizes the self-consciousness of both author and critic, arguing, in *The Beauty of Inflections: Literary Investigations in Historical Method*, that the best authors and critics, aware of pressures certain discourses exert on a culture, are empowered by that awareness to help minimize the ill effects of certain cultural biases.

Clearly, then, the teacher who practices new historicism must be willing to read widely in texts from disciplines other than literature. In the study of Joyce, the histories mentioned above and the author's biography provide sufficient material to elicit discussions and paper topics on numerous cultural issues (specific suggestions from previous student papers are included in the appended syllabus). But diverse sources like social histories, textbooks, sermons, newspaper articles, and even restaurant menus might also be assembled to relocate the literary work in its historical and ideological context. Joyce's use of such disparate works as these and his insatiable, apparently indiscriminate reading habits make his writings especially rich in linguistic booty. This essay examines how students may retrieve some of that booty.

As the appended syllabus shows, the thirty-one students in my Modern Prose Fiction class (designed for English majors) have had seven class periods of lecture and discussion on the plot, themes and motifs, critical views, and historical contexts of *Ulysses* before we undertake the individual episodes (week 4). Since students have read earlier in the course several short stories by William Faulkner and two novels by Virginia Woolf, *Mrs. Dalloway* and *To the Lighthouse*, they are familiar with difficult modernist writing techniques. As I do with the Faulkner and Woolf texts, I ask my students to try to view *Ulysses* as a linguistic artifact, an enduring text offering clues to understanding the culture that produced it. But students may employ interpretive strategies from all the critical approaches new historicism subsumes—the old New Criticism, structuralism, deconstruction, phenomenological and psychoanalytical criticism, Marxism, and feminism—while not restricting themselves to any one of them. The single mandate of new historicism is that the reader move in and *out* of the literary text to examine other cultural documents, thereby observing the power of language to make history.

In the two lectures on "Telemachus," the opening episode of *Ulysses*, I attempt to demonstrate that an "argument for position," imposed in favor of the medical profession in late-nineteenth- and early-twentieth-century Western culture, runs through the episode. (One could as easily focus on the economic inequities alluded to in the episode or to the implicit debate about the superior position of British over Irish culture as suggested in the characters of Haines, Mulligan, and Stephen.) I explain argument for position first by giving the students an example they can easily follow, that of the increasing preference for a particular style of clothes during a given period, and then by discussing the rise in status of the medical profession. An argument for position involves the often subtle pressure within a culture for one value to supersede others. The current debate about the value to the individual of acquiring a suntan is another example students readily understand. Pressure from the medical community to avoid exposure to the sun is effecting a reassessment of the cosmetic value of tanning. But the willingness of many people to expose themselves to the sun potentially affects a major segment of the tourist industry, an industry that in turn makes the equation of beautiful tan with beautiful person difficult to negate. Significantly, as in the acquisition of a tan, cultural values often determine how individuals are perceived and treated, and one set of values is always related to other values that also influence attitudes and behaviors. Students easily follow the argument for position between loose and tight-fitting clothing within a given culture, an argument often having as much to do with economic debates in the fabric industry (among other concerns) as it does with the aesthetics of style or an arbitrary change in public tastes.

I explain that just as preferred clothing styles and the desirability of acquiring a tan are influenced by, and themselves influence, other debates, so the respect a culture holds for one profession over another arises from a complex discourse on wide-ranging issues. The influence, respect, and financial rewards given members of the medical profession throughout much of Western culture for the past century indicate the superior position of medicine in society. While the doctor's rise to a position of power greater than that of

priest, poet, military officer, or educator has been erratic, in the last half of
the nineteenth century medicine began to gain status over religion (to name
only one profession) at an unprecedented rate, directly related to scientific
and technological discoveries. Established religion, until then relatively powerful, began to lose ground at a similar rate and, consequently, began vigor-
ously to try to justify its place in society.

To partially re-create the rhetorical context of the medical-religious debate
in progress when *Ulysses* was conceived, written, and published, I hand out
passages from medical histories written at the time.

I choose materials from our university library and invite students to
bring in samples of their own, asking them to avoid previous research linking Joyce with the medical profession (e.g., J. B. Lyons's *James Joyce
and Medicine*). Opening the class discussion, I do note, however, the passage in Richard Ellmann's biography depicting Joyce daydreaming of himself as "Dr. Joyce, poet, epiphanist, and physician, surrounded by fair
women" (111).

I have found that reading the passages aloud—encouraging students to do
some of the reading, to ask questions, and to bring in pertinent contemporary
materials—helps create a cultural conversation that, however imperfectly,
reflects the situation of the period under scrutiny. Students reading and
responding in isolation miss the atmosphere of debate I hope to re-create by
moving the class, as a community, in and out of various texts.

The first of the following representative passages is from a collection of
addresses given during the years 1891–1922 by William Osler (author of
what has come to be considered a classic medical textbook, *Principles and
Practice of Medicine* [1892]). The second passage, discovered by a student,
is from a history of "the physician throughout the ages," published in 1928.
The third excerpt is from a general history of medicine published in 1943,
and the fourth, which quotes Louis Pasteur and was contributed by another
student, is from a 1968 medical history for students.

> [In] the wonderful nineteenth century . . . [p]olitically, socially, and
> morally, the race had improved, but . . . for the individual, there was
> little hope. Cold philosophy shed a glimmer of light on his path, religion
> in its various guises illumined his sad heart, but neither availed to lift
> the curse of suffering from the sin-begotten son of Adam[; however,]
> in the fulness of time [came science,] the great boon of this wonderful
> century . . . for the healing of nations. Measure as we may the progress
> of the world—materially . . . sociologically . . . intellectually . . . mor-
> ally, in a possibly higher standard of ethics—there is no one measure
> which can compare with the decrease of physical suffering. . . . This
> is the one fact of supreme personal import to every one of us. This is
> the Promethean gift of the century to man.
>
> (Osler 230; first delivered to the Johns Hopkins Historical Club,
> Jan. 1901, and published in the *New York Sun*)

Man is a religious and social being who is vitally interested in his fellows. The physician is, always has been, and will be one of the greatest ameliorators of his sorrows and a great friend. His is the oldest and the most esteemed and essential of the professions. Before the priest, politician, and lawyer began their practices, the doctor pursued his noble calling and exercised the principal power in the community. (Selwyn-Brown, Foreword)

Modernization of medicine began in the nineteenth century with the extension of physics, chemistry and biology, all branches of medicine and surgery developed with rapid strides. . . . The nineteenth century was an era of almost incredible accomplishments. . . . The last half [was] a period that we may justly characterize as the glitter time of medicine. (Massengill 209–10)

Louis Pasteur (1822–1895) . . . taught that the areas of religion and science "are distinct, and woe to him who tries to let them trespass on each other in the so imperfect state of human knowledge." As a scientist he claimed absolute liberty of research. (Green 147–48)

I initiate class discussion of the historical and attitudinal implications of these texts by suggesting that the passages, mixing religious exhortation with a rhetoric that diminishes the power of religion while elevating that of medicine, convey a proud evangelical tone. After some debate, I read aloud the opening passage of "Telemachus," concluding with Mulligan's words, "Silence, all" (1.1–23). Soliciting comments on the possible arguments being established in the scene, I have students draw from their previously assigned reading about Joyce's background, Irish history, Oliver St. John Gogarty (the real-life model for Buck Mulligan), and the medical history excerpts just discussed. (See the appendix for the schedule of assignments.) My questions lead students into a discussion of the relative positions of Mulligan and Stephen. Typically, students point out that even the physical positions— Mulligan above the stairs and Stephen below them—indicate a cultural classification system. The narrator's description of Mulligan, "stately, plump," and Mulligan's seriocomic, coarse but solemn, preacherlike attitude recall for some students the tone of the medical-history passages.

Reminding the students that Mulligan, like his prototype, Oliver St. John Gogarty, was a medical student and "Anglo-Irish Catholic who [had] had the social advantages of a Protestant education" (Platt 77),[2] I ask them to consider whether the text of "Telemachus" makes implications about Mulligan's status. Noting such references as those to Mulligan's crossed razor and mirror and his ungirdled dressing gown, as well as his comments about "body and soul and blood and ouns [and] white corpuscles" (1.21–23), students most often conclude that he plays the role of both doctor and priest. But the students usually realize that Mulligan is only a sham priest who, like Gogarty, is studying, more or less seriously, to be a real doctor. Addressing Stephen as a "fearful jesuit" (1.8), Mulligan implies, in the opinion of several students, that Stephen in some way takes the role of priest too seriously. At this point in our discussion, a student once quoted a passage from *Ireland's Disease* that possibly explained Stephen's fearful attitude and perhaps negated the premise that doctors were gaining power greater than that of priests in Joyce's Ireland:

> [The authority of the priest] is that of a patriarch, who not only wields spiritual power, but . . . social and political power. . . . The faith of the Irish peasant is entire, unquestioning, absolute as that of a thirteenth century's serf.   (Daryl 227)

It is just such contradictions within discourses in contemporaneous texts that I wish to make students aware of. The contradictory arguments of *Ulysses* thus become for them part of a larger debate that, as students note, continues even in our own culture. When we return to "Telemachus," it seems appropriate to stop at Stephen's observation about Mulligan, "He fears the lancet of my art as I fear that of his" (1.152–53), a line implying a power play between doctor and writer. Here a student once observed that in fact the writer whose works have become "canonized"—as Joyce's have—has more lasting influence than an individual doctor. College students are required to study Joyce's works and consciously debate the questions implied there, one student said, while most patients accept their doctor's prescriptions and diagnoses without hesitation. Other students were not quite so willing to accept such a simple answer to the power question.

To anchor the text of "Telemachus" in the realities of Gogarty's and Joyce's lives, I submit a brief passage from Gogarty's memoir:

> Joyce and I used to go see how the actors were getting on with John Elwood, a medical student, who enjoyed the license allowed to medical students by the tolerant goodwill of a people to whom Medicine with its traffic in Life and Death had something of the mysterious and magical about it. To be a medical student's pal by virtue of the glamour that surrounded a student of medicine was almost a profession in itself. Joyce was the best example of a medical student's pal Dublin produced, or rather the best example of the type, extinct since the middle ages, of a Goliard, a wandering scholar.   (293)

Students place this subjective-factual passage from Gogarty's autobiography in relation to the fictional piece from "Telemachus" and the objective-factual comments in the medical texts quoted above. The physician as "great friend" depicted in the Selwyn-Brown passage especially seems to echo Gogarty's words and Mulligan's behavior. Students can now draw tentative conclusions about the attitudes of Stephen, Mulligan, Joyce, Gogarty, the Irish, and Western societies generally toward doctors just after the turn of the century. I suggest that the "glamour" surrounding the medical student Gogarty mentions is reflected in the medical histories that refer to the "Promethean gift" of healing, "the glitter time of medicine," and the doctor as "the principal power in the community." In "Telemachus," Mulligan is unmistakably glamorous with his "white teeth glistening," "wellfed voice," and "wellknit trunk" (1.25, 107, 132–33). Stephen, by contrast, according to Mulligan, is a "jejune jesuit," a "lovely mummer," and a "dreadful bard" (1.45, 97, 134). The condescending tone of these apparently well intentioned jibes, one student has observed, echoes the tone of Osler's references to philosophy and religion. Students may find, too, that Mulligan's overall confident tone matches Gogarty's, Selwyn-Brown's, and Pasteur's.

For most students Stephen's ambiguous position intensifies the confidence Mulligan projects. Neither priest nor committed nonbeliever, Stephen is not even a full-fledged artist. By his own admission, he is a "dogsbody to rid of vermin" (1.137). One thing about Stephen is generally clear to my students, however. He resents Mulligan's condescending attitude, an attitude that is linked in the text to Mulligan's "scientific" and apparently enlightened view of death. The exchange between Stephen and Mulligan concerning their responses to the death of Stephen's mother (1.180–220) is usually seen as epitomizing Stephen's resentment. I interject that the passage also reinforces my reading of the medical profession's increasing power in Western culture. Mulligan clearly expresses the notion that death has nothing to do with religion but is simply a "beastly thing. . . . Her cerebral lobes are not functioning" (1.206–11). Once again moving out of the text of "Telemachus" to explore how Mulligan's attitude may have been formed, I read from a medical history, this one published in 1929:

> The publication of such works as Helmholtz's *Conservation of Energy* (1847) and Darwin's *Origin of the Species* [sic] did away forever with the silly antropomorphisms [sic] and appeals to human conceit which have always hampered the true advancement of medicine in the past. . . . [P]hysics, chemistry, and biology came to be studied as objective laboratory sciences, dissociated from the usual subjective human prepossessions. Hardly anyone today doubts the theorem sustained by Emile Littré that the real advancement of biological and medical science has nothing to do with theological dogma or metaphysical speculation, but simply depends upon collateral improvements in physical and chemical procedure. (Garrison 407)

Students tend to agree that Mulligan's attitude toward Mrs. Dedalus's dying condition is similar to the stand taken in this passage. They see, too, that the resistance to such a view, as represented by Stephen, is weak and unsure.

But not all are convinced that we must necessarily conclude that religion was losing ground to medicine in Ireland. One student offered in opposition to such a view a passage from Paul-Dubois's *Contemporary Ireland*: "Few race characteristics are so profoundly marked as is the intensity of religious feeling in the Celtic races, and, above all, in the Irish race" (491). Here I suggest that Stephen's ambiguity may reflect an overall weakening in the argument against medicine's rise to power in the nineteenth century. But we also see that our intense focus on the medical-religious debate cannot bring into view *all* the facets of Stephen's character or account fully for Stephen's resentment of Mulligan, any more than a single argument for position can account for any deeply ingrained cultural attitude.

Nonetheless, for most students, the passage where Stephen observes the old milk woman respond to Mulligan as medical student decisively locates "Telemachus" in the debate about medicine versus religion as well as in the conflict about British patronage of Ireland:

> Stephen listened in scornful silence. She bows her old head to a voice that speaks to her loudly, her bonesetter, her medicineman: me she slights. To the voice that will shrive and oil for the grave. . . . And to the loud voice that now bids her be silent with wondering unsteady eyes.   (1.418–23)

Explaining the notion of the "Shan Van Vocht," the old woman as symbol of Ireland, I indicate how the passage represents an Ireland that pays homage to "her bonesetter, her medicineman" and to "the voice that will shrive and oil [her] for the grave" rather than to her writers. The subtly shifting hierarchy of doctor over priest is suggested in Stephen's repeated mention of the "loud" voice of the medicine man in contrast to, simply, the voice of the priest. Again, Stephen's resentment and apparent impotence are clear. In the context I have been re-creating, Stephen's "Usurper" label for Mulligan, with which "Telemachus" ends, seems to apply to Mulligan as a member of the profession that is usurping the power of priest, writer, and most other respected professionals of the day.

In my concluding remarks for these two or three class periods, I remind students that no single cultural debate can "explain" *Ulysses* any more than it can explain the mores of an entire society. I also admit that we have not examined religious texts that may dispute medicine's claim to power. I point out that most critics recognize an emphasis on *three* powerful voices in "Telemachus"—the doctor, the priest, and the British (in the character of Haines)—while our analysis has been limited to two professions that have been in contention outside as well as inside Ireland throughout the nineteenth and twentieth centuries. Because I believe the jockeying for power between these two professions, depicted with great subtlety and complexity by Joyce, is an important subject of discussion for my students, I encourage them to continue seeking evidence for and against the medical profession's argument for position throughout *Ulysses*, especially in the "Oxen of the Sun" episode. I reiterate that, as clever as Joyce's representation of the conflict is, some of the attitudes established in *Ulysses* may have been imposed on the text, not consciously inscribed there. Following such advice, one student turned in a paper on "Oxen," treating it as a history of obstetrics from the height of midwifery to the idealization of the obstetrician.

The approach I advocate in this essay may be modified to accommodate other cultural arguments apparent in *Ulysses*. For example, a teacher may want to foreground the argument, implicit in *Ulysses*, that mothers are uniquely responsible for a family's stability. This notion was being challenged at the turn of the century and again in the interwar years when *Ulysses* was being written. The debate surfaces especially in those episodes that describe the Dedalus family disintegrating after the death of Mrs. Dedalus. The histories of Ireland I have listed often credit the Irish mother for ensuring family stability, while articles in avant-garde journals outside Ireland, like the *Egoist*, view such credit as, in fact, an unfair imposition of responsibility.

Any of the sample topics listed in the appendix may be used in tandem with the contemporaneous texts cited in the essay. Three of the topics have been successfully written on by students. Such students, who have first encountered *Ulysses* by way of new historicism, invariably become sensitive to the connectedness of all facets of Irish culture. Since students themselves must lead all class discussions after the model lecture-discussion on "Telemachus," they have the opportunity to influence significantly the direction of the discourse as I did in the model situation. Thus, the course design reflects as closely as possible the constant rise and fall of influential voices in the cultural conversation.

NOTES

[1] For another model new-historicist reading, see Thomas's article "Preserving and Keeping Order by Killing Time in *Heart of Darkness*" and Ross C. Murfin's introduction to Thomas's article, "What Is the New Historicism?"

[2] As an alternative to the reading I suggest, Platt's article may act as a model new-historicist reading of "Telemachus."

Appendix: Sample Syllabus for Teaching *Ulysses* Using New Historicism

On Reserve

General overviews
Harry Blamires. *The New Bloomsday Book: A Guide through* Ulysses.
Zack Bowen. *"Ulysses."*
Richard Ellmann. *James Joyce.*

Patrick A. McCarthy. Ulysses: *Portals of Discovery*.
J. W. Moody and F. X. Martin, eds. *The Course of Irish History*.

Varieties of historical or cultural criticism
Richard Brown. *James Joyce and Sexuality*.
Cheryl Herr. *Joyce's Anatomy of Culture*.
Dominic Manganiello. *Joyce's Politics*.
L. H. Platt. "The Buckeen and the Dogsbody: Aspects of History and Culture in 'Telemachus.' "

Texts contemporaneous with Joyce
Phillippe Daryl. *Ireland's Disease*.
Michael Davitt. *The Fall of Feudalism in Ireland*.
Emily Lawless. *The Story of Ireland*.
L. Paul-Dubois. *Contemporary Ireland*.
Horace Plunkett. *Ireland in the New Century*.

Week 1. Read or have read the first 9 episodes of *Ulysses*. Read Blamires, the "Ulysses" entry in *A Companion to Joyce Studies* through "Nausicaa," and McCarthy through 67. The plot, main characters, and connections with the *Odyssey* will be discussed.

Week 2. Read Blamires, Bowen, and McCarthy to end. Biases and contributions of various critical approaches will be discussed. Take-home essay quiz assigned.

Week 3. Complete the reading of *Ulysses*. Read Ellmann 389–526, Moody 294–312, and introductions to Brown, Herr, and Manganiello. The interrelatedness of biography, history, and literature will be discussed.

Week 4. Read Platt. The article as a model of new-historicist criticism will be discussed. Take-home essay quiz assigned. New-historicist lecture-discussion on "Telemachus" begins.

Week 5. Lecture-discussion of "Telemachus" continues.

Weeks 6–7. Working in teams, students will lead discussion of remaining episodes as assigned. Discussions must be led *through* the episode to extratextual materials as demonstrated in the "Telemachus" lecture-discussion. Discussion leaders must provide excerpts of extratextual materials for all class members.

Final Paper Requirements

The paper is to focus on a single episode, character, or ideological "track" in *Ulysses* but must, at the same time, show how the episode, etc., has been significantly shaped by outside influences.

Besides *Ulysses* itself, the works-cited list must include at least five additional sources, including a biographical work, a history of Ireland written during Joyce's lifetime, and one other work written during Joyce's lifetime.

Paper-Topic Ideas

All topics listed are covered to some extent in the works on reserve.

1. Participation in Sports as a Determinant of Good Character in *Ulysses* and Irish Culture

2. Musical Taste and Status in Molly Bloom's Ireland
3. Large versus Small Families: Who Were the Good Citizens of *Ulysses?*
4. Broken Homes and Mothers Who Failed in *Ulysses*
5. The Case of the Disappearing Midwife in "Oxen of the Sun"
6. The Power of the Press in "Aeolus" and Dublin
7. Model Dublin Schoolboys in *Ulysses*
8. Molly Malaprop: Uneducated Womanspeak in "Penelope"

Understanding *Ulysses* through Irish and British Popular Culture

Joseph Heininger

This essay describes the methods and materials I use to teach *Ulysses* in an upper-level undergraduate course on Joyce. The group of fifteen to twenty seniors, most of them English majors, meets for three fifty-minute classes each week, a format I find more effective than two ninety-minute meetings. About a third of the students have read some *Dubliners* stories and *Portrait* before beginning the course, a few have read *Ulysses*, and one or two have even looked into *Finnegans Wake*. Most students have not read any Joyce. Because of this disparity and because I want to establish everyone on a firm footing, I assume that students have some knowledge of Joyce and his work but that they require the instructor's skill and direction in helping them to discover this rich literature.

By the time we start *Ulysses*, about five weeks into the semester, we have read *Dubliners*, *Portrait*, and some lyric poems by Joyce and Yeats. We have also seen John Huston's film version of "The Dead" (Vestron, 1987) and the excellent three-hour Radio Telefís Eireann (RTE) film on Joyce's career, *Is There One Who Understands Me?* With these readings and films as a base, the students begin to acquire a sense of Joyce's historical and urban setting and the "nets" of "nationality, language, [and] religion" (*Portrait* 203) that define his characters. Then we take seven weeks to read and explore *Ulysses*. Classes alternate between student-led presentations (twenty-minute oral reports, sometimes with video- or audiotape accompaniment) on topics concerning *Ulysses*, its art, and its times and discussion of the individual episodes and the themes of the novel. At semester's end, we spend only a week reading and hearing selections from *Finnegans Wake*.

The approach we adopt for reading *Ulysses* is to investigate the various contexts *Ulysses* occupies in Ireland's social, political, and cultural history. Together, we examine selected primary and secondary materials in class and then discuss the connections between these contexts and the novel's themes. This parallel-reading technique depends absolutely on taking the time to read *Ulysses* slowly, so that we cover an episode (more or less) in each class meeting over seven weeks. As we proceed episode by episode, we also read and discuss these other texts, looking for exchanges and correspondences between the novel and the historical sources that can stimulate greater understanding of Joyce's art. In addition, this strategy yields good topics for student presentations, such as the style of "Aeolus" in relation to the language and layout of the contemporary British and Irish press; advertising styles in "Nausicaa" and the economic and cultural roles of advertising in 1904 and in the 1990s; and the relations between "Cyclops," Joyce's politics, and the political rhetoric of some 1904 Irish nationalists. To read *Ulysses* in this way, combining traditional approaches to literary and social history with some applications of cultural studies methods, we use photographs, music, and texts from Irish literature, history, popular culture, and mass culture.

Before I describe the plan for parallel reading in detail, I wish to emphasize that students have found that learning to read a variety of cultural texts does not distract them from confronting the specific concerns and themes of the novel. Rather, this perspective becomes part of the experience of reading *Ulysses* and helps students to place *Ulysses* in its historical era and to acknowledge Joyce's narrative doubling. They see how *Ulysses* is both a retelling of Homer's epic of exile, wandering, and return and a modern story steeped in the artistic, economic, and civic life of turn-of-the-century Dublin. Although we have copies of the Homeric correspondences as schematized by Stuart Gilbert and Richard Ellmann at our side as we read, our interest is more steadily focused on what I call the contemporary Irish and English correspondences: on the characters' engagements with those "nets" Stephen Dedalus has identified in chapter 5 of *Portrait*. Then, once our sense of the realistic and symbolic potentialities of the text is alive, we explore how the classical and contemporary dimensions of the book are established in "Telemachus." This attention to contexts opens the way to consider important issues in the novel as they arise: character development, the repetition and expansion of motifs and themes, the resolution (or nonresolution) of plot, and Joyce's increasingly original stylistic experiments in the second half of the novel.

When we read "Telemachus," I provide orientation and strategies for exploring the first half of the book. According to chronology and thematic continuity, "Telemachus" presents Stephen Dedalus, whom we last saw dedicating himself to a high destiny at the end of *Portrait*, now back in Dublin after two less-than-satisfying trips to Paris. I describe *Ulysses* as a novel that draws its narrative and stylistic power from the juxtaposition of two primary sources: the classical, represented by Homer's *Odyssey* (and secondarily by the plays of Shakespeare), and the demotic, represented by the Irish and British popular and mass culture of Joyce's time. Although we look primarily to sources in Joyce's Irish culture, we do not slight the classical parallels, for the Homeric correspondences certainly show students one way in which Joyce himself suggested interpretation of *Ulysses*. Yet the astonishing variety of materials from Irish life and culture, materials Joyce incorporated in every episode, clearly indicates that *Ulysses* owes as much of its verbal and narrative energies to popular sources as to classical models.

As we read with our eyes on Irish cultural contexts, we need to clarify the difference between popular culture and mass culture. A simplified but correct distinction is that popular culture generates artistic forms and texts that come from the interests of the people, while mass culture produces forms and texts that reveal the interests of social and religious institutions and commercial organizations. In the historical Dublin of 1904 and in Joyce's

Ulysses, popular culture includes most types of songs, such as Bloom's favorite opera arias from *Martha*; folk ballads ("The Croppy Boy"); concert hall, music hall, and pantomime songs ("Seaside Girls," "Love's Old Sweet Song," "I Am the Boy That Can Enjoy Invisibility"); and street literature (the "Agendath Netaim" and "Elijah is coming!" throwaways). Whereas popular culture is by definition ancient and traditional, mass culture is a phenomenon arising in its familiar modern forms in Europe between 1850 and 1900, with the advent of the mass market and the dominance of capitalism. The increasingly more sophisticated language of mass culture is advertising, especially advertising for national brands of commodities. Although the Irish economy was depressed and poverty was widespread in Ireland in late Victorian and Edwardian times, the competition for markets and the growing importance of mass culture were exemplified in Ireland by the advertising that many English firms used to market national brands, including patent medicines, soap, cigarettes, many types of clothing, and mineral waters, beer, ale, and tea.

In *Ulysses*, we discover that mass culture continually takes form in the physical surroundings and mental worlds of Bloom, Molly, and Stephen. The point of our investigation of these cultural representations is to demonstrate to students that Joyce portrays with care and subtlety how such material, everyday changes in the urban scene contribute to perception, to changes in human personality and consciousness. These material forms include commercial photography, advertising posters, advertising jingles, even the resounding names of Dublin's modern electrified tramways and their routes, as named in "Aeolus." These forms certainly also comprehend the repeated features of mass-circulation newspapers and magazines: advice columns such as that of "Vera Verity" on beauty, which Gerty MacDowell reads in "Nausicaa"; serial fictions such as "Matcham's Masterstroke" in magazines like *Tit-Bits* and *Pearson's Weekly*; consumer-product advertising (Cantrell and Cochrane mineral waters, Mermaid cigarettes, Pears's and Sunlight soaps, and, most famous, "Plumtree's Potted Meat"); and illustrated weekly papers, such as the respectable, ubiquitous *Illustrated London News* and the more titillating *Photo-Bits* (the source of the "Bath of the Nymph" reproduction that Bloom admires in "Calypso").

The best way for students to immerse themselves in Joyce's world is by looking at photographs. As they read "Telemachus" (or earlier, while reading *Dubliners*), I exhibit photographs of the 1904 Dublin Joyce knew: the Joyce-Gogarty Martello tower, the Custom House, the churches, pubs, theaters, streets, trams, quays, and cemeteries. We spend time acquainting ourselves with the look of the houses and tenements in Dublin, the rich and poor shop fronts and shopping districts, the pubs, the breweries and distilleries, the newspaper offices, and the two colleges. We distinguish different types of clothing and dress worn on the street and point out the advertising "sandwichmen" (8.123) trudging along the Dublin curbsides (Hickey 10; Anderson

30–31). This visual inspection of photographs of Dublin's streets and people in Joyce's time is indispensable; it can only be improved on by a student's visiting Dublin itself. Even then, as Robert Nicholson reports in his new Ulysses *Guide*, the remnants of Joyce's physical Dublin are slowly disappearing, so that assimilating the look of things as they were from about 1895 to 1905 from the many excellent collections of photographs is of primary importance.

In the first week of reading *Ulysses*, I circulate the books of Irish photographs assembled by Maurice Gorham and Kieran Hickey and the illustrated books about Joyce by Chester Anderson, Cyril Pearl, and Bruce Bidwell and Linda Heffer. Then, as we read "Calypso" and the other episodes in the first half, which are filled with visual images of Dublin's urban landscape—"Lotus-eaters," "Hades," "Aeolus," "Lestrygonians," "Scylla and Charybdis," and the pivotal "Wandering Rocks"—we are prepared to associate Joyce's words on the page with the black-and-white images in the books. In "Lestrygonians," for example, Joyce describes Bloom's responses to the merchandise and human scenes of Grafton Street:

> Grafton street gay with housed awnings lured his senses. Muslin prints, silkdames and dowagers, jingle of harnesses, hoofthuds lowringing in the baking causeway. . . .
> He passed, dallying, the windows of Brown Thomas, silk mercers. Cascades of ribbons. Flimsy China silks. A tilted urn poured from its mouth a flood of bloodhued poplin: lustrous blood. The huguenots brought that here. . . .
> Gleaming silks, petticoats on slim brass rails, rays of flat silk stockings. Useless to go back. Had to be. Tell me all.
> High voices. Sunwarm silk. Jingling harnesses. All for a woman, home and houses, silkwebs, silver, rich fruits spicy from Jaffa. Agendath Netaim. Wealth of the world.
> A warm human plumpness settled down on his brain. His brain yielded. Perfume of embraces all him assailed. With hungered flesh obscurely, he mutely craved to adore.   (8.614–39)

Of course, no photograph of Grafton Street's awnings, shop fronts, and window displays can convey as much about Bloom's *states of mind* as these few lines of Joyce's prose, but a photograph can give the essential visual information about the look of Grafton Street, the premier shopping street for quality goods in Joyce's Dublin, and the well-to-do appearance of the people who pass, dallying, enjoying the shops' sensual appeal. There is a photograph of the breadth and length of Grafton Street in Anderson (31) and several of Grafton Street shop fronts, including a remarkable image of well-dressed pedestrians passing an opulent window display, in Hickey (72).

I use photographs as the primary entryway to the Irish cultural contexts of parallel reading. But beyond the look of the buildings and streets, the landscape of 1904 Dublin presents other features important to Joyce's portrait of city life. We therefore also inspect photographs and other examples of the advertisements, theater posters, magazines, and newspapers of the period, so that students can assimilate the designs and the mentalities of the communications media represented in *Ulysses*. "Calypso," "Lotus-eaters," and "Lestrygonians," in which we discover Bloom's propensity to respond to the images and language of popular urban life in magazines, handbills, posters, and advertising, all become more concrete portraits of the Dublin environment at a particular time when we examine some Victorian and Edwardian advertisements. We consider their styles, messages, and probable audiences and compare the products they tout with those Joyce chooses for thematic purposes in *Ulysses*, such as Plumtree's Potted Meat (this meat product was manufactured in Dublin, and the jingle is probably a Joycean invention, but Fritz Senn [656] claims that we can never be sure) and Bloom's pocketed piece of soap (not the ubiquitous British Pears's, or even the Dublin-made Sunlight, but Sweny's custom-made blend).

More generally, we contrast advertisements in *Ulysses* with those we see now in American magazines and newspapers, and sometimes we discuss the arguments of John Berger's *Ways of Seeing*, John Fiske's *Understanding Popular Culture*, or Stuart Ewen's *All-Consuming Images*. We recognize that contemporary television commercials are a special postmodern form because of their medium and audience. At some point in the novel, however, our reading engenders questions about and criticisms of the powers of advertisers, advertising's overt and subliminal messages, and the codes of advertising in cultural communication. Usually, students select for discussion some key passages featuring Bloom's advertising activities from "Lotus-eaters" or "Aeolus" or "Lestrygonians," and a full airing of these issues is stimulated when they encounter the language and the mentalities that portray Gerty MacDowell and Bloom in "Nausicaa."

A valuable source for well-reproduced magazine and newspaper advertisements with special relevance to the goods referred to in *Ulysses* is Robert Opie's book *Rule Britannia: Trading on the British Image*. Opie's well-chosen ads feature mass-produced and mass-marketed British products, including many that found their way to Ireland in this period. Many of these ads and products are identifiable in *Ulysses*, and their words and images often enlarge the rich storehouse of Irish-English mass-cultural symbols. Some English products become mass-marketed "massproduct[s]" (17.369) in Joyce's Ireland: soap, tea, mineral waters, cigarettes, cocoa. Examples in Opie's illustrations (see esp. 32–33) are Pears's soap, Sunlight soap, Player's Navy Cut tobacco, Bovril, and many cocoas, elixirs, and "universal embrocations" (patent medicines). Epps's cocoa, the "massproduct" Bloom and Stephen drink in "Ithaca," is represented by a politically provocative ad (the show card of a smiling John Bull sitting on top of the world [31]). Another useful source of Victorian advertisements, especially of patent medicines and beauty products such as Gerty MacDowell's "Beetham's Larola," is Thomas Richards's illustrated study *The Commodity Culture of Victorian England*. Richards makes a sophisticated analysis of the social history of "the seaside girl" by examining the advertising language of "Nausicaa," and students may be interested by the ways in which he reads ads as a "specifically capitalist form of representation" (1).

To show students how the narrative techniques of the episodes combine elements of classical culture, popular culture, and Bloom's advertising-man mass culture, I focus first on the Irish artistic and political situation in "Telemachus." Clearly, this episode prepares the ground for Joyce's portrayal of Stephen's artistic and filial problems by raising the classical ghosts of Telemachus and Hamlet through allusion and analogy. But "Telemachus" (following *Portrait* in this respect) also indicates quite specifically how Stephen's close engagements with Irish art, Irish music, and Irish poetry have shaped him, especially the art of Thomas Moore, W. B. Yeats, and Oscar Wilde.

As evidence of Stephen's Irish cultural matrix and his problems with those he calls usurpers, I bring to class either the 1903 Macmillan edition or the 1971 Cuala Press reprint of Yeats's 1903 poems, *In the Seven Woods*. We note especially the colophon, which states that the book was finished "the sixteenth day of July in the year of the big wind, 1903." In "Telemachus," Buck Mulligan speaks to Haines in Stephen's hearing, echoes this Yeatsian phrase, and mentions "the folk and the fishgods of Dundrum," thus mocking in one stroke Yeats's recent poems of the Celtic "folk" and Yeats's sisters' ("the weird sisters") newly founded revivalist projects of printing and weaving at Dundrum. Buck, of course, lumps all this cultural revivalism in a typically satirical and dismissive speech (1.365–67). By examining the reprint volume of Yeats, students can not only see Yeats's folk-inspired poems but also read them as excellent examples of the cultural projects of the Celtic revival. The satirical context in which Buck dismisses them discloses how the problem of properly rendering Ireland's realities in art feeds the rivalries in "Telemachus" between Yeats, Mulligan, Haines, and Dedalus. One of many Celtic allusions and motifs in "Telemachus," Yeats's book of folk poems exemplifies the contemporary renaissance of Irish popular culture. But its presence also reveals how frequently Joyce satirizes various types and figures of the Celtic revival in *Ulysses* (Æ and his followers in "Scylla and Charybdis," for example).

Of course, many illustrations of Bloom's physical and mental world also touch on Irish art and art's relations to nationalism and politics. With Bloom (and later, with Gerty MacDowell and Molly), the meaning of "culture" acquires a steadily wider definition than it does with Stephen in "Telemachus," "Proteus," and "Scylla and Charybdis." Bloom's sense of Irish culture is less specialized than Stephen's, as Bloom's cultural universe encompasses popular poetry, song, and folktales, the products and writing styles of newspapers and magazines, and mass-produced artifacts and advertisements. I have already referred to the many sources for reproductions of relevant ads and to the ways they may be used in class. Now I briefly mention two other sources I use to supplement our parallel reading: one is familiar to Joyce teachers, one relatively new.

The familiar resource is recorded music. Many popular and operatic songs are threaded through the fabric of *Ulysses*, and some of them, such as "M'appari," "The Croppy Boy," and "Love's Old Sweet Song," become motifs and establish themes central to the novel. Listening to taped and recorded music is crucial to students' full appreciation of *Ulysses*, especially its re-creation of the musical atmosphere of 1904 Dublin. For "Sirens" and "Cyclops," in which voices are so important, I have found that playing the tapes of the Irish actors' reading of *Ulysses* produced and broadcast by RTE in June 1982 is the ideal way to engage the sounds of those voices. We listen to the reading and singing of "Sirens," from 11.419 to 11.766, a selection that features Simon Dedalus's singing of "M'appari" (Leopold's song from *Martha*) against the background of Bloom's thoughts of Molly, himself, and Boylan.

At the appropriate points in our reading, we also hear selections from *The Joyce of Music*, including "Seaside Girls," "Love's Old Sweet Song," and "In Old Madrid." We listen to a recording of John McCormack singing "Love's Old Sweet Song," which preserves the sounds of an Irish tenor voice closely linked to Joyce's own, as Ellmann's biography informs us. (A recording by Maura O'Connell is also available.) And we look at the illustration on the cover of the *Radio Times* for 21 December 1923 (Maltby 63), which depicts a domestic scene of a British middle-class family gathered in their parlor listening to the radio together. The caption is "Just a Song at Twilight," a phrase borrowed from Joyce's and Bloom's favorite sentimental song.

I want to turn now from musical to printed source materials. The availability of a facsimile of the *Freeman's Journal* makes it possible for students to use a splendid visual, stylistic, and historical-political source as they draw their mental maps of Joyce's Dublin. Reading "Aeolus" can be a slow and confusing business to those students who are unprepared to have their conventional expectations of novelistic narrative frustrated, even when they have grown accustomed to the interior monologues and the shifts from third-person to stream-of-consciousness styles in the first six episodes. Although students still need Gifford and Seidman's extremely helpful notes in Ulysses *Annotated*, the *Freeman's* facsimile gives them another text to compare with Joyce's narrative in "Aeolus," his newspaper in the making.

Reading "Aeolus" alongside the facsimile of the *Freeman's Journal* for 16 June 1904 shows students in dramatic fashion two ways in which the events of the day were reported and represented: one is conventional, journalistic;

the other, Joyce's, is both realistic and symbolic. And beyond being able to compare these perspectives and representational ideas, students get to see a historically valuable example of the appearance, verbal style, organization, and editorial mentality of an important contemporary Irish newspaper. For instance, with almost no news but many small advertisements on the front page, it is not surprising that newspapers like the *Freeman's* and the *Irish Times* were commercially successful. It is also not surprising that, in Joyce's extremely factual fiction, Bloom's eye fell on the ad for Plumtree's Potted Meat when "he unrolled the newspaper baton idly and read idly" (5.143).

Given the importance of all the interpolated headings to the text of "Aeolus" and to its nuances of meaning and tone, I encourage my students to scrutinize the layout, headline style, and contents of the *Freeman's* facsimile and to note the range of foreign and domestic news, including the full reports of bicycle racing and other sports. When we move from textual comparisons to thematic and interpretive ideas, we look at how "Aeolus" imitates the fixed patterns of a newspaper but also parodies its layout and organization. Later, students can consider how the writing styles of different departments of the newspaper are typified and made the subjects of extended parodies and pastiches in "Cyclops."

The approach through popular and mass culture provides the class with an adaptable method of parallel reading and of interpretation to deal with the complexities of *Ulysses*. Students speak about the ways Joyce's forms of social communication relate to their experiences of contemporary advertising, music, videos, speeches, newspapers, television, and films. They recognize the major influences these forms of communication and culture have on everyday life. Our thinking about modern cultural forms and how they are made and perceived usually takes us into discussions of the major concerns of the novel: how characters and plots develop, how surface relates to symbol, how readers can discriminate between truth, fantasy, and reality as they receive messages from various media and share in human acts of communication. Students also discover, when reading "Aeolus," "Wandering Rocks," and "Sirens," that Joyce is in part writing a reflexive novel, a fiction about the making of fiction. They find that when Joyce self-consciously rewrites the styles of earlier novelists, he does so by incorporating popular cultural forms into the traditional narrative forms of English fiction, and he both echoes and strays from the formal patterns of Homer's *Odyssey*.

The pedagogical aim of dealing with the pervasive presence of popular art and culture in *Ulysses* is to maintain the focus of investigation on the essential doubleness of the text. When we examine the text of *Ulysses* to see how Joyce uses popular and mass-produced forms of social communication to shape the worlds of the characters, we ground ourselves in the Irish historical dimensions of the book. At the same time, we read these facts and these specific cultural products for their symbolic and mythic values. This attention to the objects and messages of everyday life teaches students that Joyce's method is to be contemporary and at the same time to reshape the classic.

As students undertake the odyssey of reading *Ulysses*, they must follow interpretive paths among the Homeric correspondences, the Dublin idioms, the names of places, and the artifacts of Irish and British culture. This means of supplementing the reading of the novel with related texts and materials enables students to make connections and view relations in fresh ways. The approach has worked well for my senior students, and I believe it can be a useful pedagogical tool for other teachers in their classes.

Reading *Ulysses* within the History of Its Production and Reception

Kathleen McCormick

Teaching *Ulysses* often poses a double-edged problem. If students are asked to read and respond to the the text without the assistance of guides or notes, they may be overwhelmed and intimidated because they lack sufficient literary and historical background to enjoy or even get through it. If, in contrast, the teacher attempts to provide as much authoritative guidance as possible—whether in the form of plot summaries, close textual analyses, or historical information—the students may still be intimidated. While such interventions can help the student read *Ulysses*, they can easily reinforce feelings of insecurity about reading the literature of "high" culture, encourage intellectual passivity, and strengthen traditional notions of literature as something secret, sprung mysteriously from a transcendent or otherworldly "genius."

I offer here a theoretical orientation and a pedagogical practice that can empower students to teach themselves and one another about the historical conditions in which *Ulysses* was written and has been interpreted. Students thus learn to formulate their own questions and to situate culturally and historically the interpretations they develop. No form of reading is ideologically neutral, and I introduce students to a way of reading *Ulysses* that underscores the interconnectedness of social conditions and reading and writing practices: students learn to read *Ulysses* from the standpoint of its production and reception. This approach contends that texts are not transcendent, stable entities with universal significances but material objects produced and reproduced under changing historical and ideological conditions. Likewise, readers and authors are not unique individuals who spontaneously create their own texts or meanings but subjects in history who are also traversed by a variety of complex and often conflicting discourses.

While this view of literature and the reader might initially shock students accustomed to being told that good readers should be able to develop simultaneously "original" and "universal" interpretations of literary texts, it ultimately helps to explain why students sometimes cannot generate automatic interpretations of *Ulysses*. This perspective assumes that *Ulysses* was produced in a particular social and literary formation quite different from the present one and that students can only read and respond to the text after first learning something about the formation in which it was written. Further, readers must also analyze the history of the reception of *Ulysses*— its continuing (re)production throughout its subsequent history. According to this perspective, contemporary readers—including students—are part of this history; they make active interventions into the process of the text's reception, not as individuals somehow able to stand outside the history of the text's criticism, but as subjects constituted by and in history. The theoretical—and pedagogical—rationale for reading *Ulysses* within the context of its production and reception is that students can apprehend and defend the critical and ideological significances of their readings of *Ulysses* only if they can begin to place them, even cursorily, within the complex history of the text.

Although teaching *Ulysses* in the context of its production and reception might initially look like a mixture of old-fashioned source or background study and a study of the history of criticism, this approach stands in theoretical and methodological opposition to such older perspectives. They saw the past as something that could be objectively reconstituted from a vantage point outside history and treated the text as something whose "transcendent truth" could be revealed by such investigations. Production and reception theory, in contrast, insists that the past is constructed only from the perspectives of the (changing) present and therefore that it is not objectively recoverable: as the questions one asks of the past change with the changing of the present horizon, so too do the answers which that past yields. Similarly, the literary text, far from being a self-contained given, actively changes depending on the historical circumstances in which it is read.

My emphasis on studying the historical circumstances surrounding the production of *Ulysses* parallels the work of Mary Lowe-Evans and Joseph Heininger (both in this volume), but I complement this focus by a study of reception. My students are required to develop most of the analyses of the production and reception of *Ulysses* themselves because I believe that this way of reading *Ulysses* is not only an end in itself but a means by which students can become empowered to develop historically informed and culturally situated positions of their own about *Ulysses*.

The course in which I have taught *Ulysses*, The Production and Reception of the Modern Novel, is generally composed of twenty to twenty-five junior and senior English majors. We spend four weeks on theories of production and reception, two weeks studying explicit contexts of the production of *Ulysses*, and four weeks reading *Ulysses* within the history of its reception; then we repeat the process with another novel. The theoretical readings are drawn from new-historicist and certain Marxist approaches, as well as from critics who explicitly address the question of reception. To analyze the material conditions informing the production of a text, I find it useful to have students read Terry Eagleton's *Criticism and Ideology* (chs. 2, 3, and 5) and Pierre Macherey's *A Theory of Literary Production* (esp. 69–101). Macherey develops a theory of reading literary texts to make them reveal the larger ideological forces silently underlying them.

When we turn to issues of textual reception, we begin with Hans Robert Jauss's "Literary History as a Challenge to Literary Theory." While Jauss's work tends to concentrate too exclusively on aesthetic history, it provides the most extensive model and rationale for historical study of the reception of literary texts. We then read Tony Bennett's essay "Texts in History," in which he introduces the concept of the reading formation to describe the relation among texts, readers, and contexts that determines the dominant ways texts will be read and received at any particular point in history. Bennett's concept bridges theories of cultural production and Jauss's theory of reception because it recognizes that a study of literary production is necessary to, but in itself not sufficient for, a materialist analysis of the literary text and because it advocates a study of the history of the text's reception along with the political, institutional, and ideological contexts in which that reception occurred. Finally, we read Dave Morley's "Texts, Readers, Subjects" for a discussion of the role of the reader as a subject in history.

The teacher could select different texts for this introductory unit depending on the level of the course and the familiarity of the students with theory. Chapter 2 of *Reading Texts*, a book I cowrote with Gary Waller and Linda Flower, provides an introductory discussion of many of these concepts. Robert Holub's *Reception Theory: A Critical Introduction* contains a useful and readable summary and analysis of reception theory, including a substantive discussion of Jauss's early work (53–82). Bennett's *Marxism and Formalism*, particularly chapters 5 through 8, furnishes a clear overview of Marxist theories of production and outlines the beginnings of a Marxist theory of reception.

When introducing these theories to the class (and I initially have to do a fair amount of explication), I suggest that they have the potential to alter both the traditional relations between a literary text and a reader and the traditional relations between teachers and students. Theories of production and reception can empower students to read even a text as difficult as *Ulysses* with critical and historical awareness. The process occurs in three stages that, in practice, often overlap. First, students construct a—necessarily perspectival—reading of the historical formation in which *Ulysses* was produced. They do this not simply to gain "background" information about the personages, political events, religious practices, and so on—those supposedly stable entities to which the text "refers"—but rather to examine the text *symptomatically*, that is, to look for "symptoms" of the tensions or contradictions of the social formation in which the text was produced and that are reproduced, often unconsciously, within the text.

In the second stage of reading, students study the reception of *Ulysses* and directly confront the variability of its meanings. They explore how and why different reading formations have asked different questions of *Ulysses*— how they have used or appropriated the text, often unwittingly, for particular ideological ends. Such an investigation involves examining the text in the context of both literary and larger social forces that have produced successive rereadings of it.

At the third stage of reading students self-consciously read *Ulysses* from the perspective of the current social formation: they ask questions of the novel that could not have been asked at the moment of its production but that can be asked now, and they develop their own interpretations of the text. They attempt to analyze the dialectical relation of their interpretations to those of the past and to situate their positions within the context of their current reading formation. I emphasize that in posing such "later" questions—and in reconstructing prior reading formations—students will always be repositioning and reappropriating *Ulysses* to make it address their historical condition, not discovering transcendent truths about its "original" meanings and subsequent, secondary readings.

Theories of production and reception can also help to change classroom relations between students and teachers. For if interpretations of texts are always historically situated, then the knowledge teachers have about a particular text, while likely to exceed that of their students, should not be considered by either teachers or students as transcendent; teachers know particular things because they have read, thought, and sometimes written about them, not because their positions inherently give them access to secret truths. My primary role in this course is thus to serve as what Paulo Freire calls a problem poser, who helps students gain access to the texts surrounding *Ulysses* so they can begin to take part in the continual process of its reinterpretation. The theory of the course, therefore, functions in part for pedagogical ends—to establish a situation in which the teacher and students can engage in a dialogue that enables students to develop the critical thinking and reading skills necessary to participate both in creating new knowledge and in actively directing the focus of much of the course (see Freire 66–74).

To this end, I assign two essay projects of five to six pages that students distribute at least one class period prior to discussion and that are graded by all class members. These essays serve as our primary resource material throughout the course. For the first assignment, groups of three students write collaborative essays on contexts for the production of *Ulysses*, including such areas as modernism, Irish politics, the Irish literary revival, Irish popular culture, Joyce's politics, and the status of women in turn-of-the-century Dublin. For the second essay, each student writes individually on the reception of one chapter of *Ulysses*. (The second essay is individually written only because I do not have enough students for all essays to be collaborative. For those teaching larger classes, I recommend that these essays be collaborative as well, since I find that students learn more and take more interpretive chances when they are doing research and writing in a group.) Although students do other writing in the course—notes on the theoretical essays, a journal on their reading of *Ulysses*, and a final paper—I focus here on the short essays because they direct our reading of *Ulysses*.

These short papers are not traditional background studies. The focus on production and reception requires students not just to reproduce what has already been said about a given topic. Rather, they must critically assess both their sources by situating them in larger contexts and their own places in the history of *Ulysses* criticism by performing symptomatic readings of all the texts they encounter—*Ulysses*, Irish histories, and criticism alike. Most important, students must attempt to use their understanding of historical difference to examine the cultural situatedness of their own position.

The first assignment, for groups of three students, is as follows:

Short Collaborative Background Essays

In five to six pages give the class an overview and introductory analysis of what you feel to be key aspects of your particular background area of research. Remember that since we perceive the past through the present, all histories are perspectival—whether they are about modernism or the rise of Parnell. Look for points of contradiction and tension in the accounts that you read to help you locate how these perspectives may be changing over time. Work as much as possible to suggest linkages among literary, political, and cultural forces, especially as you imagine they might impinge on our reading of *Ulysses*. Consult your syllabus for material on your topic that is on reserve in the library. Feel free to use other sources as well, and feel free to consult me.

Let me give an example of a group of students who, in the process of doing their research on the status of women in turn-of-the-century Ireland, "discovered" a concrete example of one of the theoretical premises of the course: that the past is repeatedly reconstructed from the perspective of the present. In reading various histories of Ireland, the students observed that many fairly traditional histories, particularly older ones, simply fail to talk at all about the cultural positions of women, or else they portray women as politically insignificant. Had the students read these books before learning about theories of production and reception, they might simply have dismissed the histories as having nothing to say about their topic. They now, however, began to read them "symptomatically" and asked whether the silence of these history books on the subject of women said as much—if not more—about women's status at the time the books were written as it did about women's status at the turn of the century. Students, of course, also had to acknowledge that their seemingly "natural" interest in women's social roles derived in large part from their particular place in history, in which feminism has legitimized such concerns and brought them, to some extent, into the popular consciousness.

The students found that a number of more recent histories not only assume that women's roles in society are important to investigate but also contend that women played more active roles in turn-of-the-century Dublin than they have often been credited with (see, e.g., Murphy). The students' paper thus focused on examples of historical difference—not only between the students' positions as women and those of Irish women at the turn of the century (as I had expected) but also between older and more recent historical accounts of Irish women.

While such differences in the representation of women arise from changing, historically explicable questions, confronting these differences among various histories was a jarring experience for the students writing the paper; the most pressing implication for them was that contemporary representations of women—and men—were conflicting and "unreliable." The students thus ended their paper by asking the class to question some of the ways in which women and men are depicted in contemporary culture, to explore some of the contradictions in those representations, and to imagine some of the effects of those representations. These issues took the class in a direction that I had not anticipated but that ultimately led to significant insights about the culturally inscribed nature of gender, as well as to some concrete analysis of the conflicting representations of women in turn-of-the-century Dublin. We found that we returned to this discussion when we read the "Penelope" chapter, not only to consider why Molly Bloom is presented as she is—in bed, menstruating, as a singer, frequently misinformed, and so on—but also as a way to begin to analyze and historically situate critics' contradictory interpretations of Molly (see Herring, "Bedsteadfastness" 57–59; Lammer 500–01; McCormick, "Reproducing").

This paper, therefore, was successful pedagogically as well as theoretically. The students began to find in the history books illustrations of the theoretical premises they had been studying, and they took control of their knowledge in a way they could not when they were simply reading and trying to understand the theorists. While theory is crucial to a framework for reading and research, it is only when students are asked to put that theory into practice and to share the responsibilities for teaching and learning that they are able to shift from passive learners to active producers of knowledge. The same holds true, I contend below, when the students read *Ulysses*.

Not all "production" papers are as insightful as this one, but they almost always bring new knowledge into the class, which the students generally feel freer to discuss, question, and supplement because it is presented by other students rather than the teacher. Further, when students have read books or articles I have not, I am able to ask them questions from the perspective of a learner rather than a teacher. As the course develops and more students undertake projects and gain expertise in particular areas, we can establish a learning situation in which, as Freire writes, "the teacher is no longer merely the-one-who-teaches, but one who is himself taught in dialogue with the students, who in turn while being taught also teach" (67).

By the time the students study *Ulysses* in class, therefore, they have already learned—primarily from one another—that any accounts of the contexts in which the novel was produced are always constructed, not "objective." They can now try to read *Ulysses* symptomatically because they have begun to learn how to construct a perspectival reading of the contexts in which it was written. When students write papers on the history of the reception of individual chapters, they not only read criticism on the chapters, but they also investigate the constructed nature of the criticism by researching and developing accounts—albeit in abbreviated form and necessarily perspectival—of the reading formations out of which that criticism has been produced. When students make their contribution to the reception of *Ulysses* by posing new questions to the text and developing their own readings, which they explore in detail in their final papers, they try to historicize their positions by examining their readings as a process of production in dialectical relation to other readings of the past and to their current reading formation.

The second essay assignment, to be written individually, is as follows:

Short Essays on Chapters of *Ulysses*

In five to six pages give the class an overview and introductory analysis of what you feel to be key aspects of the history of the reception of your assigned chapter. Begin by reading the chapter in its entirety, jotting down issues that you would most like to address. Then read the chapter with the *Notes* (Gifford and Seidman). This will give you vast information about politics, literary movements, and popular culture and help you get the jokes, translate the foreign expressions, and so on and perhaps give you a sense of some of the tensions within the chapter's original reading formation. From your reading of the *Notes*, decide on one passage (about twenty lines) that you feel is particularly important—because of its style, use of language, political references, jokes, or other features—for us to read together closely in class. Include the line numbers of the passage at the beginning of your essay. Consult various histories and references from the collaborative essays for any further information you may need on the general and literary ideologies informing the original reading formation of the chapter (e.g., some aspect of Irish politics that is particularly relevant, information on popular operas, Irish newspapers, Æ, etc.). See the syllabus for sources of further information on Joyce's production (writing and publishing); the early reception of drafts by friends of Joyce, publishers, and other modernists; early reviews; and criticism from the thirties to the present. Feel free to use sources not on reserve in the library and to meet with me at any point.

You can spend one paragraph giving a plot summary of the chapter, with, say, an overview of dominant mythic references, but the rest of the essay should provide information on and analysis of issues relevant to the history of the reception of the chapter. Make clear what questions *you* want to pose to the text, remembering that your position exists in a dialectical relation to past readings and is motivated by your place in a particular social formation. You obviously can't write about all that you will have discovered and all that you think, so don't try to include everything. Decide what information and which of your ideas would be most useful to the class, and put those in your essay. You can tell us about the rest in class.

For the example of a "production" essay, I discussed a paper that followed the assignment and clearly illustrated some of the theoretical premises of the course. I want now to look at a "reception" essay that inhabited the classroom situation more dialectically.

A student writing on "Nausicaa" asserted that the "text itself" is inherently feminist in impulse because, in giving Gerty MacDowell the sentimental "feminine" language of pulp fiction and women's magazines, Joyce was "obviously" satirizing the society that constructed female subjectivity in such a manner. The student briefly reviewed, but quickly dismissed, most of what critics writing before 1980 had to say about the chapter. The class made two basic responses to the student's interpretation. The first, and by far the stronger, claimed that by merging her position with the text's, the student failed to account both for the historical difference between past readings and her reading and for the critical and political significances of her position within the current reading formation, thus undercutting the radical potential of her own argument. The second response, which was less clearly articulated but which helped us to restore a more dialectical attitude toward reading, suggested that while the student did not in fact historicize her position (and hence did not quite "fulfill the assignment"), she did attempt to make the text address her historical condition, and her strategies—feminist critique combined with the language of objectivity—made the presentation both powerful and convincing, particularly given her institutional position as a student and the dominant style of writing she encountered in the criticism.

Let us look at each response in more detail. The first response was sparked by a relatively simple question by a single student, who remarked on the need to historicize one's response to a text: "How can someone say that the chapter is 'really a feminist text' if nobody thought it was until recently?" Once this question was raised, the class asked the student to review the history of the chapter's reception and to talk about the political climate in which Joyce wrote *Ulysses*—which she was capable of doing. The student's research on the reception of the chapter, supplemented by my comments, indicated that early readers indeed had seen nothing inherently feminist about it nor did they conceive of problematizing Gerty's discourse conventions. While most critics generally recognized the parallels of style between the first half of "Nausicaa" and Maria Cummings's popular novel *The Lamplighter*, there was little attempt until the 1980s to distance an analysis of Gerty from an analysis of this style. Thus Richard Kain speaks of Gerty's "cheap sentimentality" (*Fabulous Voyager* 44); Stanley Sultan contends that Gerty is a parody of all "the mass of people blighted by self-deluding sentimentality" (273), readers, characters, and authors alike; and Robert Adams finds the "perhaps overextended parody" of "Nausicaa" to be directed primarily at "Lady novelists" (224). It is only the more recent feminist critics such as Suzette Henke or Bonnie Kime Scott who explore the complex relation between Gerty's language and the society that constructed her (Henke 153–72; Scott, *James Joyce* 62–7). In tracing and discussing this history, the class reconfirmed a number of the theoretical tenets of the course: that it is not enough to ask whether a reading is "correct" with reference to the text (since all these critics were presumably expert readers of *Ulysses*); that one must attempt to ask what relation these readings have to their particular reading formations; that when constructing an interpretation, it is necessary to explore the tensions and dynamics of one's own social formation to ask what interpretations seem not only possible but responsible to take up.

It was perhaps here in the discussion that an alternative response to the student's paper began to take shape. For while the student did not analyze the history of the reception of the chapter in any detail, her position was clearly informed by that history and was written in opposition to it. Further, not only did the student's basic premise seem "responsible" to take up, but it also addressed her historical condition and spoke to that of other women in the class. Her strategy of making the text speak to, indeed, "be about," her position as a gendered subject was a powerful way for her to assert and legitimize her historicity. Given most of the criticism the students had read and most of the training they have received in school, attributing meanings or intentions to "the text itself" was—despite the work we had done in this course on production and reception—the interpretive strategy historically most available to them and institutionally the one that is still accorded the most status. Although I would stop short of saying that in embracing the legitimizing force of "the text itself" the student's essay constituted an intentional act of resistance to the dominant theoretical discourse developed in this course, the essay nonetheless helped us recognize the potential of any theory—even a supposedly dialectical theory of production and reception—to normalize responses and, paradoxically, to inhibit our thinking historically and dialogically.

My discussion here is certainly more abstract than what occurred in the classroom, but that my students could raise such issues about the "Nausicaa" chapter suggests that, when allowed to take up the role of teacher as well as learner and when given some theoretical tools for critical and historical investigation, students can become intellectually and emotionally engaged with *Ulysses*, pose textual questions in dialogic relation to those of the past, and, most important, develop interpretations that make the novel address their historical condition.

In my experience, the short-essay assignments have been crucial to this inquiry. They work largely because they are collaborative in one form or another. On a practical level, researching and writing a paper in a group helps most students cope with the wealth of reference material (and, for some, with learning how to use the library extensively for the first time). It also gives students an opportunity to try out and reformulate their ideas in a small group before deciding whether to present them to the class. Most students had never written a paper collaboratively before, and almost all reported that while the process was more difficult than they had expected (they, or their sources, did not agree; they had to meet more often than planned; they were critical of one another's writing, etc.), the cowritten paper was more complex and took more interpretive risks than what each student could have written alone. Students seem to enjoy reading *Ulysses* much more when they share the responsibilities for teaching it. Writing papers—whether individually or in a group—that will serve as a resource for the entire class often motivates students to do extensive research and independent thinking about *Ulysses* because they know that their work will directly affect the way other students read the text. When undertaken from the theoretical orientation of production and reception, such collaborative work provides a site wherein students can problematize their own and others' readings in ways that allow them to confront the dialogic nature of reading and history and to perceive their status as subjects in history—specifically as subjects in the institutional setting of a classroom.

Teaching for the (W)Holes

Richard Pearce

Teachers of *Ulysses* must fill the gaps in students' knowledge: historical
background, the Homeric superstructure, literary allusions, narrative and
stylistic strategies, theories of psychological representation. We must also
make connections among many points that cannot be grasped in first readings. As a result, we may diminish the importance of initial reactions, cushion
the shocks of disruption, obscure the reality of lacunae and contradiction—
and domesticate or naturalize a book that should disturb as well as exhilarate
us.

Our problem in teaching *Ulysses* is rooted both in Joyce's conception of
his novel and in its critical history, or in the way teachers have been taught
to read it. And we can begin to help our students by explaining this problem.
Joyce began with a need to ground his view of the modern world on a classical
base (that we have almost lost), so he built a Homeric scaffolding. He also
wanted to create a complete and realistic fictional experience, or "to give a
picture of Dublin so complete that if the city one day suddenly disappeared
from the earth it could be reconstructed out of [his] book" (qtd. in Budgen
70). But in the process of his composition he took more and more joy in
parodying classical myths, creating not only ambiguity but open-endedness
and uncertainty, and in undermining the foundations of realism.

Indeed what distinguishes *Ulysses* are its disruptions, discontinuities, si-
lences, absences, holes. And as our experience comes to include the holes,
the novel becomes more inclusive, or (w)hole. For the holes derive from or
reflect the mediation of language, the materiality of the text, our separation
from what was supposed to have happened, the limitations of a character's
subjectivity, and the inability of one character to know fully the subjectivity
of an "other."

The First Day

Before I describe some of my opening moves, I want to say that in twenty
years of teaching the novel, I've never had a successful first class. I never
get much response, until one day when the students seem to click in, say
how much they like a particular chapter, and feel more or less at home in
the world of *Ulysses*. I never know when this is going to happen, or why;
it's usually after a few weeks, but once it was much later and after reading,
of all chapters, "Sirens"!

I teach *Ulysses* in a course called Modern Fiction, limited to juniors and
seniors. Before *Ulysses* they read *Portrait*, write a paper on it, and end
up feeling pretty good about Joyce. But they're wary of *Ulysses*, if not
because of what they've heard (mostly from people who haven't read it),

then from opening it at random, or even from carrying the big book home from the bookstore. We spend four weeks working very closely with the text, though I tell my students to skim or skip anything that bogs them down, especially "Scylla and Charybdis" and "Oxen of the Sun," which I just touch on. Then I give them a week off to do research and write a paper on one chapter.

Before opening the book in class I have two opposing goals. I know, not only from teaching the novel but from my own first reading of *Ulysses*, that students will be disturbed by the disruptions, or the holes, in the text. Many will feel that they are weak readers, that they are missing the connections, that they should know something or see something, or have more patience. And I think it's important to validate their reactions: to let them know that the novel is designed to generate feelings of disruption and disorientation, that these feelings result from an assault on traditional expectations, from the way thoughts leap irrationally, from the shifting perspectives, from Joyce's rejection of the assumptions and conventions of realism. Students are responding to what Scott Klein's essay in this volume shows are the very problems Stephen and Bloom (I would add Molly) have with the dominant discourses of their culture. They are responding to what constitute the novel's distinctive breadth and power.

But at the same time I feel the need to give them a sense of the whole. So I start with a little background from Frank Budgen's *James Joyce and the Making of* Ulysses. Then I write an outline on the board (see below). This outline provides a structure for me to identify the main characters, describe the very simple plot line, and establish the principal symbolic and mythic framework.

But then I draw a big X over the outline—and tell them it's all wrong.

Ulysses	*Odyssey*
Characters	*Characters*
Stephen: intellect	Telemachus: son (Hamlet)
Molly: body	Penelope: mother, wife
Bloom: unites the two	Ulysses: father (Hamlet's father)
Structure	*Structure*
Stephen leaves tower and job.	Telemachus leaves home in search of his father.
Bloom leaves home.	Ulysses travels in search of his son.
Brings Stephen home.	Father returns home, finds son, and, after killing suitors, is reunited with his wife.
Molly's monologue in bed.	No Penelope monologue in *Odyssey*.

This really jolts them, especially the assiduous note takers. And it helps me make three points: that the novel should continually jolt them with its uncertainties and contradictions; that structures of meaning (and value) are continually being established and, at the same time, undermined; and that I will be trying to teach them how to live with uncertainty and contradiction as they read *Ulysses*. The final image on the board—of the outline crossed out—is also designed to provide an image of what Joyce does constantly to his readers: generates simultaneity and contradiction, undermines what he's just created, creates a palimpsest where several layers of erased inscription can still be made out.

Shifting Perspective and the Stream (?) of Consciousness

I want to validate and reinforce the gaps and disruptions on the opening page, while establishing an image of the scene and an understanding of the allusions. So I pass around pictures of the Martello tower—but I also show students why the image did not form so clearly in their minds. Stately, plump Buck Mulligan comes up from a stairhead, peers down some dark winding stairs, and then mounts a gunrest, but these details don't add up to much, and it takes two pages before we discover that we're on a parapet overlooking Dublin Bay. And in fact the image forming in our minds is constantly deflected by Buck Mulligan's parodic rite, which only the Catholic students recognize as a mass. It is also disrupted by any number of enigmatic phrases.

The first disruption is palpable: an italicized sentence intrudes into the otherwise unnoticeable print. *"Introibo ad altare Dei"* (1.5). This is the first time the physical text intrudes into our reading experience, though we don't become fully aware of such intrusions until the newspaper headlines in "Aeolus." We become aware that the print on the page is not invisible (as it's made to seem in a "realistic" novel) but a material reality that mediates and intrudes its own meanings and values. Moreover, to most readers the Latin sentence is unintelligible, which is another reason for its being a disruption. Of course, during Joyce's time educated people understood Latin, and Catholics knew that this passage came from the beginning of the mass. But Latin was nonetheless a language of mystification, through which the Church maintained its power.

The second disruption might be the one-word sentence "Chrysostomos" (1.26). And it's disrupting for two reasons. First, because it's an erudite reference to a "golden-mouthed" Greek rhetorician and also to one of the Fathers of the early Church. It forces readers to stop and either look it up or at least momentarily feel they have lost control. I think it is important to emphasize that while this allusion disrupts the text, it also links the present with a classical past, or the intellectual and religious beginnings of Western culture. But considering that two revered figures are linked with a plump medical student mocking the mass ("One moment. A little trouble about those white corpuscles" [1.22–23]), it creates an ambiguous link—or it undermines or interrogates the very link it establishes. Throughout the novel our reverence for the biblical and classic as well as the mythic past is continually being questioned and undermined.

The one-word sentence also breaks into the narrative as Stephen's direct thought, or as a leap in perspective from third to first person that conveys to us a palpable sense of relativity, or the distance between points of view. It is a limited example of Stephen's stream of consciousness—limited because it's only a single word—but we have nonetheless shifted our focus, or leaped across the gap, from outside to inside Stephen's mind. And Stephen's thoughts have leaped from a world of public to a world of private associations. This leap is characteristic of the stream of consciousness—where thoughts move by association rather than logic. On the one hand, a character's thoughts flow from one into another, as William James said in *Principles of Psychology* when he coined the term "stream of consciousness." But, on the other hand, the reader, not being the character, experiences them as discontinuous, so this discontinuity is another way that Joyce has made us feel the difference and distance between points of view. While we may be able to fill in some links, we can never be certain of what causes a thought or links it to another, for they are overdetermined. There are too many reasons why one thought follows another; there is an overload of causes, including some that can never be known. By foregrounding the gap while proposing the possible links, the instructor maintains this uncertainty—and affirms that we cannot fully know the subjectivity of the "other." I want to emphasize the difference between the uncertainty of overdetermination and the uncertainty of ambiguity. In the 1950s, an outstanding teacher like William York Tindall would lead a very large class in generating a multiplicity of meanings and causes for a given passage. The assumption in the days of the New Criticism was that they were all related, or held together in ambiguous tension, in Joyce's "well-wrought urn." Overdetermination, to the contrary, implies that the overload of meanings cannot be held together or contained. And the well-wrought urn gives way to an open form.

Giant Steps

As we turn from chapter 1 to chapter 2 we leap from the Martello's forty-foot cliff into "You, Cochrane, what city sent for him?" (2.1). Where are we now? Who says this? Who's Cochrane? Who's the "him" that whatever city it was sent for? We can explain to our students how Stephen got from the Martello tower to the school at Dalkey and that he's now questioning his students about Pyrrhus and the Tarrentines. But it's important to confirm the students' reading experience and maintain the gap between the chapters of *Ulysses*.

Moreover, it's important to point out that, though Joyce titled some of the chapters published in the *Little Review*, he chose not to title them in the novel. Scholars and teachers restored the titles, following Stuart Gilbert. The addition reflects the need for stability, a need felt strongly when modernism was new. But, while Joyce began with the need for a Homeric superstructure (and even authorized Gilbert's Homeric schema), he was soon parodying and undermining it. By 1937 he could tell Nabokov that employing Homer was "a whim" and collaborating with Gilbert "a terrible mistake . . . an advertisement for the book. I regret it very much" (qtd. in Ellmann, *James Joyce* 616n).

There are discontinuities, palpable gaps, between all the chapters. What contributes most to the discontinuity is the shift from one style to another. There isn't much of a stylistic shift between the first two chapters. But there is between the second and the third, which begins, "Ineluctable modality of the visible: at least that if no more, thought through my eyes. Signatures of all things I am here to read . . ." (3.1–2). In the second paragraph we discover that we are in Stephen's mind, and soon we discover that we will stay there for the entire chapter. Still, we have been prepared for this experience by the growing number of interior-monologue passages in the previous chapters. And—though we make a great leap from Stephen's cerebrations into "Mr Leopold Bloom ate with relish the inner organs of beasts and fowls" (4.1–2)—we don't come to a radical stylistic shift until "Aeolus" (ch. 7).

"Wandering Rocks" (ch. 10) begins the most radical series of stylistic disruptions, breaking into the stories of Stephen and Bloom, lifting us high above Dublin to give us a bird's-eye view of the city, raising minor characters to levels of major importance, and reducing the major characters to levels of unimportance. Each chapter that follows interposes a stylistic lens between us and the narrative action, so that we have to struggle to see what is happening when the most important event (Bloom's realization, in ch. 11, that Molly and Blazes have become lovers) is almost entirely obfuscated by the dense musical style and when the union of Bloom the father and Stephen the son can only be deduced from a series of arbitrary questions and answers. Through his stylistic disruptions, foregrounding of physical print, playfulness with point of view, exploitation of sounds, and gratuitous interferences between the reader and key events, Joyce makes us conscious of language as a form of mediation, undermines realistic conventions and Western myths, and interrogates all forms of authori-ty.

Perhaps the greatest leap is between "Ithaca" and "Penelope," for this is where the story of Stephen and Bloom ends and where Molly's story begins. And Molly's story begins with a gap. Though "Ithaca" (where Bloom finally falls asleep in the fetal position next to Molly) is overloaded with details, we never hear Bloom ask Molly to bring him breakfast in bed. And it is just this apparent request that stimulates Molly's final monologue. It is just this request that leads us to think that Bloom has achieved his ("manly") identity. It is just this request that leads Molly to her affirmation of Bloom at the end of her monologue—and to an ultimate expression of universal harmony: "Yes because he never did a thing like that before as ask to get his breakfast in bed with a couple of eggs" (18.1–2).

Molly's monologue also leads us to understand another kind of gap, or hole, in *Ulysses*—which I distinguish by calling it an *absence*. For, though Molly has been present ever since she woke up at eight o'clock in the morning, she says, in a "sleepy soft grunt," little more than "Mn" (4.56–57). She has been present only in the minds of Leopold Bloom and the men he meets. Bloom continually thinks of Molly as he leaves home and wanders through Dublin. The men he meets continually ask about his wife and her singing tour and continually wonder about "who's getting it up?" (5.153). Lenehan tells the story about being lost in Molly's "milky way" (10.570); Simon Dedalus puns that "Mrs Marion Bloom has left off clothes of all descriptions" (11.496–97); the nameless narrator of "Cyclops" tells us she has "a back on her like a ballalley" (12.503–04); the men in the cabman's shelter gaze at the photo with "her fleshy charms on evidence" (16.1428); and Bloom seems to speculate about her eighteen lovers (17.2126–42). It took scholars half a century of careful reading to discover that Molly was not promiscuous, for Boylan was her first adulterous lover.

That we accepted the male point of view for so long without taking Molly's monologue seriously reflects the absence—or co-optation—of Molly's voice; it also reflects her presence as an object rather than a subject throughout the fourteen chapters in which men have been forming her image. Now she tells her own story in a narrative space and voice of her own. We see the men of Dublin from her very different, constantly changing perspective. The gap between Molly's monologue and the rest of the novel evokes the distance between Molly and the dominant society of Dublin (though the colonized Dubliners are not really dominant), between the image the men construct of her and (though she has partly internalized that construction) the multiple facets of her subjectivity, and between the ways men and women seek identity in traditional fiction. The gap may also lead us to question, even interrogate, the happy ending—or the way readers have wanted the novel to end, with at least the hope for a reconciliation between Molly and Bloom. For this "happy ending" would ultimately deny Molly her independence. It would return her to being a character in the male story, however important her role. If Molly accedes to bringing Bloom breakfast in bed, it might very well restore the Blooms to traditional roles in a patriarchal marriage.

Holes in the Structure

Ulysses tells not one story but three main stories, each contained in its own incomplete circle. Stephen leaves his home in the tower and wanders through Dublin all day, meeting a fatherly Bloom in nighttown and returning with him to 7 Eccles Street. There they talk intimately enough to discover the similarity of their temperaments and long enough to learn that in 1892 Dante moved from the Dedalus household to become a neighbor of the Blooms in the City Arms Hotel, and there Bloom (who has taken on the role of father) and Stephen (who has taken on the role of son) become close enough to urinate together under Molly's window. But Stephen refuses Bloom's offer of a bed and a room and his wife's companionship—and indeed leaves singing an anti-Semitic song.

Bloom wanders through Dublin all day so that he can be away while Molly and Blazes make love. He and Molly have not had complete carnal intercourse for ten years, five months, and eighteen days (17.2282)—yet he continually thinks of Molly, pictures their luscious first kiss on Howth (8.899–916), follows "the moving hams" of his next-door neighbor (4.172), pictures "*[t]hose lovely seaside girls*" (4.437–43), watches a stylish woman climb into a carriage (5.98–140), imagines the caretaker courting his wife in the graveyard (6.747–49), masturbates while watching Gerty McDowell lean back to see the fireworks (13.715–45), and finally returns home to kiss the "plump mellow yellow smellow melons" of Molly's rump (17.2241). The death of his twelve-day-old son is not a sufficient reason to explain his psychological or physical separation from Molly, the gap between the two characters who care so much for each other. And while he is in bed with Molly at the end of his story, they are each thinking their separate thoughts.

Molly doesn't move from her bed. At least we never witness the scenes where she dresses, moves the furniture, and makes love to Blazes. These are significant holes in her story. Hugh Kenner (in "Molly's Masterstroke") only illuminates the enigma in his ingenious explanation of how a walnut sideboard, big enough for Bloom to have bumped his head on, was moved across the room. But we see Molly as at least as complex as and more adventurous than Bloom the father and Stephen the son, who, like their Homeric predecessors, achieve their identity by traveling. In her own narrative space and through her own narrative voice Molly establishes a presence, an identity, and an otherness that was denied her by the men who limited her because of their needs and fears.

If the three stories are contained within their separate but incomplete circles, it is because the structure of the novel acknowledges gaps, or holes, as part of the (w)hole. The holes result from what cannot be known or mastered and what is affirmed in its otherness. We will never know why Bloom and Molly have not had complete carnal intercourse for ten years, five months, and eighteen days, or why Stephen left Bloom singing an anti-Semitic song, or whether Bloom asked for breakfast in bed, or the answers to any number of questions that keep us from rebuilding Dublin on 16 June 1904 from the pages of Joyce's novel. By not only recognizing but valuing the holes in the story—or the discontinuities between three independent but related stories—we attest to a relationship among independent subjects. The novel—with its overabundance of links, its historical and social density, its shifting points of view, and its explorations of subjectivity—is about multiple and continually changing relationships. But it is also about ways that characters can achieve at least provisional independence from one another's stories—as well as from the authorities of England, the Catholic church, the patriarchal family, and literary conventions that have evolved to reflect the experience and values of the dominant culture, all of which have limited the range of human possibilities.

It's been exciting to teach *Ulysses* to most students who are willing to read the assignments. And most students learn a lot about the novel and about the possibilities of fiction, whether they receive an A or a C for the course. But if this essay conveys a clear sense of direction in a teacher who's always on top of his subject as well as the class discussion, then I have failed to give you a true picture or to convey the power of Joycean uncertainty.

Searching for Lost Keys: Epic and Linguistic Dislocations in *Ulysses*

Scott W. Klein

A student's first reading of *Ulysses* is inevitably a grappling with confusion. The narrative, dense with allusive traps and philosophic references, shifts of style and ambiguous points of view, offers readers a subtle and extended exercise in disorientation. Teaching the novel for the first time is likely to be equally off-putting. In my teaching *Ulysses*—both in an advanced freshman course on the epic tradition and in a Joyce seminar for third- and fourth-year English majors—I have found, like Richard Pearce, that foregrounding themes of disorientation and difference and demonstrating their relevance to the experience of the characters provide a useful and integrative entrance to Joyce's text. But where Pearce, writing in this volume, focuses primarily on the disruptive style of the novel, I concentrate on the relation of students' reading experiences and the interpretive issues of the characters. For the experimentation of the prose is often the greatest stumbling block to a student's comprehension of Joyce's purposes, and it is therefore my primary concern to legitimize the antirealistic tendencies of the central chapters. By emphasizing Joyce's treatment of epic themes, the instructor can lead students to read *Ulysses* as a narrative that enacts a falling away of textual authority and that becomes displaced from conventions—particularly those of the epic—in the same ways that the characters have become displaced by their differences from the world around them.

I introduce *Ulysses* by working outward from an apparently minor detail toward larger interpretive corollaries. During the morning of 16 June 1904 both Stephen Dedalus and Leopold Bloom lose the keys to their homes. Stephen leaves the key to the Martello tower behind for Mulligan in an act of grudging abandonment (1.721), while Bloom discovers that he has accidentally left his house key in another pair of trousers (5.468). To lose a key, of course, is to be locked out, no longer to be able to enter where previously there was free access. But it can also be read metaphorically as the loss of another kind of "key," the kind that allows one to resolve puzzles, to grasp the answers to seemingly unanswerable questions. The intersection of these literal and figurative meanings provides first-time readers of *Ulysses* with a thematic link between their reading experiences and the interpretive issues of the characters. As Stephen and Bloom find themselves shut out from the sources of meaning and authority that informed the world of the classical epic, so readers find themselves deprived of the authority of realist prose, adrift from the linguistic "home" for which they need to locate their own interpretive keys.

Authority for these purposes is a particularly charged term (for useful treatments of the issues of home and authority in Joyce, see Law and Mahaffey). It is a term of power. To authorize is to sanction, to judge, to declare that a particular structure or procedure is legitimate and meaningful. Yet the term is also linguistic. Etymologically it shares identity with *author*. To read is therefore to trust implicitly in the authority of the printed page. The reader can assume not only that the narrative world described is, within its own terms, valid or true but that the world is described according to sets of conventions (inherited or self-created) within which the characters can enact their questings toward meaning, toward the understanding of what is valued or valuable. The reader trusts that the author is, indeed, the first mover of the text—and throughout *Ulysses* Joyce himself frequently poses an analogy between the writer and God. Authority therefore always has a linguistic component or corollary. Students can check this assertion by noting how often Stephen and Bloom think about authorship—writing—as part of their quests for authority or meaning in their lives. Stephen thinks of himself as poet (3.397–400), lecturer (9), even potential journalist (7.922–1075). Bloom thinks of writing a newspaper sketch (4.518), and we discover late in *Ulysses* that he wrote some doggerel verse during his courtship of Molly (17.392–417). If language is a source of self-discovery and definition, however, it is also a tool of repressive authority. Mulligan, Deasy, the editor Myles Crawford, even, in "Circe," the hallucinatory Bella Cohen show their authority to disturb and disrupt, manipulating Stephen and Bloom through irony, harangue, and insult. (See, e.g., ch. 1 throughout; Deasy's wresting a favor from Stephen [2.410]; the editor's rejection of Bloom [7.980–94]; the central section of "Circe" [15.2742–3490].)

Language is therefore a source of both self-definition and oppositional power, a way to define and limit value. And as this function of language is unlikely to seem evident to undergraduates, it is worth placing issues of linguistic value and meaning in the context of larger issues of meaning in the epics that act as the implicit context for *Ulysses*. A first pedagogical foray into these abstractions would be to ask a class to list what conventions or structures have acted as stable sources of meaning for the characters in the literature they have previously read.

Here one may need to lecture if students are unfamiliar with epic procedure. If they have read in Homer, Vergil, or Dante, however, they might recognize that several cultural structures are important to the hero's sense of order and self. In the *Odyssey*, for example, the gods, family (especially the paternal relationship), and home are particularly enabling for the hero. They are sources of direction; they authorize action. Anything done on their behalf is valid, just. History, as both the past and tradition, is also authoritative. The epic hero journeys to the underworld in search of advice from past voices, which provide the quester with a renewed awareness of self and the inevitability of his fate. In the *Aeneid* national identity joins and becomes inseparable from home as a necessary telos: to establish a new and safe foundation for society becomes the ultimate source of value, while the importance of religion shifts from adherence to a particular god's direction, as in Homer, to piety itself. Finally, in Dante, the epic quester's exile because of contemporary politics—a source of worldly authority—drives him to seek validation from spiritual authority, the Christian God.

Initially, then, I ask students if they see any connections between the issues of the epic and *Ulysses*, explaining Joyce's announced project of writing a "modern" epic. To present *Ulysses* as a narrative where traditional authority has become problematic, for its characters and ultimately for its language, I direct discussion of *Ulysses* toward the relations of its characters with these "epic" aspects of their worlds. I examine *Ulysses* as an "eccentric" narrative in three respects, "eccentric" in the etymological sense of "deviating from the center." First, it posits as ambiguous the roles played by traditional centers of authority, representing characters who search, as Dante did, for order in their intellectual worlds. Second, ambiguity extends to the reader of the text, who must seek an analogous coherence in a narrative whose conventions seem at times familiar, at times alien. And third, "eccentricity" provides an answer to the vexed question of the generic status of *Ulysses* as epic and novel, suggesting that it takes part in the conventions of these forms while also problematizing its foundation in them through experimentation and irony. The keys one seeks in the classroom, therefore, are the characters', the readers', and, ultimately, the text's attempts to define their attitudes toward tradition and value.

For our discussion on the early chapters, I ask students to explore Stephen's and Bloom's often strongly conflicted relationships with family, religion, history, national identity, and society. Students readily see that both characters displace themselves from the "center" of these realms of experience, much as they are displaced from their literal homes. Here it is best to move outward from the students' immediate textual and personal experiences toward more abstract concepts. Family, for instance, is a source of failed authority for Stephen and Bloom. I question students about the absence of stable family in *Ulysses*, directing attention to the analogy between the fragmentation of the Dedalus family (in which the mother is dead, the father emotionally distant from the children, and siblings present only in the narrative fragmentation of "Wandering Rocks") and the potential failures of the Bloom family (in which the son has died, the daughter, Milly, has been sent away to Mullingar, and the wife, Molly, is contemplating adultery). I further emphasize, however, the degree to which, although displaced from their families, both Bloom and Stephen yearn for or are haunted by them. Their feelings reflect a general pattern in *Ulysses*: to be excluded does not mean that one can easily elude the power that excludes.

This pattern is perhaps most clearly true of religion, which, in *Ulysses* (and, many students agree, in their own lives), is intimately related to issues of family. Stephen, who would not pray for his mother on her deathbed, tries to free himself from an authority he finds oppressive and stifling. Yet he is haunted by the forms and issues of Catholicism, as he feels haunted by his mother. He is displaced from both religion's comforts and its strictures. Bloom is analogously unsettled by his own equivocal Judaism. Conscious of his present Catholicism as a betrayal of his heritage, he feels guilt at leaving the Jewish God of his fathers. Yet, as we find late in "Ithaca," his father became a Protestant before Bloom was born (17.1636–40), and his mother was gentile, suggesting that Bloom was never technically Jewish at all. When discussing religion, I point out Mulligan's mock invocation to his shaving bowl at the opening of *Ulysses* as an example of religion's changed status in Joyce's world, from epic source of surety to subject of taunting irony. Like family, religion is a source not simply of failure but of the persistence of authority in the guise of mocking exclusion.

Such doubleness is typical of other epic categories of value and meaning, which I discuss at length in class. For Stephen history is a "nightmare" (2.377) to be eluded rather than embraced; like national identity, it is a limiting and threatening category to which he is nonetheless subject. For Bloom, similarly, these categories are areas of exclusion rather than inclusion. In society's eyes he is one of the Jews, whom, as Mr. Deasy notes, Ireland never let in (2.442); he is also a self-professed Irishman who is yet perceived by all as an ethnic foreigner. (Useful passages for an exploration of these themes are those on Stephen's ambiguous feelings about the milkwoman in "Telemachus" [1.397–423] and on Bloom's defense of his humanistic politic in "Cyclops" [14.1474–85].) Finally, there are Stephen's and Bloom's relationships to their peers, who implicitly present the values of Dublin's larger society. Being unlike most of their peers in Dublin, Stephen and Bloom are defined by others in terms of qualities of lack or difference. "Telemachus" provides a strong test case for discussion. In the opening pages, for instance, Mulligan makes fun of Stephen's name (1.34), indirectly twits Stephen for not knowing Greek (1.79–80), declares that his "jesuit strain" has been "injected the wrong way" (1.209), and, perhaps most damningly, tells him that in Haines's opinion he's "not a gentleman" (1.52) and does not live up to social or economic norms. Throughout "Telemachus" Stephen feels rightly, if self-pityingly, out of place, "usurped" of personal, aesthetic, and political rights. In class, we discuss Stephen's relationship to Mulligan and Haines and then turn analogously to Bloom to see how he fits into his social world. By "Hades" and "Aeolus" it is clear that Bloom is patronized, when he is included at all, by people toward whom he has ambivalent feelings. Students may note, for instance, that at the opening of "Hades" Bloom not only enters the carriage last but is called by his last name where Simon Dedalus is called by his first. Later, when McCoy takes attendance at the funeral, it is clear that Bloom is the only member of the circle whose "christian name" McCoy doesn't know (6.881). The passage in which Bloom tells an implicitly anti-Semitic story against the moneylender Reuben J. Dodd also helps students gauge Bloom's attitude toward both his nominal religion and his peers (6.262–91). We see how others usurp Bloom's personal authority (for Martin Cunningham tells most of the story) and how Bloom is self-critically willing to elide his differences in order to fit in. Yet he fails. Throughout *Ulysses* he is a subject of laughter and scorn often aimed at his apparent ethnicity, or his perceived lack of manliness.

Neither Bloom nor Stephen, in short, is at home in this world in a sense larger than, but including, the literal. Both suffer from displacements of identity, family, history, and society. Like Dante, Bloom is (through the agency of a popular song) "lost in the wood" (4.179), while Stephen's abandonment of his key (1.721) is a larger corollary of his unsettled sense of identity. And once students have perceived the relation between physical dislocation and spiritual or metaphysical dislocation, I begin to draw their attention back to Joyce's use of linguistic displacement as an essential part of the narrative fabric of *Ulysses*. This displacement can be seen in the experience of the characters. For Bloom and Stephen language is not only diversion but a tool of philosophic inquiry, a source of value: language provides a way to make oneself feel better and a way to get at the truth. Beyond their pretensions as writers, Stephen and Bloom deal with their metaphysical homelessness by constantly posing themselves questions of identity and meaning, questions whose keys are often thematically linguistic. Bloom sets himself puzzles as intellectual diversion (for instance, how to cross Dublin without passing a pub or how to square the circle), but they coexist in sometimes pathetic juxtaposition with profound musings about marriage and identity. For Stephen, questions of identity are wrapped up in, and occluded by, theological questions about the constituency of the Trinity (1.650–64) and the neoplatonic search for the ultimate key, the "[w]ord known to all men" (9.429–30). Yet since other categories of epic value have become ambiguous and exclusionary in *Ulysses* and language can be used to taunt and harm, can language be trusted? Stephen's philosophic musings suggest a further question. If father and son are equivocally related in the Trinity (as in the Arian and Sabellian heresies that are the subject of Stephen's ruminations [1.657–64]), what can be known of the analogous relation of language with its origin in the things of the world? If the theological relationship of son to father is ambiguous, can the relation of sign and object, which is the fallen version of the Word and the God from which the Word issues, be less so? Is there an ultimate key, which is theologically or philosophically a final authority and a "word known to all men"?

I apprise students that, in the context of the characters' other dislocations, these abstract questions do not simply spring from their immediate narrative context, but bear strongly on Joyce's textual challenge to the reader in general. For in *Ulysses* language is no longer a safe home. It can be centrifugal from its apparent referent. It can be playful or opaque, and the reader's experience of this language mirrors the characters' experience in "reality." I shift from thematic to linguistic investigation within the text by asking students how language functions for Stephen and Bloom. Stephen, for instance, submerges, under obfuscatory abstraction, his anxieties over familial and sexual relationships. This is clear in "Proteus"—but I warn students that later the text takes on some of Stephen's linguistic attributes without necessarily acting as direct reportage of his consciousness. And I note that Stephen's textual performances within *Ulysses* are quizzically uncommunicative, emblematic of *Ulysses*'s obscurities. The riddle he tells the children in the schoolroom (2.102), his "Parable of the Plums" (7.922–1027), even the whole of his lecture on Shakespeare (ch. 9) are related examples of language's inability to negotiate the distance between an individual and the world from which he is, or feels, excluded. This deficiency of language is also self-reflexively true of the narrative that includes Stephen. We may wrest meaning from these parables, but we need to interpret actively, to search for connections that can act as keys to meaning. And we may observe, as Stephen laughs nervously at the end of each of these acts of failed communication (2.116, 7.1028, 9.1016), the degree to which Stephen's language is uncommunicative, largely private. For Stephen language fails in one of its primary tasks, direct communication. We as readers are also prey to his dilemma. Stephen walks along the beach and thinks that he needs to interpret the "[s]ignatures of all things" (3.2). The most important lesson for students from "Proteus," the first chapter to unsettle profoundly their narrative preconceptions, is that we similarly need to interpret the signs of the language used to describe Stephen and his world.

Language is eccentric in Bloom's world as well, but here more publicly. Examples are comic. The physical marks of the world around him give way to linguistic disruption or misinterpretation. Students enjoy tracing these examples as they move through the early chapters—the *t* has rubbed off Bloom's hatband, leaving him with a "high grade ha" (4.69–70). Martha Clifford's letter confuses "word" with "world" (5.245–46), "wrote" with "write" (5.253). Language may, as Hebrew is, be typeset backward (7.206), while Bloom almost confuses the word "Blood" with his name on a religious throwaway (8.8–9). The written phrase "POST NO BILLS" becomes "POST 110 PILLS" (8.101). If within Stephen's world language has become obfuscatory and uncommunicative, within Bloom's world language is literally falling apart. It is wearing down from use, capable of false construction. Language no longer unequivocally represents, and by "Sirens," "Cyclops," and "Circe," *Ulysses* itself accepts and enacts that language is no longer an authoritative guide to the reality of its characters' lived experiences.

By relating the linguistic experience of the characters to their narrative experiences with value and authority, then, I connect students' experiences of reading with those of the characters. Students, as they follow characters that have lost the keys to their world, have similarly to find keys to the enigma of *Ulysses*: narrative become interpretive parable. The exact mechanism of this parallel, the points of connection between reading and character, varies of course from class to class and is less important than the fact of the parallel itself. (Pearce's essay suggests a variety of lacunae, to which could be added many more, that would be useful to point up the reader's experience of disorientation.) One may, of course, stress directly parallel points of character and reader confusion. When Bloom almost misreads his name in the throwaway (8.8–9), for instance, he undergoes the same moment of misreading that is forced on the reader when Joyce presents a second Mr. Bloom, a dentist, as a cognitive trap in "Wandering Rocks" (10.1115). But specific points of reader disorientation are less important than the general truth that there is an equivalence between the world in which Bloom and Stephen live and the text that is *Ulysses*. Both are disruptive and doubtful. Both are filled with the potential for misinterpretation and haunted by a lack of faith in singular answers. Both insist that their respective inhabitants and readers struggle with exclusion and frustration, as they work toward provisional meanings in a world, actual and linguistic, that seems to deny meaning any conclusive resolution.

Such discussions should not, of course, reduce *Ulysses* to a sterile puzzle or a monument to indeterminacy. I try to make clear the ways in which the text formally enacts the dilemma of authority and meaning experienced by the characters, implicating us as readers in their issues of difference and discomfort. We move as readers from the seemingly transparent style of the opening chapters toward the antirealism and surrealism of the central chapters, returning only at the end, in Molly's monologue, to an authoritative or realist stability. The language charts the movement of the characters— away from "home" and back again—while playing on the Dedalian-Bloomian linguistic experience. Joyce's language, like other structures of value in *Ulysses*, is a source of both power and alienation. This simultaneous enabling and constraint, which reflects the doubleness of family, religion, and history within the text, helps students see that the challenge of the main characters to make interpretive sense of their world is the reader's challenge to make sense of *Ulysses*.

This approach to *Ulysses* has several virtues. It is a frame rather than a system of reading. One may introduce the text and its idiosyncrasies without insisting that any particular school of interpretation holds the authoritative key to the text or even that the text admits of ultimate "solution" for either reader or characters. (A student may finish the book and be, like Bloom, a reasonably satisfied "competent keyless citizen" [17.1019].) This perspective also legitimizes the difficulties of *Ulysses* by demonstrating that they develop from the characters' ambiguous attitudes toward culture and language. Finally, it can be used as a rationale for the generic ambiguity of *Ulysses*, often of concern to students who read Joyce in the context of the epic or the history of the novel. For paradoxically *Ulysses* can be understood as epic and novel, antiepic and antinovel, simultaneously ironizing the conventions of form while drawing seriously on them, exactly as Stephen and Bloom both are and are not Catholic and Jew, are and are not Irishmen and the captives of traditions they may wish to revise but cannot elude. Students may therefore read the book as enacting the doubleness of authority in convention and value as that doubleness is enacted in the characters' lives, in *Ulysses's* linguistic texture, and in its genre. For the keys to *Ulysses* are not, as the end of *Finnegans Wake* claims of itself, "Given!" The reader in the classroom must seek an understanding of the text through a recognition of the intentional difficulties and disorientations implicit in Joyce's treatment of authority and by accepting the challenge of its linguistic and interpretive corollaries.

Point of View, the Narrator(s), and the Stream of Consciousness

Erwin R. Steinberg

The narrator in *Ulysses* evokes considerable comment from students, who raise questions like, Whose voice is heard in "Proteus" or in "Calypso"? Why do there appear to be several—perhaps many—voices in such chapters as "Oxen of the Sun" and "Cyclops"? To help students begin to understand what Hugh Kenner calls "Joyce's voices," I show them examples of intrusive comments by nineteenth-century novelists—the conclusion, for instance, of Sir Walter Scott's *The Heart of Midlothian*:

> READER—This tale will not be told in vain, if it shall be found to illustrate the great truth, that guilt, though it may attain temporal splendor, can never confer real happiness; that the evil consequences of our crimes long survive their commission, and, like the ghosts of the murdered, for ever haunt the steps of the malefactor; and that the paths of virtue, though seldom those of worldly greatness, are always those of pleasantness and peace.

Or that of William Makepeace Thackeray's *Vanity Fair*:

> Ah! *Vanitas Vanitatum!* which of us is happy in this world? Which of us has his desire? or, having it, is satisfied?—Come children, let us shut up the box and the puppets, for our play is played out.

Trollope's novels also provide many examples.

Students often find these intrusions amusing. Many remember and quote Joyce's statement, in *A Portrait of the Artist as a Young Man*, "The artist, like the God of the creation, remains within or behind or above his handiwork, invisible, refined out of existence, indifferent, paring his fingernails" (215). To promote further discussion, I cite Henry James's analysis of Trollope:

> In a digression, a parenthesis or an aside, he concedes to the reader that he and his trusting friends are only "making believe." He admits that the events he narrates have not really happened, and that he can give his narrative any turn the reader may like best. Such a betrayal of a sacred office seems to me, I confess, a terrible crime.
>
> (*Art of Fiction* 5)

At this point, students may simply take sides for or against the propositions; but when I propose that we accept Joyce's and James's statements as working hypotheses to test or as ways of thinking about various voices as they appear in *Ulysses*, students generally agree.

I then turn to the concept of point of view. Take, for example, Dickens's *Bleak House*. Chapter 12 closes with an omniscient author's description of the foreboding pas de deux played by Lady Dedlock and Mr. Tulkington:

> . . . Lady Dedlock is always the same exhausted deity, surrounded by worshippers, and terribly liable to be bored to death, even when presiding at her own shrine. Mr. Tulkington is always the same speechless repository of noble consequences; so oddly out of place, and yet so perfectly at home. . . .

Chapter 13, the first of ten chapters scattered through the novel titled "Esther's Narrative," begins:

> We held many consultations about what Richard was to be; first, without Mr. Jarndyce, as he had requested, and afterwards with him; but it was a long time before we seemed to make progress. . . .

I ask a student who has read the novel to sketch the plot to that point, or I do it myself. Then I ask if Joyce's statement about the God-like invisible artist is in any way relevant. Someone may comment that shifting points of view from one paragraph to the next, even though a chapter break intervenes, makes the reader aware of the author and thus violates Joyce's prescription.

If no one offers that opinion, I read from Henry James's preface to *The Ambassadors*, in which James discusses how, in writing the novel, he remembers "employing but one centre and keeping it all within [his] hero's compass":

> Other persons in no small number were to people the scene, and each with his or her axe to grind, his or her own situation to treat, his or her coherency not to fail of, his or her relation to my leading motive, in a word, to establish and carry on. But Strether's sense of these things, and Strether's only, should avail me for showing them; I should know them but through his more or less groping for knowledge of them, since his very gropings would figure among his most interesting motions. . . . It would give me a large unity . . . and the grace of intensity. . . .   (*Art of the Novel* 317)

And again I invite the class to consider the possibilities of a novelist telling the story from a single point of view. There are always some students who put Joyce's and James's statements together and argue for filtering a story through a single consciousness so as not to interfere with the "transparency" of the novel, not to disengage the reader from the story by changes that make his or her world. Other students counter that seeing a story from

multiple points of view is more profitable, that in fact they "read" the world
by seeing and hearing multiple views and adjudicating them. Creative writing students often have thought these matters through in some detail, and I
encourage them to tell us their experiences.

I don't take sides, but I do play devil's advocate from time to time if an
argument is not presented adequately. Eventually I point out that the class
has been involved in a discussion central to modernism, which is good
experience for reading *Ulysses*. For those who want to read more on the
topic, I suggest Henry James's prefaces to the New York edition of his works
(1908–09), edited by Richard P. Blackmur as *The Art of the Novel*; *The
Psychological Novel, 1900–1950*, by Leon Edel; and *An Introduction to the
Study of the Novel*, by Jacques Souvage.

We proceed to apply these concepts to *Ulysses*. Who, I ask, is describing
Buck Mulligan on the first page (1.1–34)? The students generally respond in
chorus: an omniscient narrator. They are not disturbed by the narrator's
characterizations of Mulligan: "The plump shadowed face and sullen oval
jowl recalled a prelate, patron of arts in the middle ages" (1.31–33). They are
used to a narrator's putting a spin on a description—even being judgmental.

Soon, however, Mulligan leaves the scene, and we are given Stephen's
thoughts as he views the bay (1.242). What's happening here, I ask? Again
the answer comes with little trouble: Joyce is presenting the scene from
Stephen's point of view. Yes, I say, but then I ask the class to consider the
following passage:

> White breast of the dim sea. The twining tresses, two by two. . . . Her
> door was open: she wanted to hear my music. . . . For those words,
> Stephen: love's bitter mystery. . . . Her secrets: old featherfans, tas-
> selled dancecards, powdered with must, a gaud of amber beads in her
> locked drawer.   (1.244–56)

Are these words floating through Stephen's mind? My question evokes all
sorts of answers—this is Stephen's point of view, we're looking through
Stephen's eyes, we're inside Stephen's head—and someone usually mentions
stream of consciousness. (The term has often surfaced earlier, but I post-
poned discussing it until now.)

To help students examine the concept, I ask them to close their eyes and
imagine picking up a tennis racket, walking on to a tennis court, and facing
an opponent. Here comes the ball! Swing! Then we talk about what they
"saw" and felt. Most students say that they "see" the ball coming (visual
imagery). Some attest to feeling the swing in their muscles (kinesthetic
imagery). We talk about imagining the use of other senses: smelling vinegar,
tasting a lemon, touching sandpaper, hearing a parent or a friend call; and I
lead them to the awareness of the multidimensionality of the stream of

consciousness—most of them simultaneously "saw" the court and the ball in three dimensions and "felt" the swing in their muscles.

Since we have mentioned Henry James, I read from his brother William James's *The Principles of Psychology* (224–90) or *Talks to Teachers on Psychology* (17). James says that the complex fields of the stream of consciousness

> contain sensations of our bodies and of objects around us, memories of past experiences and thoughts of distant things, feelings of satisfaction and dissatisfaction, desires and aversions, and other emotional conditions, together with determinations of the will, in every variety of permutation and combination.
>
> (*Talks* 17; for a fuller discussion, see ch. 2 in my *Stream of Consciousness*)

A quotation from Lewis Carroll's *Alice's Adventures in Wonderland* helps raise the problem of how an author can reproduce the stream of consciousness, which is multidimensional, with language, which is linear.

> "Did you say 'pig' or 'fig'?" said the Cat.
> "I said 'pig,' " replied Alice; "and I wish you wouldn't keep appearing and vanishing so suddenly: you make one quite giddy!"
> "All right," said the Cat; and this time it vanished quite slowly, beginning with the end of the tail, and ending with the grin, which remained some time after the rest of it had gone.   (ch. 6)

We discuss the possibility of a cat disappearing and leaving its grin behind; and then I write on the board, "The cat with a grin." After we ponder the phrase for a moment, I erase the middle three words, leaving "The grin." I have deleted the cat and left the grin. That action leads to a consideration of the linearity of language. When we speak or write, listen or read, we deal with strings of words: word + word + word. As we read, such strings accumulate into multidimensional understanding, such as a visual image of Bloom giving Molly her breakfast in bed; but as soon as we try to explain that understanding, we are forced to retranslate from multidimensionality to the linearity of language.

I remind the students of what they saw and felt when I asked them to imagine they were swinging a tennis racket, and I comment that those who are writers would have to translate such a multidimensional memory into the linearity of language. The scene in "Lestrygonians" in which Bloom worries that Boylan will infect Molly nicely demonstrates such simulation:

> Some chap with a dose burning him.
> If he ....?
> O!

Eh?

No ...... No.

No, no. I don't believe it. He wouldn't surely?

No, no.

Mr Bloom moved forward, raising his troubled eyes.

(8.101–08)

Those ejaculations are the closest Joyce can get to the rush of worry, the lurch of the stomach, the sharp intake of breath that accompany Bloom's sudden realization and concern.

A return to Stephen's first stream-of-consciousness passages, in "Telemachus" (1.242–79), furthers discussion of Joyce's use of the technique. The students notice that, in the first three chapters, Joyce relies increasingly on stream of consciousness, and by "Proteus," aside from some necessary omniscient author/narrator's sentences, we are entirely in Stephen's mind. Here, too, I offer readings: Dorrit Cohn, *Transparent Minds: Narrative Modes for Presenting Consciousness in Fiction*; Melvin J. Friedman, *Stream of Consciousness: A Study in Literary Method*; and Steinberg, ed., *The Stream-of-Consciousness Technique in the Modern Novel*.

"Proteus" again raises the question of the narrator. I point to some of the third-person statements early in the chapter, emphasizing certain words and sounds (italicized below):

Stephen closed his eyes to hear his boots *crush crackling* wrack and shells. (3.10)

They came down the steps from Leahy's terrace *prudently, Frauenzimmer*: and down the *shelving shore flabbily*, their splayed feet *sinking* in the *silted sand*. (3.29)

Airs *romped* around him, *nipping and eager airs*. (3.55)

I ask, Do narrators usually talk that way? Is the concept of the invisibility of the author relevant here? Most students had not noticed the language, while some—often creative writing majors—had. A few shrug off the problem: Joyce is entitled to do anything he wants. Still others grope for something approximating Kenner's "Uncle Charles Principle: *the narrative idiom need not be the narrator's*":

Writing fiction, [Joyce] played parts, and referred stylistic decisions to the taste of the person he was playing. The Uncle Charles Principle entails writing about someone much as that someone would choose to be written about. So it requires a knowledge of the character at which no one would arrive by "observation," and yet its application to the

> character seems as external as costume, since it does not entail re-
> cording spoken words. (We hear Gerty McDowell speak just two short
> sentences.)   (*Joyce's Voices* 18, 21)

I ask the class to test each chapter with the Kenner statement. When we
reach "Calypso," students generally comment that the point of view has
changed: the language describing Bloom's actions doesn't sound anything
like the language in "Proteus." I recall the single-consciousness approach of
Henry James and the passage from *Portrait* (215) in which Stephen proposes
the invisible author, and we wonder together why Joyce violated it in *Ulysses*.
When we reach no firm conclusion, I promise that we will return to the
question later.

The problem does not rise again until we get to "Sirens": How does the
Uncle Charles Principle explain the opening page and a half of that chapter?
Discussion flounders as students try—and fail—to make Kenner's principle
apply. The class cannot agree on whether a narrator presents that opening
material; and among those who think so, there is no agreement on who, if
anyone, is being written about. I promise that later chapters, "Cyclops" in
particular, offer further opportunities to examine the problem, and we move
on. The discussion of "Cyclops," however, does not lead to satisfactory
answers either, and when it flags, I offer four additional principles:

1. David Hayman's "arranger" theory:

> The asides [in "Cyclops"] belong to a nocturnal decorum generated by
> a single impulse if not a single persona, a resourceful clown of many
> masks, a figure apparently poles apart from the self-effacing narrator.
> This figure may be thought of as an *arranger*, a nameless and whimsical-
> seeming authorial projection whose presence is first strongly felt in
> "Aeolus," where he starts usurping the prerogatives of the objective
> narrator by interjecting the frequently intrusive mocking headlines. To
> "Scylla and Charybdis," "Wandering Rocks," and "Sirens" he contrib-
> utes less obvious but more whimsical effects. Finally, in "Cyclops,"
> where his prime effects are juxtaposed as asides to the predictable
> voice of the outcast narrator, he comes into his own, obliging us to
> equate his presence with the diminution of lucidity, the assertion of
> the unconscious and instinctual side of experience, the inexplicable
> realm of darkness through which light ultimately shines darkly.
>   (265–66)

"Ultimately," Hayman concludes, "we might attribute to him the very chapter shifts, inexplicable naturalistically and only partly related to the *Odyssey*
parallels" ("Cyclops" 266n15). Hayman's comment on chapter shifts and
changes in point of view offers an interesting opportunity to return to the

discussion of Joyce's apparent violation of Henry James's doctrine of writing a novel from a single point of view.

2. The Benstock principle:

> *Fictional texts that exploit free indirect speech* (the narrative mode most common to *Ulysses*) *establish the contextual supremacy of subject matter, which influences the direction, tone, pace, point of view, and method of narration.* . . . For instance, the catechism of "Ithaca" provides a metaphysic *category* in which subject and style are wedded at various levels: catechism is obviously the method of narration; it is also its subject, in all the various forms in which "catechism" can exist (method of colloquy, ritualization of concepts, educational process, mnemonic device, a structuring of facts, and so forth); but more importantly, the "subjects" of the catechism cannot be extrapolated from the catechism because they exist in that context at this moment.
>
> (Benstock and Benstock 18–19)

3. My own contention of Joyce as intrusive author:

> There is . . . an even simpler explanation [than the ones offered by Kenner, Hayman, and the Benstocks], an explanation inherent in Hayman's statement that the arranger is "*A nameless and whimsical-seeming authorial projection*" (italics added), in Kenner's statement that "Writing fictions, [Joyce] played parts," and in the title of Kenner's book, *Joyce's Voices* (*Joyce's* voices).
>
> Kenner explains that "We find Ulysses in *Ulysses* because the author told us to" [*Voices* 60]. Indeed. One also reads there "James Joyce." We have with us in *Ulysses* our old friend "the intrusive author," familiar to all readers of nineteenth-century fiction and widely discussed by critics and scholars writing about the history of the novel and the rhetoric of fiction. ("Author!" 421–22)

Joyce has given up his avowal in *Portrait* that the author should be invisible and has come cavorting on stage as the obvious perpetrator of the opening of "Sirens," the gleeful jokester giving us the outrageous—but very funny—extrapolations in "Cyclops," and the overly sober catechist of "Ithaca."

4. The possibility that Joyce is struggling between the "classic" and "romantic" tempers he describes in *Stephen Hero*, sometimes the control of the classic temper bending the language to its will and other times the impatience and adventuresomeness of the romantic temper bursting through those controls:

A classical style . . . is the syllogism of art, the only legitimate process from one world to another. Classicism is not the manner of any fixed age or of any fixed country: it is a constant state of the artistic mind. It is a temper of security and satisfaction and patience. The romantic temper, so often and so grievously misinterpreted and not more by others than by its own, is an insecure, unsatisfied, impatient temper which sees no fit abode here for its ideals and chooses therefore to behold them under insensible figures. . . . Its figures are blown to wild adventures. . . .   (*Hero* 78)

Passages useful to test this principle are those in which Joyce shifts from the constraints of realism to various kinds of extravagance: the ending of "Lestrygonians," with its simulation of Bloom's agitated stream of consciousness (8.1168), and the opening pages of "Scylla and Charybdis," especially 9.5–6, 12–13, 29–31; the last two paragraphs of "Cyclops" (12.1906–18); or the last lines of "Wandering Rocks" (10.1270) and the opening page and a half of "Sirens" (11.1–63). The difference between principles 3 and 4 is that principle 3 has Joyce consciously breaking loose, materialized into existence, deliberately—perhaps gleefully—violating a once soberly held, youthful belief; whereas principle 4 has Joyce simply responding, less consciously, to the tension between the two "tempers" of his own artistic impulse—and, indeed, to the two tempers between which artists and the arts continue to respond over time. As Joyce explains in *Stephen Hero*, "Between these two conflicting schools the city of the arts had become marvelously unpeaceful" (79).

With five hypotheses on the table, we finish the novel. The exercise can be completed either with group presentations, in which five students each make a six-minute argument in support of one hypothesis, followed by class discussion; or with a paper, in which each student defends the hypothesis he or she finds most convincing.

When asking the class to consider Joyce's shifts from realism to what I describe as various kinds of extravagance, I also have them examine Joyce's virtuosity with language. Students need to look carefully at the various voices in the extrapolations in "Cyclops": the takeoffs on Irish folklore (12.67–99, 12.151–55, 12.280–99, 12.1438–64); on the wide interest in Mme Blavatsky and her kind (12.338–76); on medical writing (12.468–78); on newspaper reporting (12.897–938); on the Apostle's Creed (12.1354–59); on sacred writings—pre-Christian (12.1111–40), Christian (12.1676–1739), and Old Testament (12.1910–18). Students often need to be pointed, too, at Joyce's punning (12.556–69).

Such discussions should also examine Joyce's other linguistic experiments: the differences in the streams of consciousness and soliloquies of Stephen, Bloom, and Molly (see my *Stream of Consciousness*, pt. 2); the newspaper headlines in "Aeolus"; Joyce's simulation of the sound of the machines folding newspapers (7.174–77); his simulation of the development of the English language in "Oxen of the Sun" and the exuberance of the ending of that chapter—to name just a few. All are important aspects of Joyce's voices.

What I describe is just one of the many ways I help a class read *Ulysses*. Class members also pursue, for example, feminist readings, problems of discontinuities and ambiguities in the text, and differences in the reading of *Ulysses* over time. The mix and focus depend on the class. Even when a class is very interested in Joyce's narrative voices, that interest does not surface every day and occupies few whole sessions. It often waxes as students watch the growth in Joyce's use of the stream-of-consciousness technique in the opening chapters, wanes as they become accustomed to the technique, and picks up again as Joyce undertakes a variety of experiments starting with "Scylla and Charybdis."

Students generally profit from the approach I sketch for several reasons. Those who have not attempted to write fiction find it informative to look at a novel from the writer's point of view. English majors apply what they learn to other readings. And creative writing majors gain new insight into a tool they could use only clumsily before. Indeed, when I teach *Ulysses*, my creative writing colleagues complain good-naturedly of receiving a rash of stream-of-consciousness stories. I acknowledge their discomfort with a Cheshire-cat grin.

Discovering *Ulysses*: The "Immersive" Experience

Weldon Thornton

Should new readers of Joyce's *Ulysses* wrestle unaided with the text or should they resort immediately to the various annotations, commentaries, and critical discussions of the novel? This question has become more salient in recent decades because such secondary material has proliferated and because Joycean criticism has become more theoretically charged. Many professors introduce Joyce by situating him within contemporary critical ideologies—even using his writings as exemplifications of theoretical modes such as structuralism or deconstruction. Joyce's works, more than those of D. H. Lawrence or William Faulkner, have become the terrain of contemporary ideational battles. First-time readers of *Ulysses* are also more likely to turn to secondary literature owing to requirements that undergraduates study literary theory.

What is at stake is both the quality of each individual's experience of the novel and the continuing health and resilience of critical debate over the book. My preference is for first-time readers of *Ulysses* to immerse themselves in the text before turning to any secondary materials. Having devoted many years to writing *Allusions in* Ulysses, I believe the various annotations and summaries play an important role, and I recommend several to my students, but only after they have first engaged the novel for themselves. (Among others, I recommend the books by Blamires, Gifford and Seidman, McCarthy, Schwarz, and Thornton.) Having an *experience* with a literary work is the necessary touchstone for all reflections on and discussions of the text. Reading *Ulysses* should be a wholistic experience that involves readers' emotions and values fully as much as their ideas and concepts; without that affective experience as a point d'appui, discussion of the novel floats about unanchored like the island of Laputa or (to shift the metaphor) is likely to be taken captive by the various ideologies that vie for authority in the modernist intellectual milieu.

I feel the same about a first reading of *Finnegans Wake*. I am not so much a purist, however, as to advocate the approach of Roland McHugh, who toiled single-handedly with *Finnegans Wake* for three years before turning to secondary material (Finnegans Wake *Experience*). Nor do I concur with Derek Attridge's disdain of all attempts to paraphrase (or, it seems, even to interpret) *Finnegans Wake*—what he satirically refers to as backboning, or filleting, the text ("Backbone").

In support of affective engagement with the text, I invoke D. H. Lawrence, whose essay on John Galsworthy begins with a declaration we teachers of literature need to keep in mind:

> Literary criticism can be no more than a reasoned account of the feeling produced upon the critic by the book he is criticizing. Criticism can never be a science: it is in the first place, much too personal, and in the second, it is concerned with values that science ignores. The

touchstone is emotion, not reason. We judge a work by its effect on our sincere and vital emotion, and nothing else. All the critical twiddle-twaddle about style and form, all this pseudo-scientific classifying and analysing of books in an imitation-botanical fashion, is mere impertinence and mostly dull jargon.

A critic must be able to *feel* the impact of a work of art in all its complexity and its force. To do so, he must be a man of force and complexity himself, which few critics are. A man with a paltry, impudent nature will never write anything but paltry, impudent criticism. And a person who is *emotionally* educated is rare as a phoenix.

(539)

I am not so naive as to believe in an utterly spontaneous or value-free reading of any literary text, especially by present-day university students, who necessarily come to *Ulysses* with considerable cultural and literary experience. I hope, furthermore, that they would have read Joyce's earlier works—especially *A Portrait of the Artist*—and acquired background knowledge about Joyce's biography and literary milieu. And I am not in principle opposed to explication or interpretation of these texts. Articulation of our feelings and ideas about literary works, in class discussion or in print, is necessary to our total relationship with them, extending and enhancing our understanding in ways that nothing else can. But as Lawrence points out, critical discussion should articulate an *experience*, and without that affective base, we are working in a vacuum; our experience of the work serves both as the foundation for our own nascent response and as a gauge of the validity of others' responses.

I use this pedagogic principle whether I am teaching Robert Frost's "West-Running Brook" or Joyce's "The Dead" or *Ulysses*. I ask my students to read the text as fully as possible for themselves before we begin to discuss it, so that they will already have *engaged* the work from their own perspective. When teaching a long text such as *Ulysses*, I prepare the class for our discussion by raising a number of heuristic questions, asking the students to read most of the work before we discuss it. With *Ulysses* I pose questions about the distinctive qualities of the central characters: What does it reveal about Joyce's motivations that he created characters with these particular virtues and flaws and built his book around them? What is it about Stephen, Bloom, and Molly that renders them worthy of the author's interest or makes them appropriate "modern" characters? Does Joyce focus most on Stephen's seriousness and responsiveness to moral issues, his sense of his calling as a writer, or his attempt to maintain complete conscious control over his destiny? What does it suggest about Joyce's underlying artistic intentions that he concentrates on so ordinary, marginal, and semisuccessful a central character as the Jewish advertising salesman Leopold Bloom? In what ways is (and is not) Bloom a "typical Dubliner"? What seems to be Joyce's purpose in evoking a series of mythic and literary parallels throughout the novel, not only with Homer's *Odyssey* but with texts from every level of Western culture?

While these questions are obviously not "value free," in raising them I try to avoid either presanctioning or undermining the valuational assertions that I or the class members will later put forward. Rather, my goal is to sharpen the students' interests as they engage the novel, thus providing a firmer basis for their judging the specific interpretive and valuational claims that emerge in our discussion. One of my aims in teaching any literary text is to help the students become aware of their own wholistic responses and develop confidence in articulating their views. I suspect many of my colleagues feel similarly, but fewer might concur that this practice is sound for a text as daunting as *Ulysses*. Yet it is even more important to invoke this principle with such a complex work, because there is greater risk of the reader's affective response being fragmented or dispersed.

I recommend that my students' initial reading of *Ulysses* be done quickly and intensively and in large segments, so that they can get the feel of the various episodes of the book as well as a tangible sense of how it is like and unlike other novels they have read. My own first reading of *Ulysses* in the spring of 1956 was done in three days, without any support texts. I had just left graduate study in chemistry for the study of English, and I was unfamiliar with any of Joyce's other works. There is no question I missed a great deal, and I do not recommend so contextless a reading for my students—though the concentration of the experience still seems worth emulating. Ill-prepared as I was, the book nevertheless made a strong impression on me. It was unlike any other novel I had ever read. While I was intimidated, even infuriated, by the book, I was also enthralled, and I knew then that coming to terms with it would form a large part of my subsequent intellectual life. My term paper, "Liberty and License in Joyce's *Ulysses*," argued that by asking far more of the reader than he had any right to do, Joyce repeatedly and willfully violated the implicit contract that should exist between any writer and an audience. The essay threw my instructor into consternation, and, after some wavering, he awarded it a D −. That I wrote a dissertation on the uses of allusions in *Ulysses* and spent the first seven years of my academic career writing *Allusions in* Ulysses—a book designed to provide for the reader much of what Joyce chose not to provide—testifies, rather ironically, to the hold the novel had on me.

My ideas about the importance of experiencing the book are grounded in my belief (by no means concurred in by all Joyceans) that *Ulysses* is a novel. By this I mean that it presents itself to us primarily in terms of character, motive, event, tone, and atmosphere—that is, as an affective-aesthetic-valuational-cognitive experience. Only after students have read a number of episodes on their own—ideally, the whole novel—do I have them turn to annotations or critical commentaries, since these, however clarifying, always

involve some intervention between reader and text. The problem with annotations is not that they impose a theoretical frame of reference that may
override the reader's own nascent response but that they fragment the experience of reading and consequently interfere especially with our sense of
tonal and affective continuities. Even veteran readers of *Ulysses* can sense
this fragmentation if they go back through an episode of *Ulysses* keeping
Gifford and Seidman's Ulysses *Annotated* or my *Allusions in* Ulysses open
beside them; you cannot attend to each and every allusion and retain any
sense of the affective quality or continuity of the episode as a whole. A
scrutiny with annotations in hand serves one purpose; a more engaged reading quite another. And I presume that other experienced readers of *Ulysses*
feel, as I do, the need for occasionally reading the episodes quickly and
"immersively," to renew their sense of the episodes' tenor and texture, to
see what qualitative changes in those aspects of the work can be detected
since the last such reading.

I employ the full range of critical materials once the students have im-
mersed themselves in the novel. One way I encourage them to draw on the
insights afforded by annotation and criticism is to have them undertake
detailed scrutiny of one-page passages from an early Stephen episode (e.g.,
"Proteus") and an early Bloom episode (e.g., "Calypso" or "Lotus-eaters").
(If time permits, I let each student choose passages to work up, and they
come to the office to discuss them with me; this requires *at least* one hour
per passage per student. The alternative is to assign passages to the class as
a whole and then devote one full class meeting to each passage.) Availing
themselves of all the scholarly and critical tools relevant to their passages—
including Steppe and Gabler's indispensable *Handlist to James Joyce's* Ulysses—the students try to pin down every allusion, the meaning of every
phrase, the basis of every psychological association. The aim is for them
to experience the various textures of the prose—psychological, imagistic,
thematic. The questions they are to ask about every phrase, every image
include the following: How does this element link up with what precedes
and follows it? What is the nature of the continuity that holds this sentence
or this paragraph together? Does this passage connect to other passages in
the novel?

My questions are designed to bring to light the various kinds of continuity
that weave the texture of the novel, including its impressive degree of
psychological coherence, not simply on the conscious level of the characters'
psychologies but on the subconscious level as well. If we are scrutinizing
page 47 of "Calypso," the student may or may not have discovered that
Bloom's phrase "Kind of stuff you read: in the track of the sun. Sunburst on
the title page" (4.99–100) refers to a book entitled *In the Track of the Sun*
that Bloom has on his shelf, as we learn on 17.1395. But we learn that the
title page of his copy is missing. Research reveals that the book's actual
title page depicts not a sunburst but an Oriental girl playing a stringed

instrument—something that links up subconsciously with the "girl playing one of those instruments what do you call them: dulcimers" that Bloom had thought about in the preceding line (4.97–98; see Thornton, *Allusions* 69–70). Similar scrutiny of pages 34–35 in "Proteus" uncovers a variety of subconscious and apparently prelinguistic links in Stephen's thought chains regarding the Pigeonhouse (i.e., the Dublin powerhouse) which he glimpses as he walks; the "pigeon" on whom Mary blames her pregnancy, in the quote from Leo Taxil; the "wildgoose" Kevin Egan; and Columbanus, whose name means "dove" (see Michels). This detailed attention to brief passages complements the students' wholistic reading of the novel and gives them a chance to see how densely textured it is in virtually every passage.

In "Teaching for the (W)Holes" in this volume Richard Pearce speaks of the disconcerting gap caused by the reader's encountering unfamiliar allusions, such as that to Chrysostomos on the first page. But the degree to which we feel such material as a gap is a function of how we approach the text. The "gap" is exacerbated if we regard the book primarily as an intellectual challenge or as a puzzle we must solve by having every piece in place. If we are attending to the affective dimension of the novel—in "Telemachus," to the distinctive psychological tenor of the two main characters and their uneasy relationship with each other—unknown items, while not trivial, recede into the distance. If we are attending to a character's personality, the penchant for abstruse allusions itself comes into play as a significant personal trait—arcane allusions are characteristic of Stephen's psyche but not of Bloom's or of Molly's. Even when we do not understand the allusions, they help us develop our sense of how characters differ from one another.

To establish the relevant context for discussion of the novel's themes, I try to evoke a sense of the distinctive psychological tenor of the various characters and episodes rather than introduce abstract philosophical ideas. "Telemachus" has a distinctive tenor of tension, rivalry, and defensiveness, stemming from the very different personalities and values of Buck and Stephen and from the resultant conflict between them. Once we recognize and respond to that psychological milieu, we can engage the emergent themes of the episode. The issue of the real power behind the world and the question of who is its true priest underlies the rivalry between Stephen and Mulligan, as well as Stephen's defensive resentment of Haines. If bodily vigor (exemplified by Mulligan) is the most real thing in the world, then the medical doctor is the truest priest we can have. If political and economic power are the most substantial forces we can know, then Haines and the British empire must be deferred to. But the tenor of Stephen's attitude in this episode reflects his defensive and as yet unjustified belief that, as the poet, he embodies that more substantial spiritual power the old milkwoman (and Ireland) should acknowledge and turn to. In Stephen's view, this power has been challenged and usurped by Mulligan, by Haines, and by the Roman Catholic priests, all of whom represent more tangible but less substantial modes of power than he does.

All these themes are embodied in an affective, value-charged psychological situation and can only be apprehended if we respond to them in that novelistic context. We cannot discuss the theme of modes of power as if it were some abstract philosophical issue. To talk meaningfully about this theme in *Ulysses*, we must engage it in terms established by this and other analogous contexts in the novel. We must have responded to the psychological tenor of rivalry and defensiveness that "Telemachus" invokes, appreciating that modes of power involve a serious conflict of values among the characters in the episode.

Similarly, the class discusses the broad theme of identity or the self not in abstract terms but in the context of the tangible personal selfhoods, problems, and interrelationships of characters such as Stephen, Bloom, Mulligan, Molly, and Simon Dedalus. Since *Ulysses* is a novel, these affective contexts are not irrelevant to or discontinuous with the themes of the book—on the contrary, they embody them.

First-time readers who experience the text before reading secondary materials will also have a basis for seeing through the inappropriate or distortive ideas or values (or, more likely, lack of values) some critics attribute to Joyce. The first-time reader who goes through the novel trying to see what problems are most cogent to Stephen, Bloom, and Molly and how they respond to these problems as *Ulysses* unfolds implicitly relies on the continuity of the selves of these three characters. The "Bloom" who, in "Ithaca," suggests that "Stephen" spend the night at 7 Eccles Street is experienced as the same "Bloom" who took Molly her breakfast in "Calypso," and "Stephen" is the same "Stephen" who worried about his possible betrayal of his mother in "Telemachus." The reader who has experienced the continuity of the characters in the novel can better judge the various critical claims about the theme of the self in *Ulysses*—such as the claim that Joyce set out to undermine the notion of the self. My concern is to show the discrepancy between the inherently valuational nature of an affective reading and the Pyrrhonic claims of many critics that Joyce lacks values. One example is Steven Helmling's "Joyce: Autobiography, History, Narrative." On the assumption that Joyce had no interest in the novelistic aspects of his works, Helmling attributes to him pessimism and determinism about the whole range of human values. When I read Helmling's account of *Ulysses* and *Finnegans Wake*, I feel that he is describing utterly different books from the ones I have read.

I regard *Ulysses* as one of the great novels of our tradition, and I want readers to experience it directly before their responses become fragmented by annotations or overridden by critical pronouncements. I am concerned as well for the health of Joycean criticism and scholarship—for the ability of literary criticism to continue to play the role it should play vis-à-vis this great text. Our best safeguard against the danger that Joyce's works will become the province of any one critical school or mode or will be taken captive by any one ideology is to cultivate new generations of readers whose primary experience is of the texts themselves rather than of abstract, tendentious theoretical assertions. Our best protection against hegemonic stances is to afford first-time readers of *Ulysses* an opportunity to experience the text for themselves as fully as possible.

SUCCESSFUL CLASSROOM STRATEGIES AND TECHNIQUES

Some Points of Departure for Teaching *Ulysses*

Morris Beja

When we set out to teach *Ulysses*, its reputation works for and against us. It works for us because it often attracts students who are eager to confront the book; it works against us because students may feel daunted—even fearful. More than with perhaps any other work in the modernist canon, the instructor must lessen the sense of intimidation without destroying the sense of excitement. In my experience, much of that task is achieved if students are helped along before they start the novel.

To get students into the novel and into each chapter, I distribute a document I call "Some Points of Departure for James Joyce's *Ulysses*." That undramatic title is carefully chosen: it is emphatically not a summary of the book or anything remotely like one. I have no pedagogical or moral objections to what Harry Blamires does in *The Bloomsday Book*, which I put on reserve, but it is not something I am personally interested in providing, nor is it something I think is truly needed.

My document provides students with a way of orienting themselves—in regard to time, to geography, and to the narrative situation—as they come to each chapter of the novel. Each section sets up the context at the start of the relevant chapter of *Ulysses*: it tells who the chief characters are, where they (and we) are, what time it is, and so on. Except for a few bare indications,

I do not specify much of what occurs. Students still have to read the book to find out about the argument in "Circe" or about Stephen's thesis on Shakespeare and *Hamlet* in "Scylla and Charybdis." My goal is to help students start to read the book—not to read it for them.

"Some Points of Departure" is more selective than a summary would be—and no more neutral. Any selection entails interpretation. Still, I try not to overload the document with my interpretations. I do include interpretive material that comes from Joyce himself—information about the "correspondences" and the two versions of his "schema." Even those references are selective. (I used to supply copies of the schemas among the various materials with which I tend to burden my students, until students complained that the schemas confused them more than the book did.) Joyce himself decided that readers would not need his charts; no doubt more reluctantly than I should have, I have concluded that he was right—mostly. It helps to know that the correspondence for Stephen, say, is Telemachus—not Ulysses. I base decisions about inclusion on my experience of what helps intelligent and advanced undergraduate students as they come to *Ulysses*. We are not helpful to students if we do not select from all we could throw at them.

What follows is the material I distribute to students a few weeks before we start our class discussions. The target class is an advanced undergraduate course in twentieth-century British and Irish fiction, primarily consisting of English majors; I also distribute the document to graduate students coming to *Ulysses* for the first time. In addition, I try to prepare students in some of the standard ways—I have a shelf of books on reserve at the library, for example—and I make available materials I compiled through my familiarity with Dublin, where I once lived and taught: maps, and hundreds of slides following Joyce's works from *Dubliners* through *Portrait* to *Ulysses* and *Finnegans Wake*. (I assign only *Ulysses* in the undergraduate course, but I talk about the *Wake* and assume a knowledge of *Portrait* and some *Dubliners* stories.)

Throughout our discussions I always make explicit Beja's First Law of Literary Criticism: If you know all the answers, you aren't asking the right questions.

Some Points of Departure for James Joyce's *Ulysses*: A Handout for Students

Many first-time readers of *Ulysses*, although they do not really need a guide, feel more comfortable with one. This document isn't an alternative to reading the novel, and it doesn't summarize each chapter. Rather, it attempts to facilitate your initial approach by indicating a few aspects of the external setting and situation of each chapter and listing some of the major Homeric correspondences—the associations between *Ulysses* and the *Odyssey*.

All the Homeric "correspondences" (Joyce's term) come from the "schema" Joyce prepared for the novel, a chart that exists in two versions (see Stuart Gilbert's *James Joyce's* Ulysses and Richard Ellmann's Ulysses *on the Liffey* for the complete charts). Each version provides useful and critically influential information about the novel and Joyce's conception of it: the titles for the chapters, for example; the times at which the action takes place; and the colors, symbols, techniques ("technics"), aspects of science and art, and, even, bodily organs particularly associated with each chapter.

The schema deals only with the Homeric correspondences, while it is arguable that others about which Joyce was less explicit—biblical, historical, Shakespearean, and so on—are just as important. Moreover the Homeric parallels are indirect and subtle rather than direct and literal; of chief importance is what is happening to Bloom as Bloom, to Stephen as Stephen, and so on, here and now—"here" being Dublin and "now" being 16 June 1904 (a Thursday).

Although I provide Joyce's references and Homeric correspondences for your information, they should not be taken with worshipful seriousness. They were important to Joyce, so presumably they are of some interest to his readers. But they are not necessarily of overriding value, and if overemphasized, they may prove a burden.

Chapter 1: "Telemachus"

It is around 8:00 a.m. The setting is the Martello tower, in Sandycove, on Dublin Bay, a few miles south of the center of Dublin. Stephen Dedalus, age twenty-two, has been living in the tower with Malachi ("Buck") Mulligan, a medical student, and Haines, a young Englishman. A year has passed since the death of Stephen's mother, which brought him home from Paris; it is about two years since the end of *A Portrait of the Artist as a Young Man.* One version of the schema gives the technique of the chapter as "narrative (young)."

> The Homeric correspondence for Stephen is Telemachus, son of Odysseus, and for Mulligan it is Antinous, one of the suitors of Penelope (Telemachus's mother and Odysseus's wife); Antinous and the other suitors took over Odysseus's palace and attempted to usurp his (and, consequently, Telemachus's) role. The symbol of the chapter, in one version of the schema, is "heir."

Chapter 2: "Nestor"

It is around 10:00 a.m. Stephen is teaching a class of boys in a school in Dalkey, a suburb south of Dublin not far from the Martello tower. The headmaster of the school is Garrett Deasy, who asks Stephen to help him place a letter to the editor (on foot-and-mouth disease) in a newspaper. The schemas list "history" as the art of the chapter; the technique, in one version, is "catechism (personal)" (contrast with the technique for chapter 17).

> *Nestor, a king noted for his wisdom, befriended young Telemachus and offered him counsel. Here, however, the correspondence for Nestor is Deasy. Helen of Troy corresponds to Mrs. O'Shea (see ch. 6 notes on Charles Stewart Parnell).*

Chapter 3: "Proteus"

At around 11:00 a.m. Stephen walks along the strand at Sandymount, between Dalkey and Dublin. His stream of consciousness is presented through an extended interior monologue; Joyce identified the technique of the chapter as "monologue (male)"; the art of the chapter is "philology."

> *Proteus, an elusive god of the sea, had the ability to change his shape at will.*

Chapter 4: "Calypso"

We are back between 8:00 and 9:00 a.m. again, at 7 Eccles Street, north of the River Liffey in Dublin, the home of Mr. and Mrs. Leopold Bloom. Leopold, age thirty-eight, is an advertising canvaser, and his wife Marion ("Molly"), age thirty-three, is a concert singer. They have a daughter, Milly, age fifteen, who has a job in another town (Mullingar); Bloom receives a letter from her. Their only other child, a boy given the name Rudy (after Bloom's father, Rudolph Bloom, born Rudolph Virag), died shortly after birth, almost eleven years ago. Another letter, for Molly, is from Hugh ("Blazes") Boylan, who is arranging a concert tour for her—as well as an appointment to be her lover this afternoon, as Bloom is silently aware. Although he has been baptized into the Catholic church, Bloom was born of a Jewish father and is regarded by everyone in the novel as a Jew. He leaves home to buy a kidney (the organ for this chapter) for his breakfast, and he also serves Molly her breakfast. The technique of the chapter is "narrative (mature)," in contrast to the "narrative (young)" of chapter 1.

> *Joyce indicated that a correspondence for Calypso is the nymph in the picture hanging above the Blooms' bed (the symbol for the chapter in one schema is "nymph"; the alternative version lists other symbols as well, including "vagina," "exile," and "Israel in bondage"). In Homer, Calypso held Odysseus captive on her island for seven years, until ordered by the gods to release him. As a correspondence for "the recall" itself—the summons issued by Hermes for Odysseus to return home to Ithaca—Joyce cited Dlugacz, the apparently Jewish butcher from whom Bloom buys the kidney; the correspondence for Ithaca is "Zion."*

Chapter 5: "Lotus-eaters"

It is around 10:00 a.m. Bloom walks through areas south of the River Liffey (which crosses the center of Dublin, west to east) to the baths, near Trinity College. (His home at 7 Eccles Street does not have a bath.) One schema lists the organ of the chapter as "genitals"; in the other it is "skin." On his way, Bloom stops at a post office and picks up a letter from a Martha Clifford, who had once answered an advertisement he had placed under the name "Henry Flower." We discover later that when Bloom tells Bantam Lyons to keep the newspaper Bloom was going to throw away anyway, Lyons believes Bloom is giving him a tip on Throwaway, a horse running in the Gold Cup at Ascot—a long shot that, it later turns out, wins.

> The title "Lotus-eaters" refers to the incident in which members of Odysseus's crew ate the lotus, a drug that made them forget their homes and all desires save the wish to remain where they were.

Chapter 6: "Hades"

It is between 11:00 a.m. and noon; Bloom attends the funeral of Patrick ("Paddy") Dignam, along with other Dublin acquaintances, among whom is Simon Dedalus, Stephen's father. The funeral carriages go from Dignam's home in Sandymount, south of Dublin, to Glasnevin cemetery, north of the city. At the cemetery, the mourners stop for a moment at the grave of Charles Stewart Parnell (1846–91), who fell from leadership of the cause of Irish freedom after being named in a divorce case involving his lover ("Kitty" O'Shea) and her husband.

> Joyce associated the caretaker of the cemetery, John O'Connell, with Hades, god of the underworld, whose realm Odysseus visited. The River Dodder, the Grand and Royal Canals, and the River Liffey correspond to the four rivers of the realm of Hades. While in Hades Odysseus promised the shade of Elpenor (a member of his crew and here the parallel for Dignam) that his body would be given a proper burial. Other correspondences include those of Parnell with Agamemnon (the slain Greek king), Menton with Ajax (whom Odysseus saw in Hades but who, out of an old resentment, refused to speak with him), and Cunningham with Sisyphus (condemned forever to push a boulder up a hill, only to see it roll down again).

Chapter 7: "Aeolus"

It is around noon, in the offices of a Dublin newspaper, the *Freeman* (that is, the *Freeman's Journal and National Press* and the *Weekly Freeman and National Press*), in the center of Dublin, just off O'Connell Street and near the General Post Office. Bloom comes there regarding an advertisement for Alexander Keyes; Stephen comes (separately) because he has promised to try to get the letter Deasy has written into a newspaper. The art of the chapter is "rhetoric," and the organ is "lungs."

> *Aeolus (here corresponding to Myles Crawford, the editor of the news-paper), the keeper of the winds, was hospitable to Odysseus and gave him a sealed bag containing all the winds except the one that would blow his ship home. Odysseus's men opened the bag, and the released winds blew their ship off course; angered at the sailors' disobedience, Aeolus refused Odysseus's second plea for help.*

Chapter 8: "Lestrygonians"

It is between 1:00 and 2:00 p.m., lunchtime in Dublin. Bloom walks south from O'Connell Street across the river to Duke Street, where he has lunch at Davy Byrne's pub (the organ here is the "esophagus," the technique, "peristaltic prose"), and then to the National Museum (next to the National Library—the setting for the next chapter).

> *The Lestrygonians were giant cannibals who devoured many of Odysseus's men; the leader of the Lestrygonians was Antiphates (associated in a schema with "hunger"), whose daughter lured the men into his trap (as "decoy," she is connected in a schema with "food").*

Chapter 9: "Scylla and Charybdis"

We are at the National Library, between 2:00 and 3:00 p.m. Stephen has a discussion of *Hamlet* with several acquaintances, a number of whom are based on (and given the names of) actual Dublin literary figures of the time. Prominent among them are Æ (George Russell), a poet with an interest in mysticism; Richard I. Best, assistant director of the library; John Eglinton (William K. Magee), assistant librarian and author; and Thomas W. Lyster, "Quaker librarian." The art of the chapter is "literature." The symbol in one schema is "London and Stratford," and in the other Joyce adds more pairings: "Scholasticism and Mysticism," "Plato and Aristotle," "Youth and Maturity."

> *Scylla and Charybdis were the dual perils through which Odysseus had to pass: Scylla was a six-headed monster who dwelt on a rock; Charybdis was a nearby whirlpool. Joyce associates "the rock" with "Aristotle, Dogma, Stratford" and the "whirlpool" with "Plato, Mysti-cism, London." In this chapter the figure of Ulysses is associated with "Socrates, Jesus, Shakespeare."*

Chapter 10: "Wandering Rocks"

In nineteen brief sections taking place between 3:00 and 4:00 p.m., we see glimpses of Dublin life occurring in various parts of the city and involving various people. (In one schema the symbol is "citizens.") The first and longest section follows the Reverend John Conmee, SJ, who was rector at Clongowes Wood College when Stephen was a student there (in *Portrait*); it was to him that Stephen appealed his unjust pandying by Father Dolan. Now attached to St. Francis Xavier's Church, in Dublin, Father Conmee is associated with the "Asiatic bank" (of the Black Sea; see the Homeric correspondences below); the viceroy—whose procession passes in scenes throughout the chapter—is associated with the "European bank."

> *Joyce associated the groups of Dublin citizens with the Wandering Rocks (the Symplegades, near the entrance to the Black Sea, between Europe and Asia)—which are mentioned but do not actually appear in the* Odyssey, *although they do figure in Vergil's* Aeneid. *They were two huge floating rocks that crushed ships attempting to pass between them.*

Chapter 11: "Sirens"

It is around 4:00 p.m. This chapter contains many approaches and techniques based on the art of music (the art in the schema is "music"; the technique is the "Fuga per canonem," or fugue according to rule); the organ is "ear." Bloom walks to a bar (the Concert Room of the Ormond Hotel, on the quay of the Liffey). He sits with Richie Goulding (Stephen's uncle—his mother's brother) in a room apart from the one patronized by a group of men around the piano: Simon Dedalus, "Father" Bob Cowley, and Ben Dollard. Also among the patrons is Blazes Boylan, who is on his way to his appointment with Molly at 7 Eccles Street.

> *The barmaids, Lydia Douce and Mina Kennedy, correspond to the Sirens, whose song lured sailors to shipwreck on the rocks. Odysseus had his crew put wax in their ears so that they would not hear the song, but he had himself lashed to the mast, so that he could hear the Sirens but could not yield to their song.*

Chapter 12: "Cyclops"

The scene is Barney Kiernan's pub, around 5:00 p.m., near the Four Courts, the legal center of Dublin. There is a dual, interchanging narration here: one is by an unnamed patron of the pub, the other is in a series of adopted styles. One schema specifies the technique as "gigantism," the other, as "alternating asymmetry." Because of the tip Bloom is supposed to have given

Bantam Lyons on Throwaway, the men in the pub mistakenly come to believe Bloom has won money on a long shot.

The Citizen corresponds to the Cyclops, Polyphemus, a one-eyed giant who ate some of Odysseus's men; in escaping from him, Odysseus blinded him with a heated stake (cf. Bloom's cigar).

Chapter 13: "Nausicaa"

Two or three hours have passed; it is between 8:00 and 9:00 p.m., at the strand in Sandymount. Bloom, alone, has come from his visit with Martin Cunningham to Paddy Dignam's widow, whose home is nearby. Half the chapter presents the point of view of Gerty MacDowell, a young woman who is sitting on the rocks of the strand; the other half, after Gerty leaves, comprises the thoughts of Bloom, who has been watching her. The symbol in one schema is "virgin"; the other lists three symbols: "onanism," "female," and "hypocrisy." One version of the schema gives the technique as "tumescence" and "detumescence," the other, as "retrogressive progression."

Gerty corresponds to Nausicaa, the princess of Phaeacia who found Odysseus after he had been washed ashore on her island, naked and alone; Phaeacia is identified here with the nearby Church of Mary, Star of the Sea.

Chapter 14: "Oxen of the Sun"

The scene is the maternity hospital on Holles Street, at 10:00 p.m. (the art is "medicine" or "physic"). For many readers, this chapter presents the greatest problems, and Joyce himself spoke of it as "the most difficult episode." The styles follow the historical development of English prose. In part, too, the development parallels the growth of an embryo during a nine-month pregnancy: the technique is identified as "embryonic development" (or "prose [Embryo-Foetus-Birth]"). The organ in one schema is "womb," in the other, "matrix" (that is, womb) and "uterus." One schema specifies the symbol as "mothers."

Bloom has come to the hospital to inquire about his friend Mina Purefoy, who is giving birth. In the commons room, he encounters Stephen Dedalus, who is getting drunk along with a number of medical-student acquaintances, among them Mulligan. They discuss various topics, including the morality of birth control. At the end, they all go to Burke's pub; Bloom goes along to keep an eye on Stephen.

Joyce associated the hospital with the island of the Oxen of the Sun, the island of Helios, the sun god (here the parallel of Dr. Horne, a director of the hospital). Odysseus warned his men not to kill the oxen, sacred symbols of fertility, but they did so, provoking Zeus to destroy their ship with a thunderbolt.

Chapter 15: "Circe"

It is around midnight in an area Joyce called Nighttown, a brothel district in the northeast section of Dublin, where Bloom, concerned about Stephen, has followed him. Stephen has been deserted by Mulligan, Haines, and the other young men except Lynch. Most of the chapter takes place in Bella Cohen's brothel. One schema gives the technique as "hallucination," the other, as "vision animated to bursting-point"; in one version the art is "magic," in the other, "dance." In the schema that lists the symbols for "Nausicaa" and "Oxen of the Sun" (chs. 13 and 14) as respectively, "virgin" and "mothers," the symbol for this chapter is "whore."

> *Bella corresponds to Circe, the enchantress who transformed Odysseus's crew into swine. Odysseus rescued them by means of a magic herb ("moly"), and they became men again.*

Chapter 16: "Eumaeus"

At around 1:00 a.m., Bloom and Stephen walk to the cabman's shelter, a pub open late for the convenience of cabmen. The pub, next to Butt Bridge, is kept by a man his customers believe is Skin-the-Goat, who was accused of being one of the "Invincibles"—the group who murdered two high British officials in Phoenix Park in 1882. In the schema that lists the technique of the first chapter ("Telemachus") as "narrative (young)" and that of the fourth chapter ("Calypso") as "narrative (mature)," the technique of this chapter is "narrative (old)."

> *Skin-the-Goat corresponds to Eumaeus, the faithful swineherd at whose hut the disguised Odysseus was given shelter when he returned to Ithaca. The schemas identify Murphy, the sailor, as "Ulysses Pseudangelos" ("Ulysses the False Messenger"). He is apparently a false or lying Odysseus—both like and unlike the (often deceptive) Homeric Odysseus.*

Chapter 17: "Ithaca"

It is around 2:00 a.m., and Stephen and Bloom walk to 7 Eccles Street, where they have cocoa and talk until Stephen leaves, although Bloom has invited him to stay the night. Joyce called the question-and-answer technique of this chapter "catechism (impersonal)" in the schema that lists the technique for chapter 2 ("Nestor") as "catechism (personal)." The art is "science," and the symbol is "comets."

Ithaca is Odysseus's home. Blazes Boylan doesn't put in an appearance, as such, but in Joyce's schema he corresponds to Eurymachus, the second suitor Odysseus kills after he returns to his palace; the first was Antinous, the parallel for Mulligan in chapter 1. In addition, Joyce associates the suitors with "scruples" and Odysseus's bow (the weapon he uses to kill the suitors) with "reason."

Chapter 18: "Penelope"

It is no particular or specified time (in one schema, the entry for time is the sign for eternity, the inverted 8, ∞). Molly Bloom is in bed. The technique is listed alternatively as "monologue (female)" or "monologue/Resigned style": there are eight long unpunctuated sentences in this chapter.

Molly corresponds to Penelope. In the schema, Penelope is associated with "Earth," which is also the symbol for the chapter.

The Importance of Playing Earnest:
The Stakes of Reading *Ulysses*

Vicki Mahaffey

The first problem for a teacher of *Ulysses* is inducing students to finish the book; the second is helping them read to the end without obedient rigidity. An instant indication of how well *Ulysses* is taught is whether or not it is read. Creases in the spine of the poorly bound 1961 Random House edition showed at a glance the extent of a student's incursion into the book, and the "used" sections of university bookstores were graveyards of abandoned copies—some with 30 pages turned, more with 200, and fewer topping out at 380, a little more than halfway through.

Ulysses seems to promise that it will open to the key of "fact"—that if we just assemble enough facts, the mysteries of the narrative can be decoded—only to make fun of our anxious reliance on such keys once they are at hand. In a first reading of "Oxen of the Sun," for example, the progression of narrative styles seems hopelessly academic and the culmination of the chapter even more pedantic, until we realize that what appeared to be the most esoteric of styles is actually no more than an unusually literal rendition of drunken pub talk at closing time. Repeatedly in this way Joyce alienates and thereby freshens the familiar and the mundane. But how do we as teachers motivate students to finish the book when their habitual ways of reading are continually frustrated? How do we transform the book from an inert, massive monument of Anglo-Irish literature into the lively, various, and personal series of dialogues with the reader (many at the reader's expense) that *Ulysses* has the capacity to become?

Perhaps the only answer is to enjoy the book ourselves, always monitoring the students' enjoyment and their discomfiture. Among the many ways to enjoy the book, the most contagious is to appreciate its humor, humor that is only fitfully apparent to a first-time reader. But a caveat: I can never read in class, without laughing too hard to continue, the scene in Beckett's *Murphy* in which Rosie Dew's dachshund eats Murphy's cookies; *Ulysses* doesn't provoke prolonged laughter of that sort (at least not in me). The humor of *Ulysses*, like much of what the book has to offer, is seldom found in the plot; it resides more in the telling than in the tale. *Ulysses* exploits the humorous incongruity of competing frames of reference, the most obvious example being the disparity or unexpected congruence between Homeric Greece and turn-of-the-century Dublin; there is humor as well in its narrative excess, a mischievous promiscuity of reference that far outdoes the notorious peccadillo of Molly Bloom. *Ulysses*, in short, plays around; the form of humor it offers is really play, but this play is structured rather than "free": humor in *Ulysses* illustrates the most productive and pleasurable strategy for reading the novel—play against resistance, the alternative to dutiful obedience.

The kind of humor *Ulysses* teases us to appreciate—for quite serious reasons—is best observed in the most elusive of Joyce's Irish precursors, Oscar Wilde. In *The Importance of Being Earnest*, both Jack and Algernon live double lives: one life, where they are known by the "ordinary" names of Jack and Algernon, is bound by familial duty and obedience; while the other life, where they both play at being "Ernest" (or what Algernon calls "Bunburying"), is one of pleasure, of play against resistance. What's interesting about Wilde's dramatization of pleasure is that it isn't opposed to seriousness; instead, seriousness (or "earnestness") is coupled with play, and the combination is presented as a much-needed counterpart to and relief from duty, as well as a means of self-realization. As Algernon tells Jack, "Well, one must be serious about something, if one wants to have any amusement in life." But to be serious about everything, as Algernon accuses Jack of being, in Hertfordshire at least, is to have "an absolutely trivial nature" (77). The wildly improbable plot shows how, by playing at being Ernest, Jack discovers that he really was Ernest/earnest all the time. The play dramatizes—in however trivial a way—the importance of playing in earnest.

When students enroll in a course on *Ulysses*, they come in as Jacks and Algernons; their ethos is obedience, their attitude dutiful and serious (what Algernon would call "absolutely trivial"), their view of *Ulysses* largely medicinal. Our challenge is to turn them into Ernests—to take them to town if their duties are in the country, to the country if their duties are in town. Only by playing at being earnest can they discover what they are really serious about and who they really are, as opposed to who they are supposed to be. Joyce knew, as Wilde came o know only belatedly and with much anguish, that what is at stake in the opposition between duty and earnest play is serious; the issue is one of authority. The authority behind duty is parental law, which swells to become social and legal rules and conventions; such law demands that we relinquish a portion of our personal responsibility, which in turn will be assumed by the parent (or the church or the state). The tendency of the law is always toward constraint, a lessening of individual agency and freedom; it pits itself against play. As children know more clearly than adults, serious play is the counterweight to law; without it, law becomes oppression. Wilde's tragedy is that despite the playful awareness of the importance of being earnest, which he dramatized in more than one way throughout his career, he didn't play seriously enough, and the law (both the written law and the law of public opinion) crushed him. The "academic" strain in *Ulysses* makes it more strenuous for the reader to follow Joyce's play; it adds weight and earnestness to what might otherwise seem gratuitous transgression, thoughtless triviality, or mere child's play. *Ulysses* gives its readers the opportunity for serious play, framing that play as an activity with political consequences: it keeps alive the capacity for resistance to law (defined as anything passed down—or on—to us from others, as opposed to what we discover by means of serious play), the awareness of individual responsibility and its relation to pleasure, the flexibility of mind needed to refine and even transform received ideas. As a counter to habits of mind that are simply obedient and reflexive, earnest play exercises ways of thinking that are not just creative but antioppressive; it is Joyce's counterpoint to sexism, racism, and prejudice of all kinds, including the prejudice that destroyed Wilde.

The necessity of playing against resistance (as opposed to "free" play) is best illustrated in *Ulysses* by the treatment of Mulligan, who encounters no resistance other than Stephen's and whose play acknowledges no limits. As attractive as Mulligan may initially seem, his brightness palls as the book progresses; Stephen not only apostrophizes him as "a gay betrayer" and a "usurper" (1.405, 744) and accuses him (in a telegram) of being a sentimentalist—*"The sentimentalist is he who would enjoy without incurring the immense debtorship for a thing done"* (9.550–51)—he also decries Mulligan's refusal to take anything seriously, as represented by Mulligan's attitude toward May Dedalus's death: "To me it's all a mockery and beastly" (1.210). Stephen has the seriousness Mulligan lacks, but he lacks playfulness, except when drunk. Stephen can only resist, and Mulligan can only play; only the narrative exhibits the capacity to play against resistance. The kinds of resistance Joyce provides are multiple, but they all counter different aspects of the reader's expectations. Many readers expect some sort of meaningful union between Stephen and Bloom or a reconciliation between Bloom and Molly—the return to a "rock" of certainty from the sea of words that Joyce floods us with throughout. Readers may expect language to be stable and transparent, the correspondences to *Hamlet* and the *Odyssey* to be clear and consistent, the virtue of classical heroism to be vindicated and resuscitated in Bloom. Often a reader expects narrative to work linearly, as an analogue of physical time, upheld and enlivened by "plot"—a record of events. *Ulysses* works with and against such expectations, accommodating them loosely but repeatedly blowing the reader off course even as he or she tries to move in an orderly way from beginning to end.

In the Telemachiad, for example, the most important "event" has happened offstage, before the book begins: the death of Stephen's mother. This event is and is not the focus of the first three chapters; it is the reality Stephen tries hardest to evade. Women and physicality (encompassing both sexuality and mortality) create resistance in Stephen; the play that counters, responds to, and covertly expresses this resistance takes the form of wordplay, a kind of extended, nongratuitous, multilingual pun on the words *mère*, *mer*, and *mare*. In "Telemachus," Mulligan's theme of the moment is the sea ("*Thalatta! Thalatta!*" [1.80]), which he develops by apostrophizing Algernon Swinburne as "Algy" (algae?) and quoting his characterization of the sea as "a great sweet mother" (1.77–78). Although Mulligan doesn't explicitly draw attention to the pun on the French words *mère* and *mer* that implicitly (and humorously) supports Swinburne's connection, the buried verbal logic is accessible to Stephen, fresh from Paris. The implied pun seems to affect Stephen subconsciously rather than consciously; it evokes in his mind a third (English) homonym, *mare*. Compounded with *night*, *mare* recalls Stephen's "nightmare" of his dead mother (*mère*) which comes to his mind's eye as across his "threadbare cuffedge he saw the sea [*mer*] hailed as a great sweet mother by the wellfed voice beside him" (1.106–07). The horse metaphor hidden in *nightmare* is reinforced when, in "Nestor," Stephen talks with Deasy, sitting at a desk with images of racehorses framed around him on the walls (an association with horses repeated in the remoter background by the Homeric image of Nestor, the charioteer), and Stephen famously proclaims, "History . . . is a nightmare from which I am trying to awake." That Stephen can hear the *mare* in nightmare becomes apparent when he asks himself, "What if that nightmare gave you a back kick?" (2.379).

These mares can be traced all across *Ulysses*. What the overlapping patterns of meaning show about Stephen and about the mare-ridden history that haunts him is how history is "his story," a man's story—on both the personal and the cultural levels. It is a story about the human "race," in which the odds would seem to favor a mare whose name signifies authority ("Sceptre"), only she doesn't win the Gold Cup; instead, the race is a "Throwaway." Never mind that there are good reasons to cheer the unexpected victory of a dark horse (Bloom) against long odds on 16 June 1904; one race against a mare is won, while the nightmare of the race goes on. We learn that racism can occasionally be beaten back, but sexism—fear of women— underpins and outlasts many other forms of prejudice. Sexism is one of the nightmares of history and of this story. This insight is dramatized partly through Joyce's treatment of Deasy, who, with his passion for racehorses and his hatred of Jews for an alleged mercantilism he himself displays most prominently ("put but money in thy purse"), aptly becomes one of the novel's most noxious proponents of "racism," a racism that fails to recall how long odds can pay off in the human race. Although Deasy's racism is readily apparent, even to Stephen, Stephen allows Deasy's sexist comments to pass unchallenged: "A woman brought sin into the world" (2.390). Deasy criticizes Helen, a criticism Stephen later echoes when, in the library, he calls Helen "the wooden mare of Troy in whom a score of heroes slept" (9.622–23). That "mare" is at once an image of the destruction of Troy, a horse (emblem of history), a mother, and a whore; the image of history as a nightmare exposes its own deep misogyny and the relation between misogyny and destruction.

On another occasion, in "Proteus," Stephen exposes his misogyny and that of his culture, linking it once again with a fear of the sea (that unknown over which Odysseus was so adept at traveling), with horses, and with the ambivalent desire for and hatred of the virgin-mother-whore figure. A thought of Deasy prompts Stephen to make up a rhyme:

Wild sea money. Dominie Deasy kens them a'.

> *Won't you come to Sandymount,*
> *Madeline the mare?*

Rhythm begins, you see. I hear. Acatalectic tetrameter of iambs
marching. No, agallop: *deline the mare.*   (3.19–24)

Woman is here a mare, a (sexual) mount, and the *mare*, which is the Latin
word for sea (an association triggered by Stephen's repetition of "deline the
mare," which resembles the injunction to "decline the noun *mare*"). From
Stephen's patriarchal perspective, woman as he invokes her here is sexual,
maternal, and poetic, inspiring and representing a "gallop" of metrical feet.
The ambivalence of Stephen's desire-repulsion is apparent partly in his use
of the name Madeline—Madeleine is French for Magdalen. Magdalen of
course recalls Mary Magdalen, the reformed harlot who, in the Gospels, is
the double and the opposite of the Virgin Mary, the Blessed Mother—the
mère whom Stephen so fears. Stephen is inviting the Magdalen to come to
him in Sandymount so that he may "ride" her (as others rode the wooden
mare of Troy), but the web of other associations for the word *mare—mère,*
mer, and *nightmare*—point to the contradiction lodged in his desire. Stephen's fear of women reaches out along the threads of association to encom-
pass a fear of both life and art. His gynophobia (like his hydrophobia, to
which it is related) makes him (in the terminal sense of the phrase) "a most
finished artist."

When, in my classes, we have started unraveling such webs of verbal
association, the exercise has invariably provoked a chorus of protest—skepti-
cism, disbelief, anger at the complicated twists and turns of stylistic and
linguistic construction; anxiety about the level of reading competence required; complaint at the effort required to achieve a modicum of sense;
boredom in the face of excess detail; frustration over Joyce's assumption of
familiarity with Irish geography and history. One difficulty I have always had
is allowing students to experience and express this frustration fully; knowing
the frustration is coming tempts the instructor to try to short-circuit it. But
I have learned, with some chagrin, that short-circuiting student frustration
is a mistake; the frustration is an essential expression of resistance to change
in one's reading habits (and in the views of the world those habits uphold).
When that resistance is discouraged, stifled, or framed as naive, students
lose the motivation to change those habits—instead they simply defer to the
teacher's authority: they shift from playful and attentive readings to obedient
ones. And if students don't learn to read differently as a result of studying
Ulysses, then *Ulysses* will be little more to them than a cultural monument
they once visited and left behind.

The very traits that were essential to the plot of Homer's *Odyssey* are
essential in reading *Ulysses*: disorientation and wandering, perseverance, an

excellent memory, and an irresistible desire to finish the imaginative journey and to vanquish the false scions of habit, usurpers of the mind. Like Joyce, I am convinced that there are no "keys" to this process, which is why I don't usually provide students with an explicit theoretical or ideological program: to announce one's approach to *Ulysses* as a feminist one, for example, is to warn them in advance to censor their criticisms of Molly Bloom. If they suppress their real reactions, they miss the opportunity to see those reactions represented and even interpreted against the background of a changing text. *Ulysses* is a book that, if read honestly and with a sense of humor (of Homer), begins to read the reader. Helping students make that discovery is an incomparable experience: I have seen students, under the influence of *Ulysses*, proclaim implicitly sexist, anti-Semitic, and homophobic attitudes only to realize, as they wander more deeply into the text with Stephen and Bloom, that these attitudes express not contempt but fear and derive from a position not of strength but of weakness. Like Bloom, who learns in "Circe" that he has "been a perfect pig," or like Claudius in *Hamlet* when he sees "The Mouse-trap" and flees the theater in guilt and fear, readers of *Ulysses* are faced with a series of mirrors—some distorted, others not—designed to catch their consciences. Style gives up its claims to innocence and omniscience and displays itself as a panoply of limited, historically and culturally bound perspectives that are often laughable when measured against a larger context. And love, the sacred cow of American and Irish romanticism, changes shape before our very eyes; Bloom's ideal of "love" for Molly unveils itself before him in "Circe," and we see it as a monstrous hybrid of worship and possessiveness, a very Minotaur that Joyce designed the verbal labyrinth of *Ulysses* to contain. Bloom, to his credit, deplores that Minotaur when, in "Circe," he begins to apprehend its hold on him, and we begin to realize, with Molly at the end of "Penelope," that Bloom is also capable of another kind of love, one that Joyce, in *Exiles*, evokes as the active willingness "to wish [another] well."

Ulysses is not only a text to be taught and so handed down intact to another generation; it also represents a pedagogical process that we can impede or facilitate. That process is most surely impeded by pretentiousness, rigidity, irresponsibility, deliberate obfuscation, or elitism on our part, but it is also a process that can be facilitated with relative ease. First, we can avoid censoring or criticizing honest reactions to any aspect of the book, although it is legitimate to question the basis of these reactions. Second, we can make *Ulysses* easier to chew and digest by provisionally accenting the divisions between chapters, hours, styles, locations, and characters. In the aggregate, *Ulysses* is overwhelming, but as I was once taught, it is like an earthworm: you can regenerate the whole from any one of its segments. Third, we can devise ways of helping the student remember the apparently random details of the first part of the book before they seem to have any order or significance (this is essential since the second half of *Ulysses* is partly a playful revision, parody of, and supplement to the conventions and techniques of the first half, an effect that is lost when we don't remember what has gone before). Required journal entries of each episode work reasonably well, although they are time-consuming for the instructor. I prefer to distribute information and question sheets on each episode. (An example of such a sheet, on "Proteus," appears in the appendix of this article.) These sheets allow me to underline imaginatively certain aspects of the book without preempting a more detailed investigation, and they free me to follow the collective interests that emerge in class discussion. Finally, we can actively demonstrate the partiality of initial responses to the book by supplying counterevidence: when a student celebrates Bloom's religious tolerance, we can ask why he starts to tell the story of Reuben J. Dodd in "Hades"; when someone calls Molly a "slut," we can ask what might have motivated her infidelity, find out which characters' perspectives we are echoing, question the philosophical premises of fidelity and the dependence of these premises on a unified model of the self, investigate the changing views of Penelope's fidelity to Odysseus in the *Odyssey*, or ask why Joyce seems to have superimposed Molly on both Penelope and Queen Gertrude of *Hamlet*. Since none of these things can be done in a cursory introduction, I never allot less than five weeks to the book, and I think it works best as the centerpiece of an entire semester. My premise is that *Ulysses* is not particularly valuable as a textual acquaintance; the virtue of the book is that of a friend, which we can come back to and measure ourselves against at different times of our lives, and in that respect it works better than any other book I know. To adapt what Joseph Frank once said about modernism, *Ulysses* is meant not to be read, only reread (19), and all my strategies of teaching are designed to promote the illusion that the first reading is a rereading, collectively performed.

I have also found it helpful to emphasize, by treating each episode separately within the context of a larger whole, that what keeps our attention in *Ulysses* is not plot or even character but the shifting contexts that significantly redefine each hour of the fictional day the characters traverse. The Homeric parallels are frequently useful for identifying a prominent "figure in the carpet" of a given episode—a paradigm that gives shape and coherence to what otherwise might seem a mass of gratuitous details—provided the parallels are viewed not as keys to the text but as intertexts illustrating a changing array of textual patterns. In *Ulysses* these patterns do everything from furnish local color and incidental humor to act as a theoretical underpinning for the thought and meaning of an entire chapter. Menelaus's encounter with Proteus serves as a complex metaphor for how to read the "signatures" of Joyce's book, as well as for how to obtain guidance from a "myriadminded" man (9.768–69) such as Bloom; and Odysseus's two passes through Scylla and Charybdis prescribe a way of successfully navigating binaries.

Emphasizing the importance of changing frames of reference accomplishes several things. It initially undermines students' subconscious expectations that the book is a vast puzzle in which each clue can be identified and put into place once and for all, producing a single interlocking design that can be recorded and filed away. Students begin to read dynamically, with many strands of narrative in their minds at the same time, some strands producing meaning now (by interacting to form patterns), some simply dangling until they make sense in relation to another part of the book or until the passages are reread. Most of us greet puns with a groan, but an ear attuned to puns fosters an awareness of the way that different contexts and usages can change and multiply the meaning of any individual element. Having primed students to look for a range of meanings instead of one, the instructor can introduce the possibility of humor, which always involves an unexpected conjunction of different perspectives or meanings (as in a pun). In addition, the multiplicity of possible connections makes our customary practice of reading in solitude less gratifying and encourages a redefinition of reading as a communal and even a social interchange. In a prefatory note to Roland Barthes's S/Z, Richard Howard urges our indictment of masturbatory reading, which Valery Larbaud called the one unpunished vice; an attention to the plurality of signification in *Ulysses* helps to bring reading out of the closet and into the classroom (as *Finnegans Wake* does more dramatically but less practically).

Alerting readers of Joyce to the several levels of significance in the narrative is more than a game designed to be fun (although it is also that): it is an ethical principle aimed at equalizing the value of competing points of view. Having recognized that we are culturally programmed to favor one perspective over its opposite, to choose between halves of a human whole, Joyce underscores the relation between such habits of mind and prejudice of all kinds. If, as Joyce suggests, we are rewarded not for absolute and self-confirming value judgments but for provisional ones based on repeated redefinitions of the changing relation between fact and circumstance, then racism and sexism cannot flourish; like his countryman Wilde, Joyce shows that there is an importance to *playing* the part of Ernest, and it requires a much more precise and flexible mind.

Appendix: Information and Question Sheet for Episode 3, "Proteus"

From Joyce's "schema" (first printed in Stuart Gilbert's *James Joyce's* Ulysses):

> Scene: The Strand. Hour: 11 a.m. Art: Philology. Colour: Green.
> Symbol: Tide. Technic: Monologue (male).
> Correspondences: *Proteus*—primal matter; *Menelaus*—Kevin Egan; *Megapenthus*—Cocklepicker. ["Megapenthus was born before the walls of Troy, the son of Menelaus by a slave girl. Megapenthus' wedding feast is being celebrated in Menelaus' mansion when Telemachus arrives there" (Gifford 32).]

From headnote in Gifford's *Notes for Joyce*:

In Book IV of *The Odyssey*, while Telemachus is at the court of Menelaus, Menelaus recounts the story of his journey home from Troy. Menelaus was becalmed in Egypt by the gods for an infraction of the rules of sacrifice. He does not know which of the gods has him "pinned down," and he does not know how to continue his voyage home. To achieve a prophecy he wrestles on the beach with Proteus, the Ancient of the Sea. Proteus has the power to "take the forms of all the beasts, and water, and blinding fire"; but, if Menelaus succeeds in holding him throughout the successive changes, Proteus will answer Menelaus' questions. Menelaus does succeed. Proteus tells him how to break the spell that binds him to Egypt and also tells him of the deaths of Agamemnon and Ajax and of the whereabouts of Odysseus, marooned on Calypso's island. (32)

Comments Joyce made about "Proteus" to Frank Budgen, as recorded in *James Joyce and the Making of* Ulysses:

"You catch the drift of the thing?" said Joyce. "It's the struggle with Proteus. Change is the theme. Everything changes—sea, sky, man, animals. The words change, too." (48)

"I haven't let this young man off very lightly, have I? Many writers have written about themselves. I wonder if any one of them has been as candid as I have?" [Joyce's comment after reading the part in which Stephen remembers receiving the telegram, "Nother dying come home father" (3.199).] (51)

"Did you see the point of that bit about the dog?" said Joyce. "He is the mummer among beasts—the Protean animal. . . . [He] mimics the other animals while Stephen is watching him. Listen." (53)

"Yes," said Joyce. "That's all in the Protean character of the thing. Everything changes: land, water, dog, time of day. Parts of speech change, too. Adverb becomes verb." (54)

Questions

1. Throughout the first twenty-eight lines, Stephen seems to be experimenting with the nature of the visible world. What is he trying to discover about his perception of visible objects? How does he go about it, and on whose authority? What does he conclude about the visible world and his perception of it, and what happens to it when he ceases to perceive it? How, then, would you characterize Stephen's philosophical position?
2. What relation is Joyce setting up between the world of appearances (the "ineluctable modality of the visible" [3.1]) and language? In describing his contemplation of visible reality, what does Stephen mean by "*Signatures* of all things I am

here to *read"* (3.2; emphasis added)? What exactly is Stephen (like Menelaus?) attempting to "grasp"?

3. Why would Joyce set this particular chapter on the seashore? What kinds of things does the sea represent to Stephen here and in previous episodes, and how can we tell?

4. Are the two women Stephen sees coming down the shore (3.29–40) really midwives? If not, why does Stephen think of them that way, "coming down to our mighty mother" (3.31–32)? What might they be thinking to deliver?

5. If Stephen thinks of the sea as a great mother (giving birth to what?), why does he also dwell on her destructive power: the "seawrack" (3.3) and the drowned man (3.322–23, 3.470–81)? What is the relation between birth and death as he conceives of it, and how do the rhymes that he experiments with (3.401–02) help to underscore this relation?

6. Where is Stephen supposed to be at half past twelve?

7. If Stephen thinks about motherhood through thinking about the sea, what (and how) does he think about fathers? What different father-and-son combinations emerge in the course of his thoughts, and how are they characterized?

8. Does Stephen go to his aunt Sara's? What then is happening in 3.70: "I pull the wheezy bell of their shuttered cottage: and wait"?

9. What memories does Stephen have of Paris? Why does he linger over his memories of Kevin Egan? What is a "wild goose"? What is the significance of Stephen's brief memory of Patrice? Finally, what does the memory of Kevin Egan suggest about Stephen's attitude toward Irish nationalism?

10. How does Stephen envision the night to come in the tower, with Mulligan and Haines? What metaphor does he use to represent the two of them, and what suggested it?

11. What is the significance (if any) of the two dogs Stephen sees in lines 286–364?

12. What did Stephen dream last night after Haines woke him?

13. What does Stephen stop to write on a torn-off corner of Deasy's letter?

14. What are Stephen's thoughts about darkness, inspired by his shadow (3.408–23), and how might they be significant?

15. What is Stephen doing in 3.453–60, and how can you tell?

Helping Students Read *Ulysses*

Austin Briggs

When I began teaching *Ulysses*, even in classes of only a dozen students, I often found myself doing all the talking, reduced to lecturing at undergraduates cowed into silence by a work that seemed to them every bit as daunting as its reputation. My students were struck doubly dumb: they could not speak because they felt too ignorant and stupid to say anything at all about a huge novel mined with enough difficulties, as Joyce boasted, "to keep the professors busy for centuries."

To the instructor who wishes to help students read and discuss *Ulysses* more confidently, I present five teaching strategies I have developed over many years. Each provides a way for anxious students to discover that they have much worth saying about a work notoriously difficult in repute and in fact. Their pride in the accomplishment soon motivates them to engage actively the complexities of language, method, and theme that *Ulysses* offers in such abundance; and the strategies are easily adapted to a variety of critical orientations.

Strategy 1: Locate the Experts in the Class

At the start of the course, ask your students to write down some information about themselves based on such questions as the following:

> Do you know any foreign languages? Do you have any particular knowledge of music or painting? modern history? psychology? feminism? colonialism? What is your concentration? Have you read the *Odyssey*? Dante? *Hamlet*? Yeats?

By using the information thus gleaned to call on the appropriate "experts" who can answer questions about Joyce's text, you can persuade students that they need not lean on you or on source materials you recommend. You may be able to make one student responsible for the *Odyssey* and another for *Hamlet*, and you may find an astronomer-astrologer to explain the nova in "Ithaca."

Once you locate your experts, you may be surprised by how much the class knows collectively. At various times in my course: a student with an interest in art history has related collage to stream of consciousness; another who knew from a religion course that the *ba* is the soul in Egyptian mythology enlightened us about the *ba/bat* that flies over Bloom at the close of "Nausicaa"; a concentrator in women's studies shared what she had learned about turn-of-the-century women's clothing—including "frillies"—from Lois Banner's *American Beauty*; and an opera fanatic explained such matters as the *voglio* from *Don Giovanni* that vexes Bloom and also spoke wonderfully of ways in which Wagner and Joyce manipulate myth for modern purposes.

Most of the information from the student experts is available to the class from you or from supplementary reading, but much is gained when it is a student who explains Siegfried's "Nothung" or translates *basta, übermensch,* and *esprit de corps.* Students realize that *Ulysses* is not sealed off from them, that together they can work through a surprising amount of arcane reference.

Be sure to ask students for expertise that they do not consider academic. Are any of them sailors or astrologers or bird-watchers? Are any of them good at crossword puzzles? What junk reading do they do? And include personal questions. "Were you educated in Catholic schools?" "Have you been bar mitzvahed?" "Do you identify your family as Irish American?"

Thanks to such questions, we once learned a good deal about the racetrack and stud jargon in *Ulysses* from a woman who had spent her girlhood mucking out stables. Another student had done a 4H project on foot-and-mouth disease. When you get to "Nausicaa," count on help from closet readers of Harlequin Romances and maybe even *Teen World.*

By encouraging students to call on personal experience, you can help them to discover the realistic world that lies beneath Joyce's shifting styles. If any of your students has been to Dublin, obviously, first-person testimony will help you set the stage for *Ulysses,* but anyone in the class who has ever passed time in a bar in the afternoon will know something about the Ormond Bar at 4:00 p.m., 16 June 1904.

One spring, when we reached "Sirens," we found ourselves learning from a student who had worked part-time for a few months as a barmaid in a London pub. Although no gent had ever asked her to "*sonnezlacloche*" with her garter, she understood the games played in the Ormond far better than I ever will, and she articulated a persuasive feminist reading of the siren myth in *Ulysses.*

Whether or not Joyce was right in believing that life offers us only a small number of possible roles, I never lack at least one student whose Jewishness, like Bloom's, is both problematic and crucial and another student who knows a great deal about the torments of Stephen's apostasy from Catholicism (one described a pandybat "firsthand"). When we come to "Oxen of the Sun," we usually hear from an expert who knows medical students as coarse as those gathered in the commons of the Holles Street Maternity Hospital, and many campuses invariably offer a Buck Mulligan or two—well-heeled, extroverted undergraduates who are cynical, foul-mouthed, and wonderfully funny.

The most confident student is likely to lose heart at the appearance of "ineluctable modality." To get into "Proteus," ask the students to imagine Stephen walking alone, stranded on a litter-strewn beach; if they can summon up the image, they usually begin to see that the dense language of "Proteus" may reflect at least in part the confusion of a lost and unhappy young man. Surprisingly often, life supplies a visual aid, a Stephen to contemplate from our classroom windows. Garbed in an outsize overcoat and a Latin Quarter hat (both from the Salvation Army), he obligingly drifts by, a lean and lonely figure suggesting unrealized talent and deep suffering—and looking in need of a bath. (Hybrids appear, of course; at twenty-two, I was a stately, plump Stephen.)

Strategy 2: Ask Students to Read Aloud

Only recently did I realize that it never even occurs to most students simply to appreciate the richness, variety, and beauty of Joyce's language. To address the problem, I now ask students to read aloud from *Ulysses* in class. Early in our discussion of each episode, I call on a student who has been assigned to prepare a selection of fifteen to twenty lines from the episode. Passages are to be chosen because they seem "wonderful"—a quality I do not attempt to define.

The results have run far beyond my expectations. Students scour their assigned episodes, and their readings usually focus on language that is indeed "wonderful"—on the language of Bloom's searing vision of the Dead Sea in "Calypso," or on the parody of Carlyle in "Oxen of the Sun," or on "the heaventree of stars hung with humid nightblue fruit" in "Ithaca."

Although I ask students to look up unfamiliar words and check the notes in Blamires and in Gifford and Seidman, they are under no obligation to explicate the passages they read aloud, let alone to defend their choices. Except for answering questions on vocabulary, they are free to "take the fifth" as soon as they finish reading, but almost never do they forgo the opportunity to discuss their passages. I read aloud a good deal myself, but students need to hear Joyce in their own accents. I cannot refrain, incidentally, from remarking on what may be a comment on the teaching of literature in general, as it surely is on my teaching: many students seem surprised at the invitation to locate language they enjoy "merely" for such qualities as musical beauty, rhetorical power, comic ingenuity, or linguistic agility.

Strategy 3: Provide Questions for Discussion

Like many teachers, I give students episode-by-episode plot summaries that incorporate Joyce's schema. I also include three or four questions for each episode. Whether we focus on the questions or not—we are under no constraint to cover them all—they help students think about *Ulysses*; and often the handout generates student questions by suggesting the sort of question that seems worth asking, at least to the instructor. In addition, the questions on the handout furnish topics for short-essay assignments, and the short essays, in turn, may provide a basis for class discussion.

Some questions are narrowly defined: two for "Nestor" ask, "How do Pyrrhic victories and 'Lycidas' relate to the concerns of the episode?" and "What do you think Stephen's schoolroom riddle means?" Some are broad: "How do the parallels (list some) between the first three episodes and the second three suggest similarities and differences between Stephen and Bloom?" and, when we come to "Cyclops," "What has the method of parody to do with the matter of *Ulysses*?" Most are as straightforward as possible, like "What is the effect of the headlines in 'Aeolus'?"

At times, however, ingenuity is helpful. Asking the class to relate "Wandering Rocks" to cinema, I propose that the episode is roughly analogous to mindlessly edited film taken by a camera that repeatedly and arbitrarily changes location and focus. We discuss the contrasting sense of order that editing conveys in a recruitment film made for our college's office of admissions. One class dreamed up a commencement sequence that produced a neat closure to an imaginary admissions film: as the choir swells to the strains of the college anthem, the honorary-degree candidates and trustees precede the faculty, who, marching by rank, lead the graduating seniors. We all agreed that a stray shot of a local Blazes Boylan must be left on the cutting-room floor; he must not appear ogling the ladies when he should be saluting the leaders of the viceregal procession metempsychosized into our board of trustees. This exercise may help students see how "Wandering Rocks" undercuts claims for the "scientific naturalism" that some think realized in the camera's impersonal mechanism. (Even as far into *Ulysses* as "Wandering Rocks," incidentally, be prepared to find a student or two maintaining that a wholly "objective" prose is possible.)

If you have begun the course with *Portrait*, you can ask students to discuss how the shift in the narrative point of view from *Portrait* to "Telemachus" reflects the obvious change in what Stephen appears to be. Later, students can compare the seashore appearances of Stephen and the bird girl in *Portrait*, Stephen in "Proteus," and Bloom and Gerty in "Nausicaa."

My final example of a discussion question is for "Ithaca": "What do you make of the giant period at the end of the episode?" The stop starts a lively discussion that can pull many things together, whether the period is seen as epic-scale punctuation; mock-heroic punctuation (how big is this giant, after all?); QED; flyspeck; printer's error; hole in the page; gate to the realm of sleep; Alice's rabbit hole; end to the world of male consciousness; menstrual period (end and beginning); "X marks the spot," self-reflexive answer to Joyce's "Where?"; or as all these things and others. The class can also relish the Joycean reductio ad absurdum of devoting considerable time to a single speck of punctuation in a fiendishly complex novel of hundreds of pages. Moreover, you neatly set up the next question, on the lack of stops in "Penelope," the chapter that waits on the overleaf, just beyond the period.

Strategy 4: Ask Students to Commit Themselves on Paper

Though barely started on *Ulysses*, undergraduates soon learn to answer with surety at least one question in *Finnegans Wake*: "You is feeling like you was lost in the bush?" The nearly invisible plot and the increasingly changeable style of *Ulysses* frustrate the students' efforts to get their bearings. How can they do anything but ask questions about so complex a work when they have not even finished it? Yet as they read they must find the courage to make assertions about *Ulysses*, even if further reading undermines many of those assertions. The alternative—to suspend judgment until the last page—is disastrous.

To help students overcome their timidity, I ask them to write three or four short essays of two to three pages each. By assigning the papers on a staggered basis, with five students at most writing on any one episode, I can read the papers almost immediately and use them as seems useful for class discussion. Sometimes I Xerox a particularly good paper for the class to comment on. More often, I ask the author to read aloud a passage I have marked because it opens up a fruitful line of inquiry. Even a student who gets back a C may find that he or she has been able to say *something* about *Ulysses* that is not foolish and that interests the rest of the class, including the teacher.

Except for the requirement that each paper focus on the assigned episode, topics are free, but most students write on one of my discussion questions. Depending on your stamina and the class size, you might assign fewer than four short essays, but I would urge asking each student to write at least two. If the first is bad, the flop will not seem a total disaster, and if the first is good, it may prove the basis for a second short essay and even for the eventual long essay. Much may be gained, moreover, by assigning short essays on each of the first five or six episodes. Students will be emboldened if they see that even early on in *Ulysses* they can commit themselves to paper, however impossible it may be to foresee what maelstroms and reefs lie ahead on the voyage to Molly's final "yes."

Strategy 5: Assign a Long Essay on One Episode

Students may find that the most important part of their introduction to *Ulysses* is writing a final essay after they finish the novel. I assign ten to fifteen pages and often get closer to twenty. Like many teachers, I ask that the final paper focus on a single episode. This assures the class of at least some experience not only rereading *Ulysses* but reading it backward as well as forward. You can also use the essay assignment to suggest background reading and criticism beyond what daily class assignments have allowed. Along with the proviso that students who have their own ideas for essays seek my assistance to work up their own topics, here, in part, are my directions for the culminating essay:

> Focusing primarily, but not exclusively, on the episode you select, discuss it in such a way that you show your reader how to approach

Ulysses, how the episode you treat relates to basic concerns and techniques of the novel as a whole. Obviously, you will have to address matters of style as well as content (a good essay does not break into two parts—one on style, one on content). And of course you will wish to show how a reader can cut into *Ulysses* at any point and discover themes that extend throughout the entire work.

Most of this is obvious, as I think it should be. What may not be obvious is the rationale for the requirement that the final essay show how an episode "relates to the concerns and techniques of the novel as a whole." The stricture encourages the student to pull together his or her reading of *Ulysses*. Without the requirement, I have found, many papers attempt little more than to explicate Joyce's text by footnoting, usually parroting outside sources.

I also ask students to pose this question to themselves as they write: "Will your reader be learning how to read *Ulysses* as a whole from your essay on a single episode?" If you find that the results justify an affirmative reply, you may rejoice; your devices and stratagems have helped the students voyage successfully through *Ulysses*.

These strategies accommodate well to a variety of critical approaches. When students identify themselves as experts, their interests can turn discussion to gender or colonialism, for example, or to consideration of *Ulysses* in relation to canonical literature, popular literature, or both. And by drawing on the "real life" experience of the students, you can raise questions about the ways in which *Ulysses* is, and is not, a realistic or naturalistic novel.

Asking students to read aloud passages of their choice not only leads to close reading but also may raise such issues as self-reflexivity and reader response. Naturally, your own critical orientation emerges in the questions you present for discussion and short papers and in any secondary reading you assign.

My concern is to promote an active participation by the undergraduate confronting Joyce's dense and intimidating work for the first time. That the strategies encourage an eclectic approach reflects my personal preference, but I believe that such an approach is especially suitable for *Ulysses*; one of my primary assumptions is that a wide variety of readers with different and even conflicting critical orientations can find *Ulysses* a singularly rewarding experience.

A Collective Exploration of *Ulysses*

James J. Murphy

Richard Ellmann comments that "we are still learning to be Joyce's contemporaries, to understand our interpreter" (*James Joyce* 3). To remember that we are still learning is good advice for teaching anything, but it is especially true for *Ulysses*. When Mr. Deasy tells Stephen, "You were not born to be a teacher," Stephen responds, "A learner rather" (2.402–03). When I teach *Ulysses* I try to keep Stephen's comment in mind by encouraging the class to become a collective of teacher-learners.

My experience has been with seminars of fifteen to eighteen undergraduates. English majors tend to dominate, but I am able to reserve one third of the seats for students from other disciplines. I find this diversity of perspectives helpful in promoting a collective reading spirit. The students have usually had minimal exposure to Joyce—they may have read a few anthologized stories or *Portrait*, but rarely have any read *Ulysses*. They are eager to read the novel, but they feel intimidated at the prospect. *Ulysses* is the kind of text that lurks on their intellectual horizons, a threatening mystery that waits to be confronted.

In an average fifteen-week semester, we cover *Dubliners* and *Portrait* during the first four to five weeks and do an extended study of *Ulysses* during the last ten weeks. By the time we begin *Ulysses* I hope to have formed a group whose parts are greater than the whole, in which each student is confident about a certain area and is willing to teach the rest of us. As the semester moves along, we share one another's expertise and thus come closer to collectively grasping the whole of *Ulysses*.

This approach is based on the premise that, as Ellmann puts it, "we" are still learning, the plurality of his pronoun reminding us of the shared nature of the process. Joyce asks a great deal of his audience, more than the solitary reader alone can offer. After over twenty-five years of effort, my own understanding remains incomplete and tentative. Imagine, then, the position of the average undergraduate, and consider that Joyce is seeking the "ideal reader suffering from an ideal insomnia" (*Wake* 120.14), one who should have knowledge of the Bible, Homer's *Odyssey*, Shakespeare, the Maynooth catechism, kidney recipes, Aristotle, classical mythology, astronomy, the Talmud, musical theory, the influence of gaslight or the light of arc and glow lamps on the growth of adjoining paraheliotropic trees . . . Canonize the reader who can handle it all, and let the rest of us join forces to explore Joyce's world. As a group we can come to know *Ulysses* more deeply than as individual readers.

In Stephen Dedalus's own classroom, in "Nestor," the process of collective learning is evident when Armstrong cannot answer a question on "the end of Pyrrhus" but Comyn is ready and eager to reply in his place: "I know, sir. Ask me, sir" (2.20). Comyn hears "Pyrrhus," Armstrong hears "piers." One responds to meaning, the other to sound, the duality of their responses a good indicator of Joyce's demands. Only teacher-learner Stephen knows that each is right. Joyce's brief picture of Stephen's classroom demonstrates in many ways what *Ulysses* requires of our own student readers. Stephen, like Joyce, spreads before the students a range of demands, so broad that no one student seems capable of mastering them all. In the space of at most a few minutes Stephen's class wanders through the identification of historical dates and figures, a quotation from the ancient past, the definition of a word (*pier*), a recitation from "Lycidas," a riddle—and the whole teaching experience ends for Stephen with a lesson in mathematics for the confused young Sargent. It's no wonder Stephen's students are grateful to be released onto the hockey field, where there is only one ball to be struck. In the classroom Stephen has had a half-dozen balls bouncing around the room, seemingly all at once, and that analogy only covers the ideas he has articulated to the class. To his students, it must appear that their teacher wants them to know almost everything, including history, literature, and mathematics, and to know it all in almost simultaneous fashion—exactly what Joyce asks of the readers of *Ulysses*.

This scene from the novel can be read as representation of the *Ulysses* classroom. In the midst of such chaos, an "incorrect" answer—Armstrong's misguided comments on "pier" rather than "Pyrrhus"—leads to Stephen's private epiphany, his recognition that for him Kingstown Pier was, indeed, "a disappointed bridge." In synthesizing various student responses, Stephen recognizes his departure from Ireland two years earlier by way of Kingstown Pier for what it really was—a Pyrrhic victory. This insight is directly traceable to the multiple voices raised in his little classroom. The trick is to unlock a similar chorus of voices in our classrooms.

In my first experiences teaching *Ulysses*, I found students reluctant to speak up and offer ideas. Even though the class was supposed to be a seminar, students held back in the face of a difficult text. Those who had responded freely in discussions of *Dubliners* and *Portrait* seemed less sure of themselves as we began to move through *Ulysses*. The overall reticence was, however, interrupted by important exceptions that helped lead me to my own epiphany and have since helped reshape my teaching. I recall one particularly quiet student who came alive as we addressed "Sirens." A gold mine of technical information on fugues and musical theory, he clearly enjoyed sharing his knowledge with us. Suddenly he felt a measure of control over the text. As it turned out, he was an accomplished pianist with extensive musical training. Having led us through the technical aspects of "Sirens," he spoke with greater confidence for the rest of the term on matters unconnected to music. I realized that, had I earlier tapped into his area of expertise and thus given him confidence, I would sooner have added an important voice to the chorus.

I have since tried to discover such areas wherever they may exist in a given class. Students know all sorts of things that can help them enter Joyce's text with assurance, and an average class contains relative experts or at least hobbyists in many pertinent fields. Students have also been in all manner of other classes. One student contributes to the discussion of constellations in "Ithaca" from having taken an astronomy class, and another has done research on *Hamlet*; someone was raised a Catholic, albeit of the modern variety, while another is Jewish; someone else knows Irish folk songs, or an opera fan wanders in. It's hard to predict what students know, but their knowledge is always wide in range and often surprising in depth. If asked "Has anyone studied *Hamlet*?" or "Does anyone play an instrument?" students gladly reveal their interests.

Each class differs, but, in addition to the connection between "Sirens" and music, the following pairings of chapters with students' areas of interest have worked well for me: "Proteus"—philosophy, Aristotle; "Aeolus"—journalism, speech; "Scylla and Charybdis"—Shakespeare, especially *Hamlet*; "Cyclops"—the epic, Irish history, patriotism; "Nausicaa" or "Penelope"—women's studies, feminism; "Oxen of the Sun"—history of the language; "Circe"—psychology, dreams.

I draw on any such areas of interest and expertise to develop confidence and authority in each student. The ideal result is a class less reticent, a place of multiple voices where each is dependent on the others for insight and all realize that collectively we can come closer to grasping Joyce's brilliance than we could individually. To encourage this spirit, I have found two assignments to be especially helpful: chapter reports and reports on scholarly books. Chapter reports make each student an "authority" on one of the eighteen chapters, while book reports ask the student to acquire some control of a single work of Joycean scholarship.

Although we spend the first few weeks on *Dubliners* and *Portrait*, I devote the first class to preparing for *Ulysses*, the essence of the course. I probe to discover those special areas of expertise that may be there—to find the musician before we get to "Sirens" two months later, to see who is studying Shakespeare. I want to gain a head start on *Ulysses* several classes before any formal study of it begins. As much as possible, I try to direct each student to a chapter that reaches out to his or her interests. After that, each student is assigned a chapter, and I usually pair students to work on some of the more difficult later chapters, especially "Oxen of the Sun" and "Circe." The assignment is to create a handout of notes, three-to-four pages long, on important aspects of the chapter. This handout is then distributed to the class before our discussion of the chapter.

At the minimum, each report should provide a brief plot outline, an explanation of the Homeric parallels, clarification of the chapter's technique, and commentary on the major motifs. As sources for students to consult in preparing these reports I place a number of standard texts on reserve in the library. Each instructor has individual preferences, but my students have found these texts especially helpful for chapter-centered reports: Robert Adams, *Surface and Symbol*; Harry Blamires, *The New Bloomsday Book*;

Richard Ellmann, Ulysses *on the Liffey*; Don Gifford, *Notes for Joyce*; Stuart Gilbert, *James Joyce's* Ulysses; Clive Hart, *James Joyce's* Ulysses; Richard Kain, *Fabulous Voyager*; Weldon Thornton, *Allusions in* Ulysses. In addition, there are several studies directed solely to single chapters: James Van Dyck Card, *An Anatomy of "Penelope"*; Robert Janusko, *Sources and Structures of Joyce's "Oxen"*; Richard Madtes, *Ithaca*.

Where possible, I also direct students to chapter-focused articles in the *James Joyce Quarterly*, the most valuable single research source for any student of Joyce and an especially useful reference for this kind of assignment. Students appreciate this kind of focused attention when they are trying to become deeply involved in a single chapter. For "Nausicaa," I suggest Margot Norris, "Modernism, Myth, and Desire in 'Nausicaa'" and John M. Warner, "Myth and History in Joyce's 'Nausicaa' Episode"; for "Eumaeus," John Hannay, "Coincidence and Fables of Identity in 'Eumaeus'" and Brook Thomas, "The Counterfeit Style of 'Eumaeus.'"

I advise students to take notes from their sources, as they would for a research paper, and I encourage them to quote from and to paraphrase freely the sources they find most helpful. The resulting handout, usually a loose compilation of ideas sewn together under a few general headings, becomes the basis for the group's exploration of the chapter. The student responsible is the guide for that exploration. For that one aspect of the text, at least, he or she has done more research than anyone else and usually feels an appropriate sense of "authority" and a corresponding eagerness to share insights with the group. Through these chapter reports I hope to build a class of mutually dependent authorities.

This strategy introduces each student to a broad range of Joyce scholarship but attempts to make it manageable by asking the student to relate the scholarship to only one segment of the text. Students often tell me that their first peek at the card catalog holdings on Joyce is intimidating. That doesn't surprise me; I found it intimidating twenty-five years ago, and that was before everything became postmodern, hermeneutic, or metawhatever and Joyceana multiplied. A student in a Joyce class today quickly realizes that Joyce's primary texts are relatively few but that the library shelves are stacked with supplementary texts. If *Ulysses* itself is daunting to an undergraduate, even more overwhelming are the number of texts explicating Joyce. I have found that students are initially troubled to discover what awaits them; unfortunately, the sheer bulk of Joycean scholarship can inhibit rather than encourage the beginning reader. Most of my students are relative novices to this world of literary scholarship, and I want to use Joyce to familiarize them with the language of scholarly inquiry and thus to encourage them to feel more comfortable joining in the various debates. Joyce is an ideal medium for this immersion, since the full scope and fury of contemporary theory have been addressed to Joyce as to no other modern writer. By confronting the concepts and vocabulary of literary scholarship, students enlarge their possible approaches to any text. A student who has dealt with five or six supplementary texts to explicate a single chapter of *Ulysses* has learned that scholarship itself is a world of voices to be accepted or rejected—one of the most valuable insights we can leave with our students.

A similar purpose underlies the report on a scholarly text. Where the chapter report uses a number of sources directed at just one portion of *Ulysses*, this assignment asks for a complete involvement in one scholarly source, which the student summarizes for the class. I choose texts that offer a wide range of perspectives, so that the collation of all the reports gives the group a good sense of the variety of studies available. A good starting list might include Marilyn French, *The Book as World*; Samuel Goldberg, *The Classical Temper*; Elliot Gose, *The Transformation Process in Joyce's* Ulysses; Karen Lawrence, *The Odyssey of Style in* Ulysses; William Schutte, *Joyce and Shakespeare*; and Bonnie Kime Scott, *Joyce and Feminism*. Such texts introduce students to the ways in which a controlling thesis can be applied not only to *Ulysses* but to all Joyce's works. If all goes according to plan, just as the class has an authority for each chapter, it also has authorities on various scholarly approaches to Joyce.

By assigning both reports at the first meeting, I leave the students four to five weeks to prepare notes before we deal with *Ulysses* in class. This assignment initially unsettles students, because they must become deeply involved with *Ulysses* while still exploring *Dubliners* and *Portrait*. A student researching "Ithaca" is completely removed from a chronological reading sequence. But the value of this approach becomes clear as students recognize their mutual dependence and take special pleasure in their growing expertise and how it increases their understanding of Joyce's world. This early engagement with *Ulysses* and associated scholarship also helps students read the earlier texts. The student researching "Cyclops" can take satisfaction in commenting that Bob Doran of "The Boarding House" reappears in *Ulysses*. That student teaches the class a great deal by citing Doran's condition as "snoring drunk blind to the world" (12.251), a far cry from the younger, conscience-stricken Doran of the short story. Polly Mooney has become "his little concubine of a wife" (12.811–12), and Mrs. Mooney is transformed into "the old prostitute of a mother" (12.814). Recognizing that many of Joyce's Dubliners reappear promotes a sense of how Joyce's works are interconnected, one of the great pleasures in reading Joyce.

Of even greater value to the class are the insights brought to bear on *Portrait* by students who draw important connections between that novel and their research on *Ulysses*. The student doing "Aeolus" may have an epiphany when reading in *Portrait* that Father Dolan unjustly calls Stephen a "lazy little schemer" (50). The student then helps the group learn something about the associative and cumulative nature of memory by commenting that in "Aeolus," Stephen recalls the insult years after it was first delivered (7.618).

The class reading of *Ulysses* itself reaps similar benefits from each student's having mastered a chapter before we tackle the whole. Students research the text in different places, so that by the time the class begins chapter 1, a chorus of experts is ready to speak and eager to watch their individual areas of expertise merge into a collectively coherent reading. In the discussion of "Telemachus," the "Circe" student comments that when Stephen confronts the ghost of his mother (15.4157–4258), Joyce repeats much of the language from Stephen's first thoughts of her (1.100–10). The "Oxen of the Sun" student points out that Bannon shows up there (14.653), and the "Calypso" student shows that Bannon's photo girl is Milly Bloom (4.407). Because each student's preliminary research has prepared us as a group to be more complete interpreters of Joyce, pieces that existed out of context now fit together in the same fashion as when the conductor in "Sirens" says "Begin" (11.63). Students thus participate in a collaborative learning process that makes *Ulysses* more accessible to them.

As instructors, we should recall the limitations we had when we were beginning readers of *Ulysses*. Let us remember Stephen in "Nestor," looking at the befuddled young Cyril Sargent and reflecting, "Like him was I . . ." (2.168). My teaching strategies today are based on memories of myself, "a good student" who could write a nice paper on paralysis in *Dubliners* or bird images in *Portrait* but who was hungry for help in dealing with Joyce's next world. After many efforts I don't yet have a complete grasp of it, but I know that, for whatever control I do have, I owe a great deal to other readers. I imagine that ideally I might have done it all on my own—but certainly not in a semester. At the heart of my teaching strategy is the desire for the students to learn from one another and thus to experience Joyce more fully than they might have done as solitary readers.

CONTRIBUTORS AND
SURVEY PARTICIPANTS

Listed below are the contributors to this volume and the teachers of *Ulysses* who agreed to participate in the survey of teaching practices. We are grateful to them for their time and invaluable assistance in helping us to organize this project.

Derek Attridge, *Rutgers University, New Brunswick*
Rosemarie Battaglia, *Michigan State University*
Michael Begnall, *Penn State University, University Park*
Morris Beja, *Ohio State University, Columbus*
John Boggs, *University of Richmond*
Zack Bowen, *University of Miami, Coral Gables*
Austin Briggs, *Hamilton College*
Sheldon Brivic, *Temple University*
William S. Brockman, *University of Illinois, Urbana*
James Cahalan, *Indiana University of Pennsylvania*
Chris Connell, *University of Iowa*
Sidney Feshbach, *City College, City University of New York*
Alice Gasque, *University of South Dakota*
Thomas Giannotti, *University of California, Riverside*
John Gordon, *Connecticut College*
John Hawley, *Santa Clara University*
Joseph Heininger, *University of Michigan, Ann Arbor*
Cheryl Herr, *University of Iowa*
William Keen, *Washington and Jefferson College*
Hugh Kenner, *Johns Hopkins University*
Jean Kimball, *University of Northern Iowa*
Scott Klein, *Cornell College*
Morton Levitt, *Temple University*
Mary Lowe-Evans, *University of West Florida*
Vicki Mahaffey, *University of Pennsylvania*
Paul Morrison, *Brandeis University*
Patrick Morrow, *Auburn University*
James J. Murphy, *Villanova University*
Richard Pearce, *Wheaton College, MA*
Mary Power, *University of New Mexico*
Frances Restuccia, *Boston College*
Daniel Schwarz, *Cornell University*
Bonnie Kime Scott, *University of Delaware, Newark*
Jeffrey Segall, *University of California, Santa Barbara*
Craig Smith, *University of Northern Colorado*

Brian Stonehill, *Pomona College*
Ward Swinson, *Colorado State University*
Weldon Thornton, *University of North Carolina, Chapel Hill*
Robert Tracy, *University of California, Berkeley*
George Wickes, *University of Oregon*

Appendix: Conversion Formulas for Last Two US Editions of *Ulysses*

Chapter	1986/1961	Multiplier
1. Telemachus	3/3	
2. Nestor	20/24	1.200/.833
3. Proteus	31/37	1.194/.837
4. Calypso	45/55	1.222/.818
5. Lotus-eaters	58/71	1.224/.817
6. Hades	72/87	1.208/.828
7. Aeolus	96/116	1.208/.828
8. Lestrygonians	124/151	1.218/.821
9. Scylla and Charybdis	151/184	1.218/.821
10. Wandering Rocks	180/219	1.217/.822
11. Sirens	210/256	1.219/.820
12. Cyclops	240/292	1.216/.822
13. Nausicaa	284/346	1.218/.820
14. Oxen of the Sun	314/383	1.219/.820
15. Circe	350/429	1.226/.816
16. Eumaeus	501/613	1.224/.817
17. Ithaca	544/666	1.224/.817
18. Penelope	608/738	1.216/.822
[final "Yes"]	644/783	1.216/.822

Rough conversion formulas
(p. no. in 1961 ed.) × (.82) = p. no. in 1986 ed.
(p. no. in 1986 ed.) × (1.2) = p. no. in 1961 ed.

Example: "Before born babe bliss had" (ch. 14, "Oxen of the Sun")
Computed: 315 [1986] × 1.219 = 383.985 (actual p. 384 [1961])
384 [1961] × .820 = 314.88 (actual p. 315 [1986])

WORKS CITED

Writings of James Joyce

Dubliners. New York: Modern Library, 1926.

Exiles: A Play in Three Acts. New York: Viking, 1951.

Finnegans Wake. New York: Viking; London: Faber, 1939.

Letters of James Joyce. Ed. Stuart Gilbert. New York: Viking, 1957.

Letters of James Joyce. Ed. Richard Ellmann. Vols. 2–3. New York: Viking, 1966.

A Portrait of the Artist as a Young Man. New York: Viking, 1964.

Selected Letters of James Joyce. Ed. Richard Ellmann. New York: Viking, 1975.

Stephen Hero. Ed. John J. Slocum and Herbert Cahoon. New York: New Directions, 1944.

Ulysses. 1961. New York: Vintage-Random, 1990.

Ulysses. Ed. John Kidd. New York: Norton, forthcoming.

Ulysses: *A Critical and Synoptic Edition*. Ed. Hans Walter Gabler, Wolfhard Steppe, and Claus Melchior. 3 vols. New York: Garland, 1984.

Ulysses: *The Corrected Text*. Ed. Hans Walter Gabler, Wolfhard Steppe, and Claus Melchior. New York: Random, 1986.

Books and Articles

Adams, Robert. *Surface and Symbol: The Consistency of James Joyce's* Ulysses. New York: Oxford UP, 1962.

Anderson, Chester. *James Joyce and His World*. London: Thames, 1967.

Attridge, Derek. "The Backbone of *Finnegans Wake*: Narrative, Digression, and Deconstruction." *Genre* 17.4 (1984): 375–400.

———, ed. *The Cambridge Companion to James Joyce*. New York: Cambridge UP, 1990.

———. "Molly's Flow: The Writing of 'Penelope' and the Question of Women's Language." *Modern Fiction Studies* 35.3 (1989): 543–65.

Attridge, Derek, and Daniel Ferrer, eds. *Post-structuralist Joyce: Essays from the French*. New York: Cambridge UP, 1984.

Banner, Lois W. *American Beauty*. New York: Knopf, 1983.

Barthes, Roland. *S/Z*. Trans. Richard Miller. New York: Hill, 1974.

Beach, Sylvia. *Shakespeare and Company*. 1956. Lincoln: U of Nebraska P, 1980.

Beebe, Maurice. "*Ulysses* and the Age of Modernism." Staley, Ulysses 172–88.

Beja, Morris, and Shari Benstock, eds. *Coping with Joyce: Essays from the Copenhagen Symposium.* Columbus: Ohio State UP, 1989.

Ben-Merre, Diana A., and Maureen Murphy, eds. *James Joyce and His Contemporaries.* New York: Greenwood, 1989.

Bennett, Arnold. "James Joyce's *Ulysses.*" Deming 1: 219–22.

Bennett, Tony. *Marxism and Formalism.* London: Methuen, 1979.

———. "Texts in History: The Determinations of Readings and Their Texts." *Journal of the Midwest Modern Language Association* 18.1 (1983): 1–16.

Benstock, Bernard, ed. *Critical Essays on James Joyce's* Ulysses. Boston: Hall, 1989.

———, ed. *James Joyce: The Augmented Ninth.* Proceedings of the Ninth International James Joyce Symposium. Frankfurt, 1982. Syracuse: Syracuse UP, 1988.

———, ed. *The Seventh of Joyce.* Bloomington: Indiana UP, 1982.

Benstock, Bernard, and Shari Benstock. "The Benstock Principle." Benstock, *Seventh* 10–21.

Berger, John. *Ways of Seeing.* New York: Penguin, 1972.

Bidwell, Bruce, and Linda Heffer. *The Joycean Way: A Topographic Guide to* Dubliners *and* A Portrait of the Artist as a Young Man. Baltimore: Johns Hopkins UP, 1982.

Blamires, Harry. *The New Bloomsday Book: A Guide through* Ulysses. Rev. 2nd ed. London: Routledge, 1988.

Bowen, Zack. "*Ulysses.*" Bowen and Carens 421–557.

Bowen, Zack, and James Carens, eds. *A Companion to Joyce Studies.* Westport: Greenwood, 1984.

Bradbury, Malcolm, and James McFarlane, eds. *Modernism, 1890–1930.* Harmondsworth, Eng.: Penguin, 1976.

Brivic, Sheldon. *Joyce between Freud and Jung.* Port Washington: Kennikat, 1980.

———. *Joyce the Creator.* Madison: U of Wisconsin P, 1985.

Brooks, Van Wyck. *The Opinions of Olliver Allston.* New York: Dutton, 1941.

Brown, Richard. *James Joyce and Sexuality.* Cambridge: Cambridge UP, 1985.

Budgen, Frank. *James Joyce and the Making of* Ulysses *and Other Writings.* 1960. Rev. ed. Comp. Clive Hart. Oxford: Oxford UP, 1989.

Cahalan, James M. *The Irish Novel: A Critical History.* Boston: Twayne, 1988.

Card, James Van Dyck. *An Anatomy of "Penelope."* Rutherford: Fairleigh Dickinson UP, 1984.

Carroll, Lewis. *Alice's Adventures in Wonderland.* London: Macmillian, 1886.

Chace, William M. "Historical Realism: An Eco." *James Joyce Quarterly* 28.4 (1991): 889–901.

Cixous, Hélène. "Castration or Decapitation?" Trans. Annette Kuhn. *Signs* 7.1 (1981): 41–55.

———. *The Exile of James Joyce.* Trans. Sally A. J. Purcell. New York: Lewis, 1972.

Cohn, Dorrit. *Transparent Minds: Narrative Modes for Presenting Consciousness in Fiction.* Princeton: Princeton UP, 1978.

Cowley, Malcolm. *Exile's Return: A Literary Odyssey of the 1920s*. New York: Viking, 1951.

Cronin, Anthony. *A Question of Modernity*. London: Secker, 1966.

Daly, Mary E. *Dublin, the Deposed Capital: A Social and Economic History*. Cork: Cork UP, 1984.

Daryl, Phillippe. *Ireland's Disease*. London: Routledge, 1888.

Davitt, Michael. *The Fall of Feudalism in Ireland*. London: Harper, 1904.

Deane, Seamus. *Celtic Revivals: Essays in Modern Irish Literature: 1880–1980*. London: Faber, 1985.

Deming, Robert H., ed. *James Joyce: The Critical Heritage*. 2 vols. New York: Barnes, 1970.

Dickens, Charles. *Bleak House*. London: Bradbury, 1853.

———. *Nicholas Nickleby*. London: Dent; New York: Dutton, 1907.

———. *Oliver Twist*. London: Bentley, 1838.

———. *The Personal History of David Copperfield*. New York: Oxford UP, 1948.

Dunleavy, Janet, ed. *Re-viewing Classics of Joyce Criticism*. Urbana: U of Illinois P, 1991.

Eagleton, Terry. *Against the Grain: Essays, 1975–1985*. London: Verso, 1986.

———. *Criticism and Ideology: A Study in Marxist Literary Theory*. London: New Left, 1976.

Eco, Umberto. *The Aesthetics of Chaosmos: The Middle Ages of James Joyce*. Trans. Ellen Esrock. Cambridge: Harvard UP, 1989.

Edel, Leon. *The Psychological Novel, 1900–1950*. New York: Hart-Davis, 1955.

Ehrlich, Heyward, ed. *James Joyce and Modernism*. New York: New Horizon, 1984.

Eliot, T. S. *Collected Poems*. New York: Harcourt, 1963.

———. "*Ulysses*, Order, and Myth." Givens 198-202.

———. *The Use of Poetry and the Use of Criticism*. London: Faber, 1993.

Ellmann, Richard. *The Consciousness of Joyce*. New York: Oxford UP, 1977.

———. *James Joyce*. 1959. Rev. ed. New York: Oxford UP, 1982.

———. *Ulysses on the Liffey*. New York: Oxford UP, 1972.

Ellmann, Richard, and Charles Feidelson, Jr., eds. *The Modern Tradition: Backgrounds of Modern Literature*. New York: Oxford UP, 1965.

Ewen, Stuart. *All-Consuming Images: The Politics of Style in Contemporary Culture*. New York: Basic, 1988.

Fanon, Frantz. *The Wretched of the Earth*. Trans. Constance Farrington. New York: Grove, 1963.

Farrell, James T. *The League of Frightened Philistines and Other Papers*. New York: Vanguard, 1945.

———. *A Note on Literary Criticism*. New York: Vanguard, 1936.

Fiske, John. *Reading the Popular*. Boston: Unwin, 1989.

Fitch, Noel. *Sylvia Beach and the Lost Generation*. New York: Norton, 1983.

Foster, R. F., ed. *The Oxford Illustrated History of Ireland*. New York: Oxford UP, 1989.

Foucault, Michel. *The History of Sexuality*. Trans. Robert Hurley. New York: Pantheon, 1978.

Frank, Joseph. *The Widening Gyre: Crisis and Mastery in Modern Literature*. Bloomington: Indiana UP, 1963.

The Freeman's Journal *of Bloomsday*. Vol. 137. London: Chelsea, 1989.

Freire, Paulo. *Pedagogy of the Oppressed*. New York: Continuum, 1970.

French, Marilyn. *The Book as World: James Joyce's* Ulysses. Cambridge: Harvard UP, 1976.

Freud, Sigmund. "A Special Type of Object Choice Made by Men." *Sexuality and the Psychology of Love*. Collected Papers of Freud. Vol. 8. Ed. Philip Rieff. New York: Collier, 1963. 49–58.

Friedman, Melvin. *Stream of Consciousness: A Study in Literary Method*. New Haven: Yale UP, 1955.

Frost, Robert. *West-Running Brook*. New York: Holt, 1928.

Gallagher, S. F., ed. *Women in Irish Legend, Life and Literature*. Gerrards Cross: Smythe; Totowa: Barnes, 1983.

Garrison, Fielding H. *An Introduction to the History of Medicine*. 4th ed. London: Saunders, 1929.

Gaskell, Philip, and Clive Hart. Ulysses: *A Review of Three Texts. Proposals for Alterations to the Texts of 1922, 1961, and 1984.* Gerrards Cross: Smythe, 1989.

Gifford, Don. *Notes for Joyce: An Annotation of James Joyce's* Ulysses. New York: Dutton, 1974.

Gifford, Don, and Robert J. Seidman. Ulysses *Annotated: Notes for Joyce's* Ulysses. Rev. ed. Berkeley: U of California P, 1988.

Gilbert, Sandra, and Susan Gubar. *No Man's Land, Vol. 1: The War of the Words*. New Haven: Yale UP, 1987.

Gilbert, Stuart. *James Joyce's* Ulysses: *A Study*. 1930. New York: Vintage, 1958.

Gillespie, Michael Patrick. "Certitude and Circularity: The Search for *Ulysses*." *Studies in the Novel* 20.2 (1990): 216–30.

———. *Reading the Book of Himself: Narrative Strategies in the Works of James Joyce*. Columbus: Ohio State UP, 1989.

Givens, Seon, ed. *James Joyce: Two Decades of Criticism*. New York: Vanguard, 1963.

Gogarty, Oliver St. John. *As I Was Going down Sackville Street: A Phantasy in Fact*. London: Sphere, 1968.

Goldberg, Samuel. *The Classical Temper: A Study of James Joyce's* Ulysses. New York: Barnes, 1961.

Gorham, Maurice. *Ireland: From Old Photographs*. London: Batsford, 1971.

Gorman, Herbert. *James Joyce: A Definitive Biography*. London: Lane, 1941.

Gose, Elliot. *The Transformation Process in Joyce's* Ulysses. Toronto: U of Toronto P, 1980.

Gosse, Edmund. "Letter to Louis Gillet." Deming 1: 313.

Grattan, C. Hartley, ed. *The Critique of Humanism: A Symposium.* New York: Brewer, 1930.

Green, John R. *Medical History for Students.* Springfield: Thomas, 1968.

Greenblatt, Stephen. *Renaissance Self-Fashioning: From More to Shakespeare.* Chicago: U of Chicago P, 1980.

Gregory, Augusta. *Visions and Beliefs in the West of Ireland.* Collected and arranged by Lady Gregory, with two essays and notes by W. B. Yeats. 2 vols. New York: Putnam, 1920.

Groden, Michael, gen. ed. *The James Joyce Archive.* 63 vols. New York: Garland, 1977–79.

———, comp. *James Joyce's Manuscripts: An Index to the James Joyce Archive.* New York: Garland, 1980.

———. *Ulysses in Progress.* Princeton: Princeton UP, 1977.

Hannay, John. "Coincidence and Fables of Identity in 'Eumaeus.' " *James Joyce Quarterly* 21.4 (1984): 341–55.

Hart, Clive. *James Joyce's Ulysses.* Sydney: U of Sydney, 1968.

Hart, Clive, and David Hayman, eds. *James Joyce's Ulysses: Critical Essays.* Berkeley: U of California P, 1974.

Hart, Clive, and Leo Knuth. *A Topographical Guide to James Joyce's Ulysses.* Colchester: A Wake Newslitter, 1975.

Hart, Clive, and C. George Sandulescu, eds. *Assessing the 1984 Ulysses.* Totowa: Barnes, 1986.

Hayman, David. "Cyclops." Hart and Hayman 243–77.

———. *Ulysses: The Mechanics of Meaning.* Englewood Cliffs: Prentice, 1970.

Helmling, Steven. "Joyce: Autobiography, History, Narrative." *Kenyon Review* 10.3 (1988): 91–109.

Henke, Suzette. *Joyce's Moraculous Sindbook: A Study of Ulysses.* Columbus: Ohio State UP, 1978.

Henke, Suzette, and Elaine Unkeless, eds. *Women in Joyce.* Urbana: U of Illinois P, 1982.

Herr, Cheryl. *For the Land They Loved: Irish Political Melodramas, 1890–1925.* Syracuse: Syracuse UP, 1991.

———. *Joyce's Anatomy of Culture.* Urbana: U of Illinois P, 1986.

Herring, Phillip. "The Bedsteadfastness of Molly Bloom." *Modern Fiction Studies* 15.1 (1969): 49–61.

———. *Joyce's Ulysses: Notesheets in the British Museum.* Charlottesville: U of Virginia P, 1972.

———. *Joyce's Uncertainty Principle.* Princeton: Princeton UP, 1987.

Hickey, Kieran. *Faithful Departed: The Dublin of James Joyce's Ulysses.* Dublin: Ward River, 1982.

Holub, Robert C. *Reception Theory: A Critical Introduction.* London: Methuen, 1984.

Homer. *Odyssey.* Trans. William Morris. London: Longmans; New York: Green, 1901.

Howe, Irving, ed. *Literary Modernism.* Greenwich: Fawcett, 1967. Republished as *The Idea of the Modern in Literature and the Arts.* New York: Horizon, 1968.

Irigaray, Luce. *This Sex Which Is Not One.* Trans. Catherine Porter. Ithaca: Cornell UP, 1985.

Iser, Wolfgang. *The Implied Reader: Patterns of Communication in Prose Fiction from Bunyan to Beckett.* Baltimore: Johns Hopkins UP, 1974.

James, Henry. *The Art of Fiction and Other Essays.* New York: Oxford UP, 1948.

———. *The Art of the Novel.* Ed. Richard P. Blackmur. New York: Scribner's, 1934.

James, William. *The Principles of Psychology.* 1890. New York: Dover, 1950.

———. *Talks to Teachers on Psychology.* New York: Holt, 1914.

Jameson, Fredric. *The Political Unconscious: Narrative as a Socially Symbolic Act.* Ithaca: Cornell UP, 1981.

Janusko, Robert. *The Sources and Structures of James Joyce's "Oxen."* Ann Arbor: UMI Research P, 1983.

Jauss, Hans Robert. "Literary History as a Challenge to Literary Theory." *An Aesthetic of Experience and Literary Hermeneutics.* Trans. Michael Shaw. Minneapolis: U of Minnesota P, 1982. 3–45.

Jones, Ellen Carol. Introduction. Benstock, *Ninth* 77–79.

Joyce, Stanislaus. *Dublin Diary.* Ed. George Healy. Ithaca: Cornell UP, 1962.

———. *My Brother's Keeper: James Joyce's Early Years.* Ed. Richard Ellmann. New York: Viking, 1958.

Kain, Richard M. *Dublin in the Age of William Butler Yeats and James Joyce.* Norman: U of Oklahoma P, 1962.

———. *Fabulous Voyager: James Joyce's Ulysses.* New York: Viking, 1959.

Kelly, Dermot. *Narrative Strategies in Joyce's Ulysses.* Ann Arbor: UMI Research P, 1988.

Kenner, Hugh. *Dublin's Joyce.* New York: Columbia UP, 1987.

———. *Joyce's Voices.* Berkeley: U of California P, 1978.

———. "Molly's Masterstroke." *James Joyce Quarterly* 10 (1972): 19–28.

———. Ulysses. Rev. ed. Baltimore: Johns Hopkins UP, 1987.

———. *Wyndham Lewis.* Norfolk: New Directions, 1954.

Kershner, R. B. *Joyce, Bakhtin, and Popular Literature: Chronicles of Popular Disorder.* Chapel Hill: U of North Carolina P, 1989.

Kidd, John. "The Scandal of *Ulysses.*" *New York Review of Books* 30 June 1988: 32–39.

Krafft-Ebing, Richard von. *Psychopathia Sexualis.* Trans. Charles G. Chaddock. Philadelphia: Davis, 1892.

Kristeva, Julia. *The Kristeva Reader.* Ed. Toril Moi. New York: Columbia UP, 1986.

Lacan, Jacques. Ecrits: *A Selection.* Trans. Alan Sheridan. New York: Norton, 1977.

Lacan, Jacques, and the Ecole freudienne. *Feminine Sexuality.* Ed. Juliet Mitchell and Jacqueline Rose. New York: Norton, 1983.

Lammer, John. "The Archetypal Molly Bloom, Joyce's Frail Wife of Bath." *James Joyce Quarterly* 25.4 (1988): 487–502.

Larkin, Emmet. *The Roman Catholic Church in Ireland and the Fall of Parnell, 1881–1891*. Chapel Hill: U of North Carolina P, 1979.

Law, Jules David. "Joyce's 'Delicate Siamese' Equation: The Dialectic of Home in *Ulysses*." *PMLA* 102.2 (1987): 197–205.

Lawless, Emily. *The Story of Ireland*. New York: Putnam, 1892.

Lawrence, D. H. "John Galsworthy." *Phoenix: The Posthumous Papers of D. H. Lawrence*. New York: Viking, 1936. 539–50.

Lawrence, Karen. *The Odyssey of Style in* Ulysses. Princeton: Princeton UP, 1981.

Leavis, F. R. *The Great Tradition: George Eliot, Henry James, Joseph Conrad*. New York: Stewart, 1948.

Lee, Joseph. *The Modernization of Irish Society: 1848–1914*. Dublin: Gill, 1973.

Levin, Harry. *James Joyce: A Critical Introduction*. Norfolk: New Directions, 1960.

Lewis, Wyndham. "An Analysis of the Mind of James Joyce." *Time and Western Man*. 1927. Boston: Beacon, 1957. 77, 90–168.

Liddell, Henry G., and Robert Scott, eds. *Greek-English Lexicon*. Oxford: Oxford UP, 1940.

Litz, A. Walton. *The Art of James Joyce: Method and Design in* Ulysses *and* Finnegans Wake. New York: Oxford UP, 1961.

Lyons, J. B. *James Joyce and Medicine*. New York: Humanities, 1974.

MacCabe, Colin. *James Joyce and the Revolution of the Word*. London: Macmillan, 1979.

———, ed. *James Joyce: New Perspectives*. Brighton: Harvester; Bloomington: Indiana UP, 1982.

MacCurtain, Margaret. "Women, the Vote and Revolution." *Women in Irish Society: The Historical Dimension*. Westport: Greenwood P, 1979. 46–57.

Macdonald, Dwight. "Kulturbolschewismus Is Here." *Partisian Review* 8.6 (1941): 442–51.

Macherey, Pierre. *A Theory of Literary Production*. Trans. Geoffrey Wall. Boston: Routledge, 1978.

Maddox, Brenda. *Nora: The Real Life of Molly Bloom*. Boston: Houghton, 1988.

Madtes, Richard. *The "Ithaca" Chapter of Joyce's* Ulysses. Ann Arbor: UMI Research P, 1983.

Mahaffey, Vicki. *Reauthorizing Joyce*. New York: Cambridge UP, 1988.

Maltby, Richard, ed. *The Passing Parade: A History of Popular Culture in the Twentieth Century*. New York: Oxford UP, 1989.

Manganiello, Dominic. *Joyce's Politics*. London: Routledge, 1980.

Mansfield, Katherine. Extract from *Letters of Katherine Mansfield*. Deming 1: 22.

Massengill, Samuel Evans. *A Sketch of Medicine and Pharmacy*. Bristol: Massengill, 1943.

McCarthy, Patrick. Ulysses: *Portals of Discovery*. Boston: Twayne, 1990.

McCormack, W. J., and Alistair Stead, eds. *James Joyce and Modern Literature*. London: Routledge, 1982.

McCormick, Kathleen. "Reproducing Molly Bloom: A Revisionist History of the Reception of 'Penelope': 1922–1970." *The Historical and Performative Molly Bloom*. Ed. Richard Pearce. Madison: U of Wisconsin P, forthcoming.

———. Ulysses, *"Wandering Rocks," and the Reader: Multiple Pleasures in Reading*. Lewiston: Mellen, 1991.

McCormick, Kathleen, Gary Waller, and Linda Flower. *Reading Texts: Reading, Responding, Writing*. Lexington: Heath, 1987.

McDowell, Edwin. "On the Eve of 'Bloomsday': Scholars Level Attack on Corrected *Ulysses*." *New York Times* 15 June 1988: C30.

McGann, Jerome J. *The Beauty of Inflections: Literary Investigations in Historical Method and Theory*. Oxford: Clarendon–Oxford UP, 1985.

McGee, Patrick. *Paperspace: Style as Ideology in Joyce's* Ulysses. Lincoln: U of Nebraska P, 1988.

McHugh, Roland. Finnegans Wake *Experience*. Berkeley: U of California P, 1981.

Michels, James. "The Role of Language in Consciousness: A Structuralist Look at 'Proteus' in *Ulysses*." *Language and Style* 15.2 (1982): 23–32.

Miller-Budnitskaya, R. "James Joyce's *Ulysses*." *Dialectics* 5 (1938): 6–26.

Milton, John. *Paradise Lost*. Bloomington: Indiana UP, 1984.

Mirsky, D. P. "Joyce and Irish Literature." Trans. David Kinkead. *The New Masses* 10–11 (3 Apr. 1934): 31–34.

Mitchell, Juliet, ed. *The Selected Melanie Klein: The Essential Writings*. By Melanie Klein. New York: Free, 1987.

Moody, J. W. and F. X. Martin, eds. *The Course of Irish History*. Rev. ed. Cork: Weybright, 1968.

More, Paul Elmer. "The Demon of the Absolute." 1928. *American Literary Criticism, 1900–1950*. Ed. Charles I. Glicksberg. New York: Hendricks, 1951. 258–87.

———. *On Being Human*. Princeton: Princeton UP, 1936.

Morley, Dave. "Texts, Readers, Subjects." *Culture, Media, Language: Working Papers in Cultural Studies*. Ed. Stuart Hall. London: U of Birmingham P, 1980. 163–73.

Morse, J. Mitchell. *The Sympathetic Alien: James Joyce and Catholicism*. New York: New York UP, 1959.

Murfin, Ross C., ed. Heart of Darkness: *A Case Study in Contemporary Criticism*. Case Studies in Contemporary Criticism. New York: St. Martin's, 1989.

———. "What Is the New Historicism?" Murfin 3–16.

Murphy, Cliona. *The Women's Suffrage Movement and Irish Society in the Early Twentieth Century*. Philadelphia: Temple UP, 1989.

Nicholson, Robert. *The* Ulysses *Guide: Tours through Joyce's Dublin*. New York: Routledge, 1989.

Noon, William T. *Joyce and Aquinas*. 1957. Hamden: Archon, 1970.

172   WORKS CITED

Norris, Margot. "Modernism, Myth and Desire in 'Nausicaa.' " *James Joyce Quarterly* 26.1 (1988): 37–51.

O'Brien, Joseph V. *Dear Dirty Dublin: A City in Distress, 1899–1916.* Berkeley: U of California P, 1982.

O'Connor, Laurence. *Lost Ireland: A Photographic Record at the Turn of the Century.* Harmondsworth, Eng.: Penguin, 1985.

Opie, Robert. *Rule Britannia: Trading on the British Image.* New York: Viking, 1985.

Osler, William. *Aequanimitas: With Other Addresses to Medical Students, Nurses, and Practitioners of Medicine.* Philadelphia: Blakiston's, 1914.

———. *Principles and Practice of Medicine.* New York: Appleton, 1892.

"Paralysis." *Oxford English Dictionary.* 2nd ed. 1989.

Paul-Dubois, L. *Contemporary Ireland.* Dublin: Maunsel, 1908.

Pearl, Cyril. *Dublin in Bloomtime: The City James Joyce Knew.* New York: Viking, 1969.

Platt, L. H. "The Buckeen and the Dogsbody: Aspects of History and Culture in 'Telemachus.' " *James Joyce Quarterly* 27.1 (1989): 77–86.

Plunkett, Horace. *Ireland in the New Century.* London: Murray, 1904.

Poggioli, Renato. *The Theory of the Avant-Garde.* Cambridge: Harvard UP, 1968.

Pound, Ezra. *The Cantos (1–95).* New York: New Directions, 1965.

Radek, Karl. "James Joyce or Socialist Realism?" *Problems of Soviet Literature: Reports and Speeches of the First Soviet Writers' Congress.* Ed. A. Zhdanov et al. New York: International, 1935. 150–82.

Read, Forrest, ed. *Pound/Joyce: The Letters of Ezra Pound to James Joyce, with Pound's Essay on Joyce.* New York: New Directions, 1967.

Richards, Thomas. *The Commodity Culture of Victorian England: Advertising and Spectacle, 1851–1914.* Stanford: Stanford UP, 1990.

Rossman, Charles. "The New *Ulysses*: The Hidden Controversy." *New York Review of Books* 8 Dec. 1988: 53–58.

Schutte, William. *Joyce and Shakespeare: A Study of the Meaning of* Ulysses. New Haven: Yale UP, 1957.

Schwarz, Daniel. *Reading Joyce's* Ulysses. New York: St. Martin's, 1987.

Scott, Bonnie Kime, ed. *The Gender of Modernism: A Critical Anthology.* Bloomington: Indiana UP, 1990.

———. *James Joyce.* Atlantic Highlands: Humanities, 1987.

———. *Joyce and Feminism.* Bloomington: Indiana UP, 1984.

———, ed. *New Alliances in Joyce Studies: When It's Aped to Foul a Delfian.* Newark: U of Delaware P; London: Associated UP, 1988.

Scott, Sir Walter. *The Heart of Midlothian.* London: Dent, 1906.

Seidel, Michael. *Epic Geography: James Joyce's* Ulysses. Princeton: Princeton UP, 1976.

Selwyn-Brown, Arthur. *The Physician throughout the Ages.* Vol. 1. New York: Capehart-Brown, 1928.

Senn, Fritz. Rev. of Ulysses *Annotated: Notes for James Joyce's* Ulysses, by Don Gifford and Robert J. Seidman. *James Joyce Quarterly* 27.3 (1990): 653–62.

Shakespeare, William. *Hamlet.* Ed. Harold Jenkins. London: Methuen, 1982.

Shechner, Mark. *Joyce in Nighttown; A Psychoanalytic Inquiry into* Ulysses. Berkeley: U of California P, 1974.

Skeat, Walter W. *Etymological Dictionary of the English Language.* 2nd ed. Oxford: Clarendon–Oxford UP, 1893.

Souvage, Jacques. *An Introduction to the Study of the Novel.* Gent: E. Story–Scientia PVBA, 1965.

Staley, Thomas F. *An Annotated Critical Bibliography of James Joyce.* New York: St. Martin's, 1989.

———, ed. Ulysses: *Fifty Years.* Bloomington: Indiana UP, 1974.

Steinberg, Erwin. "Author! Author!" *James Joyce Quarterly* 22.4 (1985): 419–25.

———. *The Stream of Consciousness and Beyond in* Ulysses. Pittsburgh: U of Pittsburgh P, 1973.

———, ed. *The Stream-of-Consciousness Technique in the Modern Novel.* Port Washington: Kennikat, 1979.

Steppe, Wolfhard, and Hans Walter Gabler, eds. *A Handlist to James Joyce's* Ulysses: *A Complete Alphabetical Index to the Critical Reading Text.* New York: Garland, 1986.

Stoker, Bram. *Dracula.* Garden City: Garden City, 1959.

Structuralist/Reader Response Issue. Spec. issue of *James Joyce Quarterly* 16.2 (1979).

Sullivan, Kevin. *Joyce among the Jesuits.* New York: Columbia UP, 1958.

Sultan, Stanley. *The Argument of* Ulysses. Columbus: Ohio State UP, 1965.

Svevo, Italo. "James Joyce." Deming 1: 355–56.

Swift, Jonathan. *Gulliver's Travels.* New York: Pocket, 1972.

Synge, J. M. *The Playboy of the Western World. Works.* Vol. 2. Boston: Luce, 1912. 4 vols.

Thackeray, William Makepeace. *Vanity Fair: A Novel without a Hero.* London: Bradbury, 1948.

Thomas, Brook. "The Counterfeit Style of 'Eumaeus.' " *James Joyce Quarterly* 14.1 (1976): 15–24.

———. "The Historical Necessity for—and Difficulties with—New Historical Analysis in Introductory Literature Courses." *College English* 49.5 (1987): 509–21.

———. *James Joyce's* Ulysses: *A Book of Many Happy Returns.* Baton Rouge: Louisiana State UP, 1982.

———. "Preserving and Keeping Order by Killing Time in *Heart of Darkness.*" Murfin 237–58.

Thornton, Weldon. *Allusions in* Ulysses: *An Annotated List.* Chapel Hill: U of North Carolina P, 1968.

———. "Liberty and License in Joyce's *Ulysses.*" Unpublished essay.

Tindall, William York. *The Joyce Country*. University Park: Pennsylvania State UP, 1960.

———. *Reader's Guide to James Joyce*. New York: Noonday, 1959.

Trilling, Lionel. "Freud and Literature." *The Liberal Imagination: Essays on Literature and Society*. Garden City: Doubleday-Anchor, 1955.

———. "James Joyce in His Letters." *Joyce: A Collection of Critical Essays*. Ed. William M. Chace. Englewood Cliffs: Prentice, 1974. 143–65..

Van Boheemen, Christine. *The Novel as Family Romance: Language, Gender, and Authority from Fielding to Joyce*. Ithaca: Cornell UP, 1987.

Virgil. *The Aeneid*. Trans. C. Day Lewis. Garden City: Doubleday, 1953.

Warner, John M. "Myth and History in Joyce's 'Nausicaa' Episode." *James Joyce Quarterly* 24.1 (1986): 19–33.

Watson, George J. "The Politics of *Ulysses*." *Joyce's Ulysses: The Larger Perspective*. Ed. Robert D. Newman and Weldon Thornton. Newark: U of Delaware P; London: Associated UP, 1987. 39–58.

Watt, Stephen. *The Popular Theatres of Joyce, Shaw, and O'Casey*. Syracuse: Syracuse UP, 1991.

Weber, Eugen, ed. *Paths to the Present: Aspects of European Thought from Romanticism to Existentialism*. New York: Dodd, 1960.

Wells, H. G. "James Joyce." Deming 1: 86–88.

West, Rebecca. Extract from "The Strange Case of James Joyce." Deming 2: 431–32.

Wicke, Jennifer. *Advertising Fictions: Literature, Advertisements, and Social Reading*. New York: Columbia UP, 1988.

Wilde, Oscar. *The Importance of Being Earnest: A Trivial Comedy for Serious People*. Ed. Russell Jackson. London: Benn, 1980.

Wilson, Edmund. "Archibald MacLeish and 'the Word.' " *New Republic* 103.1 (1 July 1940): 30–32.

———. *Axel's Castle: A Study in the Imaginative Literature of 1870–1930*. New York: Scribner's, 1948.

———. "Mr. Brook's Second Phase." *New Republic* 103.14 (30 Sept. 1940): 452–54.

———. "Mr. More and the Mithraic Bull." *The Triple Thinkers: Ten Essays on Literature*. New York: Oxford UP, 1948. 3–14.

———. "Notes on Babbitt and More." Grattan 39–62.

Woolf, Virginia. *Diary*. Ed. Olivier Bell, assisted by Andrew McNellie. Vol. 2 (1920–24). New York: Harcourt, 1978.

———. "Modern Fiction." *The Common Reader: First and Second Series*. 2 vols. New York: Harcourt, 1948.

Wright, Elizabeth. *Psychoanalytic Criticism: Theory in Practice*. London: Methuen, 1984.

Yeats, W. B. *In the Seven Woods*. 1903. Dublin: Cuala, 1971. Rpt. in *Later Poems by W. B. Yeats*. London: Macmillian, 1922.

INDEX OF NAMES